YALE STUDIES IN RELIGIOUS EDUCATION

XIII.
TENNANT'S PHILOSOPHICAL THEOLOGY

TENNANT'S

PHILOSOPHICAL THEOLOGY

BY

DELTON LEWIS SCUDDER, Ph.D.

Assistant Professor of Ethics and Religion
in Wesleyan University

New Haven : Yale University Press

London : Humphrey Milford : Oxford University Press

1940

TO

FREDERICK ROBERT TENNANT

ABLE DEFENDER OF THEISM,
ADVOCATE OF FACT AND TRUTH

The publication of this volume has been aided by a grant from the Research Funds of Wesleyan University.

PREFACE

THE writings of Dr. Tennant are becoming increasingly important to philosophers of religion in the English-speaking world. Long an authority on the problem of evil, Dr. Tennant's work in philosophical theology is regarded by some as the best intellectual defense of theism in our time. The theological faculties of the United States are placing Tennant's writings upon the *sine qua non* lists of readings. References to Tennant appear in innumerable new books and articles. It is evident that the issues of his rigorous thinking cannot be avoided by philosophers either within or without the area of theistic conviction.

For a detailed outline of the subject matter here presented the reader may refer to the Contents. In brief summary, it may be said that Tennant's background, problem, and solution are first set forth (Introduction and Chapter I) upon the basis of all his published writings to date. Then in criticism (Chapter II), his empirical validation of theism which excludes the truth-claim of all direct religious experience is rejected because the empirical analogies, the cognitive analogies, and certain extrapolations fail to establish the case. Especially important in this context is the issue of our knowledge of one another which is critically debated in some detail. In Chapter III Tennant's seven objections to the "proof-value" of religious experience are also found inadequate to eliminate the testimony of religious experience from a comprehensive world-view. In the reconstruction of the theistic case, which follows in the concluding chapter, religious experience is given a basic, primary, but not solitary position in philosophical theology. It is contended that the task of philosophical thought is to validate true religious experience, to reveal the atheistic implications of naturalism, and to examine the evidence of an identification of the God of religious experience with the God of the cosmos.

The substance of this book constitutes "A Dissertation Presented to the Faculty of the Graduate School of Yale University in Candidacy for the degree of Doctor of Philosophy" (May, 1939). Its origin and continued inspiration reside in the vigorous mind of Professor Robert L. Calhoun of Yale, teacher, adviser, and friend. Its publication demands an expression of gratitude to Dr. Tennant for reading the manuscript, for extensive correspondence, and for suggestions which deal with the exposition of his doctrine. A word of thanks is due, also, to Professor C. D. Broad of Trinity College, Cambridge, who with Dr. Tennant gave me the benefit of wise counsel and many courtesies in England during the long-vacation term of 1936. The constant encouragement of Professor D. C. Macintosh of Yale has been as indispensable as his scholarship.

To acknowledge other sources of gracious stimulus and help is almost beyond my power. Particularly do I owe much to my parents and the pastors and friends of the Burnside Methodist Episcopal Church for my early interest in religion. To my first teachers of philosophy, Professor Cornelius Krusé and the late Andrew C. Armstrong, and of the philosophy of religion, Professor William G. Chanter, I owe the beginnings of philosophical and religious reflection as an undergraduate at Wesleyan University. To Professors L. A. Weigle, R. H. Bainton, and F. S. C. Northrop of Yale, I am indebted for graduate studies in religion and philosophy. To my colleagues on the faculties, as well as to many students, both at the American University of Beirut, Syria, and at Wesleyan University, and to the parishioners of the Durham Methodist Episcopal Church, I owe the development that comes only in the mutual sharing and criticism of concepts and ideals. Grateful also am I to my adviser and friend, Professor Thomas W. Bussom, and to President James L. McConaughy, both of Wesleyan, for many kindnesses. To my wife, Inez Hamilton Scudder, I owe the unrepayable comfort and stimulus of intimate friendship and hours of laborious assistance. To my secretary, Miss Bernice Welker, I stand in debt for expert stenography, typing, and proofreading, and for the patience to bear with my idiosyncrasies. Finally, I wish to express my appreciation to the library staffs of the Hartford Seminary Foundation and Wesleyan University and to the technicians of the Yale University Press for cordial service.

D. L. S.

Middletown, Connecticut,
  February, 1940.

CONTENTS

Chapter II: A Critique of Tennant's Empirical Validation of Theism   88

CONCLUSION: The Validation of Theism   213

TENNANT'S PHILOSOPHICAL THEOLOGY

INTRODUCTION

F. R. TENNANT, HIS INTELLECTUAL BACKGROUND AND AFFILIATIONS

From Science to Theology

IT is the purpose of this introduction to portray Dr. Tennant's intellectual background and affiliations. Such an orientation will forward the understanding of his central ideas. Tennant's early interests were neither philosophical nor theological but scientific. As an undergraduate at Caius College, Cambridge (1885–89), he worked in physics, mathematics, the biological sciences, and chemistry, his principal subject in Part II of the Natural Science Tripos being chemistry. Certain lectures of Huxley delivered in 1889 called Tennant's attention to the conflict between scientists and the established principles of religion. He traced the German sources, Walter Baur and Friedrich Strauss, upon whose "Higher Criticism" many of Huxley's statements about the Bible were based. His growing interest in religion led him to prepare himself for ordination in the Church of England.

For three years (1891–94), while teaching science at his old school (Newcastle-under-Lyme), he continued both his theological and scientific studies, taking his B.Sc. at the University of London and his M.A. at Cambridge the following year. After serving as Curate of St. Matthew's, Walsall (1894–97), he took up residence at Cambridge again, now as Chaplain of Caius College, later as Curate of St. Mary the Great, and began his study of philosophy under Ward. There followed a college studentship (1899–1902) which enabled him to complete an extensive investigation of the history and development of the doctrine of the Fall and Original Sin in an attempt to bring this doctrine into line with the scientific postulate of evolution. His Hulsean Lecture (1901–2) published under the title, *The Origin and Propagation of Sin*, and his foundational research, *The Sources of the Doctrine of the Fall and Original Sin*, were the fruits of this period. The former book gives evidence of his early studies in philosophy, particularly the philosophy of Lotze, Leibniz, and Ward. His essay, *The Being of God in the Light of Physical Science* (1905), written in the early part of his service as Rector of Hockwold (1903–13), reveals a mastery of Ward's *Naturalism and Agnosticism* and an acceptance of Ward's solution of epistemological problems. With Ward, Tennant the scientist turned to psychology to obtain a factual illumination of the problem of knowing. Cambridge awarded him a B.D. in 1904, a D.D. in 1906, and called him to be University Lecturer in the Philosophy of Religion in 1907. From 1913 to his retirement[1] in 1938, he held the post of Lecturer in Theology at Trinity College. His vast learning in science and philosophy is evident in many writings,[2] the greatest of which are *Philosophical Theology* (1928 and 1930) and *Philosophy of the Sciences* (Tarner Lectures, 1932). Oxford recently bestowed an honorary D.D. upon him (1929), not without great cause.

The Cambridge Background

It is important to note that Tennant is not only a scientist in temper but also a logician. While mastering Ward's teaching, he went to school to Johnson, the logician, and worked out his philosophical and theological convictions in interaction with a circle of tough-minded Cambridge teachers (McTaggart, Russell, Hobson, Barnes, Broad, and others). It is to such a group of people that he has stated and defended his convictions on matters of religious belief. His controlling ideals have always been fact, logic, clarity, and precision, an intense hostility for rhetoric which is the befuddlement of thought and for mysticism which escapes exact definitions and sharply drawn inferences. It is not strange that his *Philosophical Theology* should receive a more cordial reception from his agnostic friends than from the theologians.

His way is the Cambridge way [writes De Burgh with admirable comprehension], scientific and abstruse, scrupulous in the use of language, reveling in fine and sometimes meticulous distinctions, above all tenacious of the actual, mistrustful of predilections for the visionary and the supersensible, and uncompromising in his intolerance of any slurring of the difference between thoughts and

1. Date of Tennant's birth, 1866.   2. See Bibliography, pp. 259 ff.

things. To follow him along the arduous and unromantic path towards his vindication of the personal and human factors in knowledge, of teleology and value, and of the noumenal ground of sensible actuality, is a task which, however difficult, is of extraordinary interest to the serious reader. We find ourselves wondering whether Cambridge philosophers, who are not as a rule prone to indulge in theological speculations, will be induced to trip it to Dr. Tennant's measure, and by inferences from premises which they share in common, to accept the articles of the Christian faith.[3]

It is this Cambridge background which illuminates many characteristics of Tennant's thought. It illuminates his wholesale rejection of religious experience as a fact which theology must accept as something in itself, and his desire to start with facts which are commonly accepted by all. It illuminates his indebtedness to Ward, Johnson, Broad, and Oman for important direct contributions to various phases of his work and to naturalistic philosophers, to McTaggart and Moore, for stimuli which only opponents at various points can give. In opposition to Moore, Tennant develops his theory of value; to McTaggart's pluralism, a part of his argument for theism as ground of the coherence and coöperation of the many toward an end; and against the naturalistic scientists who maintain the theory of materialistic mechanism, he builds his negative case against the noetic and factual assumptions of this type of thought. On the other hand, he acknowledges a debt of gratitude to Oman for his analysis of human freedom and divine grace in *Grace and Personality*, to Johnson and Broad for their work on the logic of probability and of induction, and to Ward for ideas innumerable.

The Influence of Ward

The greatest single influence upon Tennant is Ward, and through Ward, Kant is the master whose teaching controls major lines of Tennant's work. Ward spent the later years of his life in an extensive study of Kant, the results of which finally appeared in a book to which Tennant acknowledges great indebtedness.[4] Ward naturally approached Kant from the standpoint of his psychology and this same approach dominates Ten-

3. *The Journal of Philosophical Studies*, III, 538.
4. *Philosophical Theology*, I, 93 n., reference to Ward, *A Study of Kant*.

nant, though it must be fairly said that Tennant's own Kantian study is more extensive than Ward's. The writer is not aware of any published attempt on Ward's part to work out the epistemological aspects of his psychology in Kantian terms. This Tennant does in terms of a "causal," or "creational," conception of the relation of noumena to phenomena which is also stated in Wardian terms of "appearance-of-noumena-to-a-subject."

Perhaps the major attitude which Ward and Tennant bring to bear upon Kant is an emphasis upon continuity where Kant stressed disparity in the knowledge processes. Kant separates sense from understanding and understanding from reason. Ward's supreme psychological motive was that of tracing the continuous evolution of conscious processes from lowest to the highest without any break or disparateness. So great was the idea of continuity in Ward's thinking that one of his ablest disciples[5] claims that he failed to recognize the disparity between thought and sense processes and is not entitled to derive time-consciousness (eventually thought) from change in the sensory-motor continuum (a sense process). Whether this is true or not, it serves to bring out the fact that Ward was dominated by the desire to trace continuity in psychological powers and tended to derive the higher forms from the lower forms with possible neglect of disparateness. This same tendency is manifest in Tennant. Tennant too is controlled by the idea of continuity as against separation of psychological processes and Tennant too emphasizes the relation and derivation of the higher form to the lower. This constitutes his empirical standpoint which he admittedly pushes with greater rigor and consistency than Ward all the way through the various mental activities.

Points of Agreement

It is illuminating to draw up a list of the points of agreement and disagreement between Tennant and Ward, attempting at the same time to orient the list by reference to Kant:

1. Tennant agrees with Ward in psychological method. Both

---

5. Stout, *Studies in Philosophy and Psychology*, pp. 109–114. Stout's criticism is that Ward cannot derive the particularized thought of a definite past, present, and future time—*a, b, c*—from the sensing of presentations in continuous flow. Some transcendent consciousness is required to cut this sensory flow into *a, b, c.*

employ genetic and analytic techniques as opposed to Kant who analyzed developed consciousness to discover the preconditioning factors which must be operative if there is to be experience at all.

2. Tennant agrees with Ward in his psychological analysis of the genesis and the development of sensation, perception, and the operation of intersubjective intercourse in the development of the categories which constitute our knowledge of public Objects. This is opposed to Kant in several ways: (a) Kant was unaware of the function of intersubjective intercourse in the development of the categories. This lack of social psychology betrayed him into supposing that the categories are universal and necessary in some independent sense rather than in the qualified sense of universal among, and necessary to, minds embodied in human organisms and oriented by communication dependent upon and limited by organisms. (b) Kant was unprepared to admit that the formal categories arise from a direct "reading off" of relations which are given with and in the experience of sensa. He was likewise unmindful of the derivation of the categories of substance and of cause from direct experience of the embodied self and its implicit ejection into the data of sense. Because of his inadequate psychology he came to the idealistic conclusion that mind creates the relations in nature whereas these relations are only made by mind out of that which is created by objective reality.

3. Tennant agrees with Ward in his doctrine of the existence of the pure ego, the argument for which is worked out by Tennant in complete acceptance of Ward's *Study of Kant*. Ward supported the thesis that Kant's *Critique* really points to the subjective deduction of the categories or a psychological justification of their existence in terms of a real noumenal self instead of a logical analysis of the synthetic presuppositions of objects known in developed experience. In this work Ward contended that the pure ego, that unity into which the categories and through the categories all objects are apperceptively bound, is a reality and not a logical form. The "pure ego does not know itself through the categories but knows the categories and through the categories objects in the transcendental unity of apperception." That this is one important interpretation of

Kant there is no question, but that it is Kant's own interpretation or that it is the only interpretation which can be discovered
in Kant's *Critique* is problematical.[6]

4. Tennant agrees with Ward and with Kant that the pure
ego is not an object of direct experience. It is a conceptual object
from the standpoint of the knowledge process. Unlike Ward,
Tennant says that we do have immediate experience of cognitive, emotional, and conative states of consciousness. This is not
sense-experience but it is direct awareness that we are undergoing certain recognizable processes.

5. Tennant follows Ward on the following psychological
topics: memory, ideation, heredity, the subconscious—topics
which do not refer explicitly to Kant.

6. Tennant follows what he believes to be Ward's teaching on
the problem of knowledge with this one major amendment;
namely, Tennant does not think that it is necessary or valid to
deny metaphysical dualism. The metaphysical reality may be
either material or spiritual or both. He prefers to remain agnostic on this point whereas Ward was definitely committed to a
spiritualistic monadism of the Leibnizian type. We shall note
this point of difference under the list of disagreements. For the
present it is important to state the agreement. Both Tennant and
Ward agree in drawing the distinction between o (private object over against the individual subject) and O (common Object
conceptualized as social and read into o) and ω (metaphysical
thing-in-itself). Both interpret o from the standpoint of a denial
of Cartesian dualism. Whereas Descartes believed that the subject is shut up within the closed system of its own ideas and that
these ideas corresponded with metaphysical independent reality
by the operation of God, Ward and Tennant reject this idealism
as an impossible point of departure for either epistemology or
psychology. The o or private psychological object is that-which-

6. An important attempt to support the non-Wardian interpretation of Kant
in this respect is to be found in N. K. Smith's *A Commentary to Kant's Critique
of Pure Reason*, pp. l–lii, 235–239, 263 ff., 272–277, 461–462, 473–477, where it is
maintained that it is wrong to hold that Kant's postulation of synthetic processes
of consciousness means the postulation of a noumenal self. Such is a violation of
critical principles. We do not know what the synthetic processes are underlying
our consciousness of meanings and objects. We know that there are results of
synthetic processes but not that a noumenal self is there. This position represents
the fully critical aspect of Kant's teaching whereas Ward's interpretation is
based upon the semicritical or precritical strain in Kantian thought.

is-over-against-the-subject in the act of knowing; it is not a state of the subject but a metaphysical object appearing to a subject. Kant, of course, would admit a distinction between O (a public Object the sense materials of which come from an unknown cause, the forms of which come from a mind inherently socialized) and ω (a thing-per-se) which is unknown. But Tennant modifies the Kantian position at both points.

7. Tennant follows Ward in principle in his critique of naturalism (materialistic mechanism) and in his critique of pluralism. From the standpoint of psychological and epistemological analysis, science cannot know that metaphysical reality is a system of inert masses operating by impressed forces, hence naturalism is insecure when it poses as metaphysics. From the standpoint of philosophy, pluralism cannot give a sufficient reason for the world's evolutionary development. Neither Ward nor Tennant holds that pluralism is absurd or logically impossible. What they do find difficult in pluralism is that it does not give a ground for the advance from a plurality of elementary monads or entities to the higher entities discovered at the upper end of the evolutionary trend. Thus both Ward and Tennant adopt a concept of creation.

8. Tennant agrees with Ward in his concept of creation. (a) Both agree that it is necessary to complete the deficiencies of pluralism. (b) Both reject the idea of "creation" as the shaping of inert materials already existent and insist that "creation" means that the many derive their existence and continuance from God, being dependent upon God as He is not dependent upon them. (c) Both reject the idea of creation in time and insist that the world and God are coeternal; that the notion of God as existing prior to the world and bringing it into existence at a moment of time is meaningless. God is world-ground and as there can be no world without a ground, there is not to be conceived any ground without a world. This is an ultimate relationship.

9. Both Tennant and Ward maintain the distinction between certitude and certainty—certitude meaning subjective conviction or convincedness and certainty meaning an objective quality of propositions supported by reasons. Hence both insist that the idea of God must be supported by reasons. Though belief in God cannot attain such proof as to make it a logical certainty, it is a belief which is not theoretically worthless. It has some theoretical

value in explaining what pluralism omits. Whatever additional
"probability" it attains is based upon moral grounds and values.
Tennant differs on the matter of moral value as we shall note
presently, but both allow value-elements to constitute a part of
the basis of the reasonableness of theism. This integration of
theoretical and valuational elements Tennant believes to be the
essential outcome of a synthesis of the results of the Kantian
Critiques when seen as a whole.

Points of Difference

It remains to point out the major differences between Tennant and Ward. We shall give the two most important first.

1. Tennant, Ward to the contrary, does not believe that it is
necessary to establish spiritualistic pluralism before theism can
be maintained. Tennant does not believe that there is any way to
determine the exact qualitative nature of the physical world. He
believes that scientific research makes it probable beyond a reasonable doubt that there are metaphysical entities corresponding in some way to the concepts of electrons and atoms. Though
he is not prepared to accept these concepts as final photographs
of reality, he is prepared to say that they point to something real
which cannot be denied. He is prepared to admit that these entities may be spiritual monads of a certain rudimentary type or
they may be characterized by inertia and moved by impressed
forces. He believes that these are structurally patterned to give
rise to qualities known by the subject when the two are *en rapport*. As far as theism is concerned, he finds no sufficient reason
to suppose that a creator who is able to posit spiritual monads is
not also able to posit material particles characterized by inertia.
In any case, it is necessary to remain agnostic on this point at
this stage of knowledge.

2. Tennant disagrees with Ward also upon the matter of
value. He believes that Ward, in his posthumous book, *Psychology Applied to Education*, laid down the view that values,
unlike mathematical forms, are absolute in the sense that they do
not derive their truth from the human mind nor can they be explained by genetic studies. Tennant does not believe in absolute
values. To him moral standards are built psychologically by certain processes of conceptualization or abstractive idealization.
No standard evolved by man is final, completely perfect, or ab-

solute. All are subject to revision and abandonment for higher claims. "There is no eternal prius of truth, in ethics any more than in mathematics, into the realm of which we simply 'enter'; genetic studies at any rate reveal that the entities of which pure sciences are valid, such as the circle whose circumference is $2\pi r$, and the abstract good, are definitions or postulates that would not be forthcoming as ideas, were it not for subjective operations and human interest."[7]

3. Tennant disagrees with Ward upon another theological point. Ward held that mechanism is irreconcilable with teleology but Tennant does not believe this to be the case. A machine can be a mechanism and at the same time fulfill the purpose for which it was made. Tennant maintains that the world as a whole, with its intricate dovetailing of dissimilar and disparate entities so as to produce certain ends, is a mechanism comparable to Paley's watch and yet at the same time is a mechanism which fulfills a purpose, the purpose for which it was made.

4. The last point of difference between Tennant and Ward is this. Tennant maintains that we are directly acquainted with the psychological processes of attention, feeling, and conation whereas Ward contended that these are known by inference only. Tennant agrees with Ward that the pure ego is known by inference; i.e., it is a concept built up to account for certain facts, but the empirical ego is known by acquaintance, not through the senses as other objects are known, to be sure, but experienced nonetheless directly.

Eighteenth-Century Affiliations

Having noted the most important contemporary influences upon Tennant's thought, it is now fitting to note his affiliations in the history of theology and philosophy. Three guiding principles seem to be helpful here: (1) Tennant is unwilling to separate theology and philosophy; hence the history of the theologians and philosophers must be woven together. (2) Tennant is interested in modern philosophy from Descartes to Ward and in modern theology which he believes began with the Deists of the eighteenth century. (3) Within this modern history of philosophical theology, Tennant's outlook coincides with the eighteenth century and opposes the nineteenth. The eighteenth cen-

7. *Philosophical Theology*, I, 160; cf. p. 217.

tury is characterized by an emphasis upon reason and nature; the nineteenth by romanticism, feeling, mysticism, and intuition. Tennant's orientation toward these centuries can be stated in his own words:

Had Butler's suggestion been followed that probability is the guide of life; and had the deistic tenet, that revealed religion presupposes natural religion, not been evaded; the 19th century would have done better than expend much of its theological strenuousness in pursuing blind roads that had the look of short cuts, and eventually, in sheer weariness, beating the tracks of superficial pragmatism and airily nonchalant subjectivism.

If the modern demand is "back to experience," to experience by all means let us go. Genuine empiricism would go nowhere else. But it would go to experience as an unmutilated whole out of which the knowledge process has been fashioned; not to this or that analytical element in it, abstracted from setting or context. Unscared by the breakdown of rationalism, and its professedly logical proofs, empiricism would rely on "reasonableness" which the 18th century confounded with "rationality" and the 19th century, perpetuating the confusion, largely deserted for "irrationalism" that is antithesis to both.[8]

Let us glance at the eighteenth-century situation in philosophical theology as seen through Tennant's eyes. In the background is the Cartesian rationalism with its belief in reason as a *lumen naturale* and its notion of innate, self-evident, logically certified ideas. The first modern theologians were, in Tennant's mind, the Deists who set aside authority (both of Bible and of church) as a test of truth and tried to find evidence in nature and in reason for the basic religious ideas. The Deist applied the method of doubt to religious beliefs, as Descartes did to all ideas, and insisted that they be tested before the bar of reason. In a sense the Deists did not differ from other progressive minds both within and without the church. Liberal theologians and philosophers agreed that religious beliefs should be proved true and that they could be so proved. The Deists were simply more radical than their contemporaries in rejecting all revealed religion. Belief in God precedes belief in Christianity or the Bible, and

8. *Ibid.*, I, 304–305.

because of this, belief in God must be substantiated by evidence and proofs acceptable to reason. Tennant considers Tindal to be the greatest Deist, Toland second. These men were actually rational theists who saw the distinction between causes of belief and objective reasons for belief; between subjective certitude and objective certainty. As to the problem of theology; i.e., the question of the validity of theistic belief—and as to the method; i.e., the rational substantiation thereof, they were correct. Before men ever come to God, they must first believe that He is. But where the Deists erred was in their Cartesian conception of reason as the organ of self-evident, logical truth and in their conviction that a completely rational proof for theism was possible. To destroy these two convictions was the work of Hume.

Even before Hume, however, Locke rejected innate ideas and was far along the way to a conception of probable belief as the actual substitute for a priori ideas. It was Bishop Butler, however, a better Lockean than Locke, who saw that religious belief could be established only on the basis of probability, which he declared to be the "guide of life," and that no complete logical proof was forthcoming. Butler's advice ought to have been followed, but the rational theists believed in proofs and in logical certainty.

Hume led the attack upon the rationalistic conception of reason and upon proofs for the existence of God. When the work of Hume and, later, of Kant upon the shortcomings of the proofs for God's existence was finished, the belief in the provableness of theism was banished from modern philosophy forever. When Hume had finished his criticism of the category of cause, rationalism, as it had developed through Descartes, Spinoza, Leibniz, and Wolff, found itself in serious circumstances. Kant tried to meet the work of Hume preserving the truth in rationalism and the truth in empiricism, but he made the mistake of restoring the category of cause as an a priori form whereas it is anthropically derived and applied to independent reality by postulation. Facts founded upon the category of substance and cause are a matter of probability rather than self-evident certainty, and hence no category of cause is dissimilar to the category of teleology which Kant declared to be regulative. Both are regulative and probable. Thus we arrive at the situation in which we see that all knowledge, even our scientific knowledge of facts or substance-causes, is probable rather than a priori. Theism which is an hypothesis accounting for the nature of the world as a whole cannot be proved in any a priori or logically coercive fashion. Such validation as it can have must be in the realm of probability. But here it is not dissimilar to science. Probability is the common ground of both—". . . certainly one may say that Butler's analogy between natural and revealed religion might be supplemented by an analogy between natural theology and science. For inductive science has its interpretative explanation-principles and its faith elements with which the faith of natural theology is in essence continuous."[9]

Nineteenth-Century Evasions

If this be true, then there is no ground for retreating into irrational and emotional defenses for theism as the nineteenth-century theologians proceeded to do. Thinking that Hume and Kant demolished all intellectual proofs for the existence of God, they attempted to establish the basis for such belief on "immediate religious experience" and upon the valuable results for living which followed the acceptance and practice of theism. Schleiermacher and Ritschl, Coleridge and the Romanticists, Mansel and Maurice, represent those who evaded the truth which the Deists saw; namely, that religious experience depends upon the prior acceptance of the theistic idea (natural theology precedes revealed theology) and if this idea is to be substantiated, it must be substantiated by objective reasons and not asserted on the basis of subjective causes.

Schleiermacher failed to see that the object of the feeling (intuition) of dependence is only a vague Beyond unless it is interpreted by an idea derived and really engendered by philosophical research. Immediate experience of a vague Something is not an experience of God at all until God or theism is "read into" the experience. If the theistic idea is "read into" this experience, then the problem arises—is it veridical? Such a question can be answered only by considering objective public reasons for accepting it as veridical. The Deists perceived this but they did not understand the nature of reason and of the sort of proof which is open to human minds. Hume not only destroyed the idea of

9. *Philosophy of the Sciences,* p. 185.

logically coercive proofs, but he destroyed the whole rationalistic conception of reason, fact, and natural law as well. Kant's rationalism is demolished by modern genetic and social psychology. There is no need to be frightened out of a reasoned defense of theism simply because the rationalistic conception of reason and proof has had to be abandoned. A factual conception of reason and of probability to which we are actually entitled will restore the type of validation we must have and can have. Once theism is found to be "reasonably probable" Schleiermacher's interpretation of the vague Beyond is justified.

Another type of evasion of this fundamental truth is to be seen in Ritschl's theory of value-judgments and the whole pragmatic type of theology which sets forth the theory that if a theological idea has the power to promote spiritual life; i.e., if it is valuable, it is therefore true. It is a fact of common experience that multitudes of ideas which promote spiritual life do not correspond with anything actual in reality. Imaginary objects are fully as potent as actual objects in producing valuable results. It is necessary, therefore, to find reasonable evidence that the object of religious grace is an existential object and not a pure idea. This is the problem and task of the Deists over again. If we can first "prove" the object of religion veridical, we are assured that an object which is valuable for life is first and foremost objectively real.

Evasions of these two types pervade the entire thinking of the nineteenth century and betray it into religious subjectivism. Our problem now is to face the problem of the eighteenth century with a conception of reason and of proof which modern psychology permits. The nineteenth century was motivated by a sound sense of the impossibility of the rationalistic conception of reason and of a priori proofs. But "proofs" there are such as the argument from design which even Hume and Kant could not but respect in practical life.

Affinity with Butler, Paley, and Locke

Tennant is temperamentally akin to Butler. Both are characterized by that "sweet reasonableness" which pervades a common-sense point of view. On the whole, theism is probably true. The world is the theater of the moral life and, on the whole, good is sustained in the long run whereas evil is self-destructive. A quiet optimism sweeps through the thought of both men who are convinced that all things taken as a whole work together for good. The point at which Tennant and Butler disagree is this. Butler is what Broad calls a nonnaturalist in ethics, and Tennant is a naturalist. Butler believed conscience to be the voice of God, an objective demand of reality, whereas Tennant defines value in terms of social psychology and complexity of psychological processes.

In another respect, Tennant is comparable to Paley whose evidences for natural theology influenced Cambridge thinking in the latter part of the eighteenth century. Tennant believes that Paley was mistaken in his effort to liken every particular adaptation in nature to purposive design on the part of the creator. Paley was unaware of the Darwinian theory of natural selection. But in spite of all of Paley's defects, Tennant maintains that the world-as-a-whole is a mechanism comparable to Paley's watch and is legitimately conceivable as the result of external design.

From the standpoint of method, Tennant attacks the problem of knowledge from an essentially Lockean standpoint; i.e., an enquiry into the origin and development of ideas. From the standpoint of metaphysics, Tennant leans toward a pluralism of the Leibnizian–Lotzean type. He differs from Leibniz on the matter of creation in time, and a prius of law and of possibilities in the mind of God. He does believe that the principle of contradiction must hold for God as well as for man but beyond that he finds no meaning to a prius of law or of possibilities. Law and possibilities are discoverable only in reference to the actual world; hence the actual determines them and not vice versa. The actual basis of the actual lies in the divine will. It is God who determines the actual, and there is no prius of law or of possibility independent of God and determining Him. Tennant thus follows Lotze rather than Leibniz because it is only upon an ontology comparable to Lotze's[10] that the problem of evil can be handled. If the Leibnizian prius of law be admitted, evil has its source in a principle which is independent of God as well as independent of man's will. Evil is traced to metaphysical evil and moral evil is in reality given up (pp. 46–48). An ontology is

10. Cf. *The Origin and Propagation of Sin*, pp. 46–48, 62, 67, 128–129.

needed which is intermediate between Leibnizian pluralism and various kinds of pantheistic monism; between Herbartian realism and absolute idealism (p. 128). Such a system is offered by Lotze who makes place for real selfhood, for the reality of God as a ground which embraces the many and yet is distinguished from the many, for the reality of evil, and for the goodness of God. Thus it becomes evident that Tennant's mind approaches metaphysics with the results of his consideration of the problem of sin and evil in the background.

This brief statement discloses the affiliations of Tennant in the history of modern philosophy and theology. His thinking revolves about the men we have mentioned and this is important, for it tells us as much by omission as by affirmation. Ancient philosophy, Hegel, much of contemporary psychology and philosophy, is conspicuous by its absence or inadequate treatment. Needless to say, however, his work, in the judgment of some, is the ablest presentation of natural theology since Butler. If there is error in it, it is not because he has avoided the most difficult and critical analysis of those grounds upon which naturalism and antitheistic theories are based. He has given reason to men of antitheistic bias for the faith which he holds to be reasonable without any attempt to short-cut this difficult procedure by arguing from values or immediate religious experience or pragmatism alone. He has stated a position with clarity and precision. It may need modification, but no little credit must be given for a statement of this position which is rigorous and unconfused.

CHAPTER I

GENERAL EXPOSITION OF TENNANT'S PROBLEM AND HIS ANSWER

The Problem: The Validity of Theistic Belief

IN order to understand the major problem with which F. R. Tennant repeatedly wrestles throughout his published works,[1] it will be well to permit Tennant to speak for himself.

The central problem of faith, [he writes, in an essay on the famous "faith" chapter (chap. xi) in the Book of Hebrews,[2]] the problem which at times may press upon any believer and provide trial for his faith is the question whether we can justify to our reason this leap from what we deem the *terra firma* of knowledge into hope, trust, or belief, as to what we do not know and cannot rigidly prove. . . . However, the power of a great belief, once it is held with unquestioning conviction, to produce strenuous activity or spiritual endeavor is one thing; and the correspondence of the same belief with external reality or fact is another. Experience now and again enforces this distinction upon us, however ardently some have tried to annul it; for we well know that beliefs such as have proved to be not really true to fact have sometimes inspired men to do and to die. There has always lived in my memory in this connection a ballad describing how a very commonplace young man was transfigured, by his belief in the exalted nobility and purity of his lover, into a hero; yet she turned out to have been all the time a worthless and depraved woman. Spiritual efficacy, then, although a criterion of true religious belief, is by no means so exclusively a characteristic of true belief that we can infallibly or without exception infer the one from the other. None of us doubts that life is more than logic, that reality is richer than thought and unexhausted by knowledge, or that advantages of the highest and noblest kind do actually accrue from believing where we cannot see.

1. I.e., those writings in which Tennant deals with the subjects of religion, religious experience, faith, theology, etc., and not with the subject of "sin" and books or reviews on irrelevant topics.
2. *The Expository Times*, XXXII, 562–563.

But our faith will perhaps still be liable to be beset with a certain shrinking fearfulness unless we can further justify to ourselves the reasonableness of its venture or assure ourselves as to the clairvoyance of blind hope.

Again and again throughout Tennant's published works this problem is presented in a variety of forms. It is an oft-repeated theme in variations. Spiritual efficacy is not by itself a criterion of truth in religious belief; by itself it cannot verify the actuality of its supposed actual divine source or cause.[3] To assert that spiritual efficacy is sufficient to verify the supposed actuality of the divine object is to confuse the subjective state of certitude (that the idea of God corresponds with the actuality of God) with objective reasonable (common) grounds for such correspondence; the "psychic" (i.e., psychological) with the "psychological" (i.e., epistemological) ; causes with grounds; a criterion of good faith with the criterion of truth. Failure to perceive these distinctions is in Tennant's judgment an important weakness in much modern theology. In fact, the scorn of Ritschl for metaphysics and tendencies fostered by Schleiermacher and James to restrict theology to the psychology of religious experi-

3. See representative statements:
  (a) *The Journal of Theological Studies*, XVII, 207.
  (b) *Philosophical Theology*, I, 297–302.
  (c) *Philosophy of the Sciences*, p. 178. "Theological pragmatism is summed up in such a statement as that a religion under the influence of which a genuine spiritual life has flourished cannot be simply false. Now a highly developed religion is a complex thing and usually comprises ethics as well as theological or metaphysical doctrine. And inasmuch as the phrase 'spiritual life' includes ethical goodness, a religion may promote spiritual life in virtue of its purely ethical teaching. But when we speak of a religion as true, we generally mean true as to its dogma. Its ethics may be lofty, and may be moulded by worthy doctrinal ideas, and yet those ideas may conceivably have no counterpart in actuality. It must not be ignored that a person's convincedness as to the truth of a dogma is a sufficient condition of its efficacy in ministering to his spiritual life, and that the truth of the credendum is then a superfluous condition. The credendum may conceivably be ungrounded or even false. At any rate we must not confound a credendum with belief in it, nor read the causal agency involved in the promotion of spiritual life into the object believed in, without asking whether that agency may not be located in the experient's believing. Until the latter explanation is proved impossible or inadequate we have no right to assume the former to be dictated by the facts of experience.
  (d) *Mind*, XL, 93–97. Critique of Pringle-Pattison for accepting pragmatist theory of truth with respect to assertion of actuality of religious object on basis of an appeal to spiritual efficacy without prior reasonable justification.

ence is in Tennant's judgment perilously close to the Scotist reversion from Thomas and to the paradoxical state of decadent Scholasticism—shown in the doctrine of the twofold truth.[4] In the modern world, the criteria of verifiability (i.e., valid of actuality) and consistency have been exalted to the highest place,[5] and theology cannot afford to rest content with any type of verification which fails to come to terms with common reasonableness.

Conception of Religion

These statements are best clarified for further discussion by regarding Tennant's conception of "religion"[6] and of "religious experience."[7] Religion, in Tennant's work, is defined as a complex mental attitude of the whole personality to supposedly actual superhuman (personal) beings or powers involving: (a) a cognitive factor; i.e., an idea of divine power, varying from the crude notions of primitive man to the refined concept of ethical theism of modern man; (b) an emotional factor; i.e., a complex feeling response of loyalty and love, awe and adoration, etc., to the object apprehended by cognition; and (c) a volitional factor; i.e., a practical reaction to the object in terms of conduct.

Religious experience may with justice to Tennant's position be defined in some such statement as this:[8] experience which consists in a complex emotional and practical response to a superhuman (personal) object—known through interpreted-sense-data presented by the world, man, and human history to the knowing subject—is religious experience. Thus to Tennant experience is constituted religious when it is conceived as coming from a superhuman personal object in response to which emotional and practical reactions occur. From the standpoint of emotion, there is no peculiar emotion which is *sui generis* religious. Emotion is made

4. *Philosophy of the Sciences,* pp. 166–167.
5. *Ibid.,* p. 120.
6. "The Aim and Scope of the Philosophy of Religion: The Connotation of Religion," *The Expositor,* 8th ser., VI, 342–357.
7. "Theology," *Encyclopaedia Britannica* (14th ed.), XXII, 61–62; also cf. *Philosophical Theology,* Vol. I, chap. xii; *Philosophy of the Sciences,* Lecture VI; *The Journal of Theological Studies,* XIII, 312, XVI, 122, XVII, 203–209, XXIII, 204, XXXV, 401; *Mind,* XL, 93–97.
8. The writer is unable to quote a specific definition of religious experience from the sources.

religious emotion by virtue of the object which evokes it. The emotions of loyalty, love, adoration, awe, mystery, dependence are essentially similar as emotions whether they are evoked by a human object or a divine object. Love to man is no different insofar as feeling is concerned from love to God. But in the former case love is human whereas, in the latter case, love is religious. The feeling of mystery before a thunderstorm cannot be distinguished as feeling from the feeling of mystery before God; what constitutes the latter as religious is the divine object. This insistence upon the determination of the quality of the emotional and practical elements in religious experience by reference to the (religious) idea of God is of far-reaching importance for Tennant. It means that ancestor worship and animism are not to be designated by the term "religion." Reverence for dead ancestors is not different from reverence to living ancestors; in both cases the object of reverence is human and not divine. Likewise, a natural object which is regarded as being indwelt by souls of some sort is not to be called a religious object until these indwelling powers are regarded as gods (p. 347).[9] It means that Matthew Arnold's "morality touched with emotion," Spinoza's intellectual contemplation of nature (pp. 345–346, 354), "cosmic feeling" evoked by the whole universe (pp. 354, 357), and "religion without a personal object" (p. 356) cannot be honored with the term "religion" but solely as a widely prevalent "philosophy of life" (p. 355). It means that a certain common statement; i.e., the statement that theology presupposes religious experience and is the explication of it, is based on misapprehension. Tennant points out that this statement is a matter of one's starting point.[10] The theology and religious experience of Paul the Christian presuppose Christian experience, but the religious experience of Paul the Christian differs from the religious experience of Paul the Pharisee by virtue of the acquisition of the Christian religious idea. From the standpoint of genetic psychology no experience is religious until the idea of a divine object is acquired. In this sense theology precedes religious experience. Once experience which can be called religious is acquired then religious

9. All the page references in this paragraph are from *The Expositor*, 8th ser., VI.

10. See article "Theology" in *Encyclopaedia Britannica* (14th ed.), XXII, 62.

experience may enrich theology, and such enriched theology may be said to presuppose religious experience. Some such situation, Tennant suggests, holds true of historical origins; i.e., some crude notion of God must have preceded the experience of God. In this sense the idea that natural theology precedes natural religion has a basis in history. Tennant believes that there is as much truth in the statement that theological doctrine determines the quality of religious experience as there is in the statement that religious experience is presupposed by theology.[11]

One of the severest applications of this principle to a specific theological discussion appears in Tennant's critical review of Spens's *Belief and Practice*. Spens contends—and Tennant believes rightly contends—that Christian doctrine brings into being the Christian (religious) experience; but having said this, Spens then argues for the truth of the Christian doctrine (of God, in particular) on the ground that it is the explication of the Christian religious experience. It is Tennant's criticism that Spens cannot have it both ways; that when he thus argues, he assumes what needs to be proved—the truth of the doctrine which gives rise to the experience. Spens tries to substantiate his statement that this doctrine is the best explication of religious experience by appealing to consensus, to numbers of people in different points of place and time, who find that this doctrine does best explain their religious experience, but Tennant counters with the reply that the multiplication of cases does not refute the point he has made; namely, that such argument begs the question to be proved.

In the association of this insistence that the idea of God determines religious experience with the common belief of philosophical and genetic psychology that all knowledge of actuality, whether of the world, man, or God, arises in the sensorily perceptual[12]—the reasons for which belief will be presently given— Tennant finds his reasons for asserting that the idea of God arises as overbelief derived from perceptual contact with the world, man, and human history, and that such justification as it may receive must come from philosophical theology. He points

11. *Encyclopaedia Britannica* (14th ed.), XXII, 62, col. 2.
12. This phrase is understood to include "introspective" perceptual or fundamental acquaintance with elements of "consciousness."

out that in primitive stages of religion the supernatural object seems to have lodged in a natural object or phenomenon which inspired emotions and evoked worship.[13] Though Tennant does not rest his case upon speculation as to origins, he does make this suggestion as to primitive religion in conjunction with his sustained insistence that the idea of God, by which experience which is as yet "atheous"[14] is constituted religious, must from the general epistemological point of view be derived from the perceptual world. In this event natural religion or natural religious experience is the only type of religious experience which modern man can philosophically and reasonably justify as having a measure of "objective certainty." It is for this reason that Tennant insists that natural religion, or natural religious experience such as Christians may acquire today, precedes revealed religion, or such religious experience as was open only to special individuals of a former day, and that philosophical theology—such as examines the truth-claim of religious belief on basis of the common results of psychogenetic analysis of cognition—must precede revealed or dogmatic theology or that system of sciences which comprises the positive element in the philosophy of religion.

Conception of the Philosophy of Religion

Tennant's definition and analysis of "philosophy of religion," "positive philosophy of religion," "theology" (theology in general—"revealed," "dogmatic," "natural," and "philosophical" theology in particular), and "general philosophy" (its relation to theology and the sciences)[15] need to be made explicit. Tennant diagrams the situation as follows:

13. *Encyclopaedia Britannica* (14th ed.), XXII, 62.
14. Tennant says that the psychological analysis of experience proceeds without reference to a theistic object, and that such theistic inferences are drawn as are necessary to account for certain facts. In its procedure psychology is not "atheistic" but "atheous" with respect to assumption; i.e., it does not deny theism but simply suspends interpretation.
15. Sources: "The Philosophy of Religion as an Autonomous Subject," *The Expositor*, 8th ser., VI, 250 ff.; also in same issue: "The Services of Philosophy to Theology" and "The Aim and Scope of the Philosophy of Religion." "Theology" in *Encyclopaedia Britannica* (14th ed.), XXII, 61–66.
Book: *Philosophy of the Sciences.*
Review: "Studies in Philosophy of Religion," by Pringle-Pattison in *Mind*, XL, 93–97.

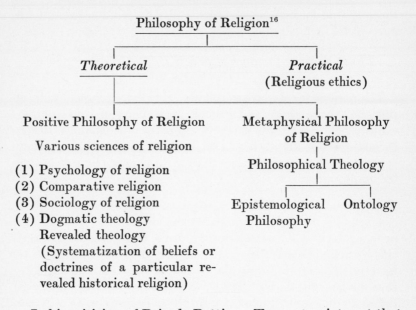

In his criticism of Pringle-Pattison, Tennant points out that the term "philosophy of religion" is used in several senses: (a) it may be used to designate the positive sciences of religion and their systematization into a body of data; (b) it may be used to designate the further attempt to examine the truth-claim of the beliefs presented by a coördinated body of religious doctrine, varying from the assemblage of doctrine of one revealed religion to the coördination of the doctrine of several such historical religions, but in so doing to make no attempt to examine that truth-claim in relation to general philosophy and to such epistemological considerations as general philosophy requires; (c) finally, it may be used to examine the truth-claim of religious doctrine by reference solely to such validation as general philosophy requires. It is in this last sense that Tennant believes the term "philosophy of religion" should be used and, to insure against misunderstanding, he has replaced it with the term[17] "philosophical theology" or philosophy of theology, i.e., "general philosophy" dealing with the truth-claim of theology, particularly "natural

16. The writer has amended Tennant's original diagram in *The Expositor*, VI, 263, in light of all source material; i.e., Point (4) under "Positive Philosophy of Religion" has been added.

17. See *Mind*, XL, 93–97.

theology" or doctrine which is controlled by relation to empirical perceptual fact.

Three Reasons for an Empirical Type of Philosophical Theology

His reasons for this are as follows: 1. Epistemological philosophy, i.e., the analytic and genetic psychology of cognition, establishes the fact that, as far as general epistemology is concerned, the sole known firsthand, original, underived immediate contact which man has with actuality is the sensorily perceptual. Tennant writes:[18]

The profane sciences . . . possess one broad characteristic in common. Their original matter, or the objective nucleus of their primary data, is the sensorily perceptual. Our percepts and their simpler religions are the sources of our ideas and universals, at least in the sense of being the occasions of our obtaining them, though once thus derived, ideas can be related without further recourse to the sensory, so as to yield the pure sciences. It is by percepts in the first instance, and then by other objects derived from or by means of them, that feeling and valuing are evoked, so that appreciation as well as cognition, and consequently the sciences of valuation, such as ethics, ultimately presuppose sensory data. Again, sense-givenness is the sole original certificate of actuality; and it is the perceptual that gives our first, our most direct, if phenomenal, touch with the real that underlies the phenomenal. If all knowledge is thus ultimately conditioned on its objective side, by sensation, it follows theology must be an outgrowth from ordinary knowledge of the world and man.

2. The second reason which Tennant gives for his argument that philosophical theology must be controlled by the sensorily perceptual and that alone, is that such experience data as are said to be original, firsthand, underived, immediate contacts with nonsensorily perceptual divine reality cannot be "proven" to be of the same order of underivedness as the sensorily given; i.e., such unique data do not appear to be of the same order of underivedness in the light of the common experience of mankind.

This is in turn supported by several reasons. (a) The "numi-

18. *Philosophy of the Sciences,* pp. 167–168.

nous presence" or specific religious quality which always pervades some visible object, which evokes a peculiar type of response, and which is said to be as clearly distinguishable as a sense-object or quality is actually vague and devoid of immediately perceived quality. Tennant says that the numinous seems to be an "agency" more analogous to Kant's "things per se," the pure ego, or to the physicist's "electrons," than to the specifically designated *qualia* of colored surfaces. The pure ego, Tennant maintains, is not known with immediacy; it has no immediately perceived quality. The *numinous* is in the same category and therefore "it is not easy to conceive of acquaintance with actual 'terms' as distinct from relations which is not correlative with presentation of some specific quality."[19]

(*b*) Moreover, if this consideration is not sufficient to indicate that so-called religious data are not as specifically discerned as sense-qualities, then Tennant holds that another is sufficient. Either all the divine powers discerned by all religions, from crude nature mythologies to advanced monotheism, are real, or the divine power has selectively indwelt many objects. If the former is true, theology is refuted, and if the latter be true, theology must admit that progress in religion has been made by successive refusals to regard various objects as indwelt by divine power. The religious object is so vague and lacking in specific quality that it can figure in all kinds of mythology and theology and in all sorts of experience, normal and mystical; it is more like a vague notion or concept of a Beyond than like a specific sense-quality.

(*c*) Furthermore, such immediate contacts cannot be readily conceptualized into common Objects as can the *idia* of sense-perception. The experience remains exclusive and private.

(*d*) Again, mysticism and intuitionist theology, both of which assert the immediacy of religious experience, fail to distinguish between immediacy of the psychic (psychological) and of the epistemological (reflective) type. From the psychic standpoint, experience of any type of object—actual, imaginal, conceptual—may be immediate and direct. But if such experience is ex-

19. *Ibid.*, p. 171. Note: Throughout this presentation the source from which this material is drawn is Tennant's latest discussion of religious experience in *Philosophy of the Sciences*, pp. 168–178.

amined reflectively and analytically after it is past, as genetic psychology sets out to do, it will be seen that the only immediate experience is the private individual's contact with an undefined sensorily presented continuum. Experience beyond this primary contact is progressively mediate; i.e., it progressively involves an increasingly complex element of imaginative synthesis of which the experient is unconscious when he affirms that he is having immediate experience of even complex perceptual objects.

All known objects beyond certain elementary perceptual contacts are ventures of what Tennant calls "anthropic analogising"[20] or interpretation of the seen by categories of the unseen, faith-ventures in interpretation of aspects immediately "read off" from actuality in perception. The religious object from the standpoint of analytic psychology is a conceptual interpretation "read in" to other conceptually complex data which are grounded in the immediately perceptual. God as an actuality is not immediately apprehended as a color is apprehended, but through a complex, mediate, interpretative synthesis of elements which are "read in" to the fundamental perceptual facts. From the standpoint of genetic psychology, the conceptions of theology are metaphysical conceptions which contain more complex ideational synthesis than the sciences, and even the sciences contain complex interpretative elements which are ventures beyond the immediate and hence do not permit science to parade in the uniform of realistic metaphysics.

"What is called God-consciousness," writes Tennant,[21] "must . . . be, like self-consciousness, an indirectly and reflectively acquired, and interpretative, kind of knowledge or belief." Hence theologians have no reasonable right to assert that they have immediate experience of God and employ as verification of this assertion the evidence of spiritual efficacy. Spiritual efficacy might be the result of ideal ethical factors in the conceptual complex which are involved in the concept of God, or it might be the outcome of pure certitude or convincedness on the part of the experient. Psychologically the religious man does experience God whom he believes to be real, and actually he may be en rapport with a real being, but inasmuch as this real being is known

20. For the meaning of "anthropic" see footnote p. 74, below.
21. *Philosophy of the Sciences,* p. 174.

only through a concept, it is necessary to give a reason for the relevance of the concept of God to the less complex concepts which are grounded in the perceptual, which in turn is known to be nonconceptual and actual. In this way the concept of God is indubitably shown to refer to the actual; religious experience is delivered of subjectivity, and its concept is "proven" to correspond to an actual reality on grounds other than spiritual efficacy. Such grounds will be a matter of "probability" rather than "certainty," but "probability" is an objective quality of the truth of propositions and not solely a subjective state of psychological convincedness. The criterion of truth is distinguished from the criterion of good faith, and philosophical theology which accepts a genuinely, profanely secular empiricism stands ready to confront the scientifically educated believer.

(e) Lastly, both intuitionalist and mystical theology appeal to a specific cognitive faculty by means of which the religious object is perceived.[22] Analytic and genetic psychology does not find any such unique faculty in the case of the milder type of religious experience, and in the case of mysticism, it is unable to distinguish this higher faculty of cognition from the subliminal functionings of the mind. Anesthetics and hypnosis both produce cosmic consciousness and metaphysical revelations. No antecedent reason is available to distinguish the latter revelations as illusory and the former as veridical. Certainly no weight can be given to the assertion of special faculty.

3. This leads to the third reason for standing by a perceptually grounded, empirical philosophical theology—namely, its apologetic value. Tennant says that a religious apologetic which endeavors to proceed on any less common[23] grounds then these is offering a statement of what is very interesting as personal biography but is unconvincing to those who do not share the apologist's faith. Such is the sharply critical comment which Tennant makes of Bishop Temple's book,[24] *Nature, Man, and God*, in which Temple states that for many of his conclusions he can give

22. *Philosophical Theology*, I, pp. 309, 323–324.
23. In *ibid.*, p. 316, Tennant points out that the mystic datum, which the mystic claims to be as immediately perceived as sense-data, is unlike sense-data because it cannot be conceptualized into common objects.
24. *The Journal of Theological Studies*, XXXVI, 316.

no conscious reasons. Tennant says that this is very interesting as personal biography but will not convince the "unfaithful." Tennant expresses deep concern for the fact that circles of educated people are alienated from the church and religious faith. Because much of the doctrinal teaching of the church cannot be assimilated by the modern mind; because "everywhere the suspicion is abroad that religious faith starts somewhere in the air and is wholly distinct, not only in degree but also in kind, from knowledge"; because the main tenets of religious belief are not interpreted in such a way as to be shown reasonable, but rather are claimed to be derived from specific emotions or instincts, or from nonreasonable, immediate, religious experience, the free thinker is led silently to ignore the truth of religious tenets, and the church's ministration comes to be concerned with the half-educated.[25] It is the office of "philosophical theology," says Tennant, "to interpret to reason the contents of religious experience"; "to show how the fundamental ideas of religion, so far from being contrary to reason, are capable of receiving rational justification in terms of philosophical principles"[26] (pp. 145–146); to translate the inadequate common-sense language of religious doctrine into language philosophically (and scientifically) adequate to express it (p. 147); to reveal the relationship of faith to knowledge (p. 148); and to indicate as accurately as possible the true nature of reasonable belief. If this is done, philosophical theology may serve apologetic purposes of the first order not only to the "unconverted" but to those of the "faithful" whose "faith will perhaps still be liable to be beset with a certain shrinking fearfulness unless 'we' can justify to 'ourselves' the reasonableness of its venture."[27] It is such "shrinking fearfulness" on the part of Tennant himself which doubtless motivates his drastic rejection of the "proof" value of mysticism and of experience *sui generis* religious, a fact which according to Canon Raven is wholesome as a reaction against a theology preoccupied with the witness of the irrational but which in Tennant's case amounts to a "prejudice."[28] Perhaps it amounts to a

25. *The Expositor,* 8th ser., VI, 150; 9th ser., II, 116; and *The Journal of Theological Studies,* XXVI, 301.
26. The references in this sentence are to *The Expositor,* 8th ser., VI.
27. Cf. quotation cited on p. 17.
28. Raven, *Jesus and the Gospel of Love,* pp. 65–66; also, see *Philosophical*

delicate sensitivity to the "suspicions" of the critically severe. In any event, Tennant sets out to ground his religious ideas in reasons which are set forth on the basis of facts and principles which are open to the inspection of any critically competent mind. Reason, to Tennant as to the Deists—though Tennant's understanding of reason differs from that of the Deists—is to be the sole instrument for the acquisition, appropriation, and judging of truth in religion as in any other field of thought.[29] No specialized religious experience is required of the reasonable mind to whom the apologia of philosophical theology is to be rendered other than the common, generalized, conceptualized experience of nature (inclusive of the onta of the world, man, and the common values of rationality, beauty, and morality). The truth of theism is dependent upon philosophical arguments and must be first established upon grounds of common reasonableness.

The Solution: Two General Channels of Demonstration

It remains now to present the lines along which such an apologia is to proceed. Such demonstration as Tennant offers advances in two general channels: (1) a demonstration of the essential continuity (from the reflective, psychogenetic, and analytic standpoint) of the faith-element in scientific "knowledge" and religious belief;[30] (2) the establishment of such objective reasonable probability as is necessary to "prove" to a reasonably critical observer the superiority of theism to other world-explanations on the basis of the principle that the world needs a sufficient reason for being what it is.[31] The former is a matter of analyzing the nature of knowledge and faith respectively as cognitive processes and the relation of knowledge to reality. The latter is a matter of facing the problem of verification in philosophical theology.

Theology, I, 315 n., in which Tennant says that his discussion of the epistemological import of mysticism is not vitiated by lack of sympathy and relevant knowledge.

29. *The Expositor,* 9th ser., II, 119.

30. *Philosophical Theology*, II, 250. Note Tennant's reëmphasis of the fact that demonstration of the reasonableness of religious belief consists in showing continuity of faith in science and theology.

31. See below, p. 78.

I. THE DEMONSTRATION OF THE FAITH-ELEMENT IN SCIENTIFIC KNOWLEDGE AND ITS CONTINUITY WITH META-PHYSICAL AND RELIGIOUS FAITH

The demonstration of the faith-element in science is exceedingly important in Tennant's system of thought. In the first place, negatively, it is considered as necessary to combat the uncritical and highly dogmatic assertions of the positivistic science out of which antitheistic tendencies spring; and, secondly, and positively, it is necessary to indicate in what way science leads up to and needs, and is continuous with, the particular faith-venture which is theological belief. The negative phase is as important as the positive phase to Tennant, for if science is permitted to proceed apart from the higher criticism of philosophy, not only is theology debarred from the intellectual stage, but the relations of the sciences to each other are hopelessly obscured and confused. We shall indicate (A) the negative aspect first and (B) the positive aspect second.[32]

A. NEGATIVE CRITIQUE OF THE POSITIVIST'S CONCEPTION OF SCIENTIFIC KNOWLEDGE

Tennant's entire life has been concerned with the implications of science. In 1904, when James Ward was crossing swords with naturalism and insisting that not until an idealistic or spiritualistic metaphysics had been established could theism be maintained, Tennant wrote his essay, "The Being of God in the Light of Physical Science,"[33] in which he too stated:

If theology argue with science on the tacit assumption that the theory of knowledge adopted by science is adequate for purposes other than those of practical life, theology will find it hard to worst its opponent. It is only by refusing to open the debate until the realistic has been exchanged for the idealistic standpoint, that theism can entertain the prospect of ultimate success. It is precisely in repudiating the epistemological presuppositions of sci-

32. See below, p. 60.
33. *Cambridge Theological Essays*, pp. 56–99.

ence that theology disarms her opponent and makes herself invulnerable.[34]

. . . Reflection (epistemological) on the results of science leads us to an idealistic conception of the universe. The step from such spiritualism or idealism to theism is still, indeed, a step; but in the light of other considerations it is relatively an easy one.[35]

This extreme demand for an idealistic metaphysics as the only approach to the establishment of theism Tennant came to relinquish. In 1918, he stated definitely that spiritualism is not the *sine qua non* for theism, that God might be conceived as the creator of matter (atoms characterized by inertia) as well as of monads and minds, and that the only realistic metaphysics which could not be allowed is mechanistic materialism.[36] This position he has maintained consistently since then in *Philosophical Theology* and in *Philosophy of the Sciences*. He is admittedly agnostic with respect to the qualitative nature of the ultimate metaphysical plurality which comprises the physical universe. Either lifeless atoms characterized by inertia or living monads there may be, but that these units are inert particles acting under mechanistic uniformity to the exclusion of living things, souls, teleology, and God, that he is concerned to deny with reasons. With empirical science as science he has no quarrel; in fact, he offers it his intense devotion; but with uncriticized empirical science masquerading as certain and positive knowledge, and with dogmatic theoretical science dictating *ex cathedra* a materialistic world-view as the ultimatum of science, he does have a combat which is determined and severe.

It will be best to quote his own caricature of the type of scientific attitude he is concerned to demolish, an attitude which he says characterized the ablest representatives of science a few decades ago and still persists in some quarters today:

Before science entered upon its recent course of self-examination, and before what has been called "the idealistic reaction against science" set in, the representatives of science were imbued with the naive assurance of the positivist. Science was regarded as a body

34. *Ibid.*, pp. 85–86.   35. *Ibid.*, p. 86.
36. "The New Realism and Its Bearing on Theism," *The Constructive Quarterly*, VI, 57 ff.

of knowledge based on observed facts or data, enriched by deductions rendered possible by the application of mathematics and possessing all the unconditional certainty or necessity which belongs to the pure sciences such as mathematics; a body of knowledge involving no taint of metaphysical speculation, no presuppositions, no unclear or treacherous categories, and always capable, unlike other kinds of so-called knowledge, of verification by appeal to direct sense-experience. As against such knowledge pure and undefiled, commanding and coercing universal consent, and wholly independent of all such subjectivity as characterizes individual opinion or human interests, stood the realm of "possible knowledge" awaiting invasion and annexation by further application of the method of positive science; and distinguished sharply from both of these, the dreamland of the unknowable, of nescience, in which metaphysic and theology were left free to expatiate fatuously and with futility.[37]

The assumptions of such positivism Tennant challenges by aligning his criticism with the work of two types of thinkers: the logicians, Johnson, Broad, Keynes on the problems of induction, uniformity of nature and probability; and the psychologists, Ward and Kant (interpreted along psychological lines) on the problem of knowledge and mind.

(1) Criticisms Based upon the Logician's Analyses of Induction and Probability

With the logicians,[38] Tennant argues that the generalizations which science draws from experienced facts are neither certain nor self-evident but rather probable and postulatory.[39]

---

37. "The Present Relations of Science and Theology: (I) The Theological Bearings of Empirical Science," *The Constructive Quarterly,* IX, 580.

38. Concerning the results of these "investigations of the indemonstrable metaphysical beliefs presupposed in the whole inductive method of science," Tennant says: "To my mind no philosophical work as significant as this for the general question of the relation of theology to science has been produced in our generation. It annihilates the old disjunction—Science is knowledge, religion is faith—and it leaves the agnostic with no more legitimate agnosticism than the theist who holds that 'probability is the guide to life' should confess." *The Journal of Theological Studies,* XXXIV, 401.

39. For textual passages see: (1) "The Being of God in Light of Physical Science," *Cambridge Theological Essays,* pp. 69 ff.; (2) "The Theological Bearings of Empirical Science," *The Constructive Quarterly,* IX, 582–583; (3) *Philosophical Theology,* chap. xi.

Broad has argued [he says] that in this principle, that every event has a cause, several postulates are concealed which assumptions "are neither self-evident nor mutually independent, nor are they capable of complete proof or disproof by experience." They bespeak the assumed existence in nature of a simple ground plan of the material world, which experience has suggested to us, such as that nature is built up of a few "natural kinds," all instances of which are exactly alike and completely permanent. How far experience is from ability to speak with certainty as to exact likeness or complete permanence, does not need pointing out. And the logical position, further to quote Prof. Broad is (a) "that those inductions which we regard as highly probable are so relatively to the belief that we really have got hold of the general groundwork of nature in the region of phenomena under investigation; (b) the evidence for this is never of the nature of a 'knock-down' proof and no numerical probability can be assigned to it. The kind of evidence is that this plan is suggested to us in a rough form by crude experience and that as we investigate nature more and more thoroughly, experience itself suggests ways in which we can state this plan with greater definiteness, and rigor, and at the same time, nature is found to accord with the more rigorous and definite plan better than it did with the crude suggestion of a plan. E.g. we believe we have got very near to the ground plan of the material world in the theory of chemical elements, in the laws of mechanics, and in Maxwell's equations, and it is relative to these beliefs that particular inductions in chemistry, electricity, etc., are practically certain. The certainty of the most certain inductions is thus relative or hypothetical, and the probability of the hypothesis is not of a kind that can be stated numerically."[40]

Tennant's statement of this major position of the Cambridge logicians with respect to the status of scientific induction is presented in *Philosophical Theology* (chap. xi) and with the same[41] object in view; namely, the disclosure of the falsity of the claim of science to absolute certainty and hence to absolute dissimi-

40. "The Theological Bearings of Empirical Science," *The Constructive Quarterly,* IX, 582–583. Tennant quotes from Broad's article in *Mind,* No. 113, p. 44.
41. By "same object" the writer does not mean that the logicians worked with this implicatory objective in view, but that Tennant uses this work with the same objective as he has used it in earlier articles.

larity to theology. It is unnecessary to repeat this argument here.[42] What it is necessary to indicate is that this criticism of induction brings out the fact that the empirical sciences make their generalizations upon the bases of postulates which are conceptions of theoretical science. Such conceptions utter judgments about the nature of reality which are not inferences directly from empirical (or sensorily perceived) fact. As concepts of this nonempirical character they must be weighed in the light of other metaphysical concepts which as concepts are of the same psychological type as these. That is to say, if all induction from empirical facts rests upon the principle of uniformity of nature and ultimate constituents of like nature, it is gross dogmatism to insist that materialistic mechanism is the only concept which explains this situation. The uniformity may be the result of divine will ordering a world of monads according to some end. The empirical facts are accounted for upon either metaphysical ground and, as far as science goes, it does not make any difference. The least that the theoretical scientist-metaphysician can do is to argue his case on metaphysical grounds and with some understanding of the epistemological status of metaphysical concepts.

Science Ignores the Human Equation

This reference to the epistemological status of metaphysical concepts brings up the whole problem of the nature of facts and concepts as employed in science and in metaphysics. It is because scientists are unconscious of the psychological constitution of facts and concepts that positivistic conceptions of the certainty of scientific knowledge grow up; for example, that facts are absolutely independent of any human mind, directly verifiable by the senses, utterly devoid of metaphysical assumptions. Unreflective science proceeds on the realistic assumption that its facts are completely objective and independent of the human equation, but it is unconscious of the mistaken presuppositions and the processes of abstraction which are involved in this assumption. Science starts with the public facts of common sense and mistakenly assumes that the scientist perceives these as data in sense-perception, but this is not true. A private individual senses cer-

42. It is impressive to note that Broad believes Tennant to be right with respect to these problems: cf. *Mind*, XXXVIII, 99.

tain sense-data privately. By virtue of communication with other
people he comes to suppose that they have similar data as well.
He thereafter conceives an object which is perceived by all men
as he perceives his own private data. This object becomes a fact
for common sense and science and is founded upon good circum-
stantial evidence, but it involves a venture of faith and results in
a mistaken notion. Because the individual supposes that other
people perceive his own sense data or the same sense-object, he
comes to think that the object exists for itself and independently
of all observers just as it is for the individual. But because science can abstract the individual subject from its facts and work
with the phenomena which are supposedly common to all, it must
not suppose that these facts are devoid of all human thinking or
that they are things-in-themselves. Undoubtedly they may be
some version of the truth about things-in-themselves, but this is
an epistemological matter and must be treated as such.

The Selective Procedure of Science

Another type of abstractive procedure is employed by empirical science on the opposite side, of which it is also often unconscious. It may be termed the artistry of concept making; that is
to say, a scientist selects from the perceptual flow of phenomenal
reality certain aspects for the purpose of description, manipulation, and control. If he is a physicist, he uses certain mathematical and formal categories to "explain" his data, but in this way
he omits a vast part of the perceptual fulness of experience and
deals solely with the quantitative aspects of things. The individuality and unique features of phenomena he omits also. The
perceptual flow of phenomena is a nonreversible, one-way passage of history, but the scientist in order to predict and manipu-
late his data selects the repeatable and uniform features of the
historical process. Such selection is due to his specific interest
and results in a simplification and reduction of the complexity
and spontaneity of the historical process.

That the historical process is discovered to confirm his selec-
tions by repeating these features in the flow of events is pragmatically true, but there is no a priori reason why this should
be so; the sufficient reason is in the actual world itself. And there
is no a priori reason, either, why reality must be composed of the

simplest terms and most easily manipulatable relations. Complexity is more likely a characteristic of the actual world than simplicity. The theoretical scientist who reduces the world to simple elements is motivated by a human, anthropomorphic interest as well as the theist, and his simplified explanation runs against this difficulty; namely, that it is possible, if one starts from the fulness of the experienced world, to pass on to the theoretical world-explanation of physical science, but, if he starts from the ground-plan of theoretical science, it is impossible to pass on to the fulness of experience. "Science might have finished its work and still be a fool."

Furthermore, the selective interest of the particular empirical scientist often causes misunderstanding between the empirical sciences themselves. It is not possible, for example, to deal with biological and psychological phenomena in the same categories one must use to deal with chemical and quantitative phenomena. A vicious process of abstraction is involved in the reduction of psychology to theoretical physics. The categories of "explanation" differ with respective sciences, and the unique categories of each are demanded for "explanation" in each.

Implications for Theology

We have noted, then, that unreflective science is involved in a twofold process of abstraction; an abstraction of the conscious subject on the one hand with its resulting positivistic realism and self-sufficient certainty, and an abstraction of the complex, historical features of the entire experienced world on the other hand with its uncautious expression of the anthropomorphic desire for simplicity of explanation. Both processes are exceedingly dangerous to theism. If the positivistic conception of the absolute certainty of scientific knowledge is true and theology is but blind, credulous faith, then natural theology is a weak type of intellectual endeavor. If the naturalistic explanation of the universe is the only explanation open to scientific men, then natural theology is unnecessary. But if science is not certain knowledge but a matter of faith and probability, faith entering into the very foundation of its so-called facts and pervading its entire generalizations, then it may be that the theistic explanation is not essentially different in type but only in degree from those theoretical and reasonable conceptions which are scientific. If naturalism is not the only possible world-explanation which is open to the philosopher who is himself anxious to stick close to scientific facts, and if perhaps it is the least adequate world-explanation when all the considerations of the world order, progressiveness, and values are taken into a synoptic account, then it may be that the theistic explanation is the most reasonable explanation available. "Certainly one may say," writes Tennant, "that Butler's analogy between natural and revealed religion might be supplemented by an analogy between natural theology and science. For inductive science has its interpretative principles and its faith-elements with which the faith of natural theology is, in essence, continuous."[43]

The Necessity for a Psychogenetic Analysis of Cognition

The demonstration of this analogy between theology and science and the revelation of the mistaken assumptions and presuppositions of science belong solely to a genetic and analytic enquiry into common knowledge by the psychology of cognition. Tennant's contention is that any other nongenetic or "epistemological" method of enquiry into the problem of knowledge is false and that the psychogenetic, or empirical, method is the only true one. The "epistemological," or rationalist, method attempts to discover what knowledge is by critically analyzing the logical preconditions which are universally and necessarily prior to any result which might be called knowledge. It first assumes or presupposes what logically perfect knowledge would be and then proceeds to examine the *ordo concipiendi* or logical steps by which this ideal goal is realized without any concern whatsoever for the actual preconditions of its premises; i.e., the connection of its premises with the sensory-perceptual and the genetic connection of thought and sense in the evolution of consciousness in the individual. It regards reason as an innate faculty possessed of native power to bring forth premises which are absolute, universal, necessary, and self-evident, apart from any experience of the actual world whatsoever. The father of this method was Plato, we are told. Kant continued it in his critique of knowl-

43. *Philosophy of the Sciences*, p. 185.

edge by bifurcating form from matter and reason from sense; and many idealists perpetuate it by emphasizing reason as an absolute faculty and by neglecting the sensory factor which constitutes the basic fundamental contact of the mind with the actual.

To Tennant this position is entirely a mistake. It assumes and presupposes too aristocratic a conception of the faculty of reason and too theoretical a conception of the perfection of the product of reason; i.e., that knowledge is universal, necessary, absolutely and logically certified to perfection. Such assumptions are pure dogmatism on the part of the rationalist, and to avoid such dogmatism it is necessary to examine the knowledge of the actual world as we have it in the nonabstract sciences and common sense, to assume that such knowledge is "presumptive" in that it claims to be some version of the truth about the actual but not absolute and perfect truth, and to undertake such examination with a noetic self-consciousness; i.e., with the tentative assumption that our knowing faculty is relatively sound, not absolute or perfect but capable of producing some sort of knowledge.

If such an enquiry is to be undertaken with these less arrogant presuppositions, it will naturally turn to the *ordo cognoscendi*, the entire knowing process from beginning to end, and not to the *ordo concipiendi*, nor to the *ordo essendi*, for the logical order avoids the sensory, empirical foundations and the metaphysical order comes last in the series of respective areas of knowledge; i.e., acquaintance with the sciences precedes metaphysical philosophizing.

The *ordo cognoscendi* is the province of psychology, because no other science isolates the area of mental facts for description and analysis; hence it is only to psychology that one can go for an analysis of the knowledge process. If someone argue[44] that the knowing upon which the science of psychology is founded is full of presuppositions, assumptions (many of which are false), and perhaps faulty processes, and that the examination of an imperfect instrument by an imperfect process will never light up the imperfections, Tennant replies that this is only part-

44. Each of the arguments cited on this and the following page are contained in *Philosophy of the Sciences,* chap. ii, where Tennant answers criticism of his method as pursued in *Philosophical Theology,* I.

truth, for any science clarifies its earlier confusions as it works them over, and such is the case with psychology. If someone argue that logic is presupposed in this psychogenetic analysis, Tennant replies that it is, but these are "only a few empty forms"[45] which offer psychology "some assistance,"[46] and which can be taken only as the rules of the game of thinking. There are no a priori premises which psychology must accept as "true no matter what." If someone object that this method involves the arrogant assumption that this is the only method, Tennant replies that this is not true, for it does not presume an absolute and perfect ideal of knowledge before it starts, and it seeks through the only science available, namely psychology, such facts as we have. If someone question whether or not psychology can give these facts, Tennant points out that the psychogenetic method which he is to pursue is neither sensationist (as the Lockean), nor associationist, nor purely genetic (James and Bradley), nor purely analytic. It avoids all abstractions such as "pure experience" and "pure data" (James and Bradley) and, by its emphasis on an objective continuum without and a subjective productive activity within, it avoids the evils of sensationist empiricism. If finally someone argue that the genesis of knowledge in no way invalidates its absolute truth, Tennant points out that this is not the case, for if the lower stages in the process of knowing involve supposition, trial and error, and pragmatic testing, the final stages cannot lose all taint of these impurities. If it is claimed that this final stage of knowledge is a matter of "immediate intuition," Tennant says that this represents an utter failure to comprehend the ambiguity of the term "immediate." All things are psychically immediate in being before the mind, but these have a prior history and are psychologically "mediate," though the mind is unaware of those mediacies because of accomplishing its operations with learned rapidity.

The Relativity of Knowledge and the Meaning of Phenomenalism

Before tracing the stages of his psychogenetic analysis as set forth in Volume I of *Philosophical Theology*, it ought to be noted that Tennant is not contending for the total subjectivity of

---

45. *Philosophy of the Sciences*, p. 30.   46. *Ibid.*, p. 48.

knowledge but for the relativity of knowledge (in all its various stages) to the mind as well as to independent reality. "The doctrine of the relativity of knowledge," he writes, "becomes a denial of realism such as would abolish the distinction between reality and appearance, and refuse to assign 'colored spectacles' to the mind. If the ontal be not known in its native purity, but only with additions or modifications due to our organs of sense and the capacities and peculiarities of our intelligence then things are not what they seem and all knowing . . . is symbolizing."[47] Knowledge then is, as he expresses it, an "emergent evolute" from which the subjective factor cannot be eliminated. It is what Ward in his unpublished lectures called impure,[48] but this does not mean that the objects of perception are subjective states or a *tertium quid* existing between independent reality and the subject.

Descartes bequeathed to Locke and Leibniz the assumption that sensa are changes in the subject, and so left to early modern philosophy a bias toward idealism. It is now known that sensa have *qualia* and relations of their own and that they are psychologically distinct from subjective modifications. If they were not, there would presumably be no real world; experience would be "absolute becoming"; and there would be no difference between percepts and images.[49]

It should be clearly understood that Tennant, as Ward before him, comes to the psychogenetic analysis of cognition convinced that the Cartesian dualism between objects of mind and things independent of mind is an impossible position into which the philosophy of Locke to Hume was driven by the logic of subjectivism. He is trying, as Ward before him, to develop a theory of "presentations" which, though similar to Cartesian and Lockean "ideas" in some respects, is nevertheless founded upon different epistemological presuppositions. The whole meaning of their method of approach will be misunderstood unless it is clearly realized that dualism is rejected for a theory of relational duality in which the entire analysis is controlled by an attempt to hold both poles of the cognitive relation—the ego and the in-

47. *Philosophical Theology*, I, 250. 48. *Ibid.*, p. 250.
49. *Ibid.*, p. 35.

dependent reality, without wholly denying the contribution of either to knowledge at whatever stage of the process we may analyze it.

"The forthcomingness of this knowledge (i.e., such knowledge of actuality as we presume to have) is a fact with which our analyses and our refined interpretations must be compatible." This is the meaning of phenomenalism, the doctrine which Tennant contends is most in accord with the known facts of the psychogenetic analysis of cognition. Neither pure subjectivism (individual and collective) nor pure realism (individual and collective) can stand before a full deliverance of the facts of the cognitive relation. Knowledge is a product of the coactivity of the conscious subject on the one hand and of the independent reality on the other. The total cause of knowledge is subject-*en-rapport*-with-reality. One cannot be separated from the other without falsifying the facts, and because of this it is impossible to identify phenomena with noumena, the product of a joint process with one of its contributing causes only. Yet at the same time it is impossible to break them utterly apart into an absolute dualism. Able thinkers such as Dawes Hicks and De Burgh interpret Tennant—as Hicks also interprets Ward—as a dualist. It may be that dualism is the inevitable logic of his position but it must be insisted upon at the outset that this is not Tennant's own approach and attitude toward the problem of cognition.

Fluctuating Emphases as the Distinction Between Phenomena and Noumena Is Applied to Opponents

The distinction between phenomena and noumena which emerges from this duality-theory, however, does appear to fluctuate according to the opponents at bay. Whenever realism attempts to construe noumena in terms of primary and secondary qualities; i.e., to make noumena identical with phenomena, then these supposed phenomena per se or noumena are shown to be mind-dependent or mind-relative and agnosticism is pressed as to the phenomenal nature of the real. Mind is real and active; phenomena are known only as experiences which are mind-produced. There is some external stimulation, it is true, for an independent reality partially causes phenomena, but science does not know (via acquaintance) this to be physical matter or a configuration of real primary qualities or of primary plus secondary qualities. Whatever this active Something, this independent source of stimulation, is in itself, its nature can only be inferred. It is not known by acquaintance, and inasmuch as it is active, such activity as it exhibits is most adequately interpreted by way of analogy, in terms of spirit, spirit being the only active cause which we know (experience from within by being a cause, or, *erleben*) noumenally.

In any case, science does not know (via acquaintance) that the ultimate, nonsubjective causes are not spiritual beings, and it would not matter to science as science if they were. In stating that the ultimate constituents are physical entities only, science, now posing not as science but as materialistic metaphysics, is ignorantly guessing or supposing, and there is no reconciliation with it until such reconciliation can be *in profundis* rather than *in excelsis;* i.e., until science will surrender its metaphysical pretensions and admit its ignorance of noumenal reality.

On the other hand, whenever there is danger that the mind-dependent nature of the knowledge product may lead to subjective idealism, or to social solipsism, or to agnosticism, emphasis is placed upon the noumenal, independent aspect of the duality relation. Berkeley and Kant were correct in emphasizing the productivity and activity of mind in experience, we are told, but phenomena are not merely mind-dependent. Solipsism is wrong in thinking that objects are states of mind; Berkeley is wrong in believing that to be is to be perceived in mind; Kant is wrong in holding that there are no forms in sensa. As a matter of fact, it is incorrect to say that we know phenomena only; we know the noumenal through the phenomenal. There is a one-to-one correspondence between the structural detail of the noumenal and the phenomenal. The forms of the understanding which Kant developed into the wider solipsism of common consciousness are grounded in the independently real. Mind, we learn, neither "creates" nor "makes" the *qualia* and relations of sensa themselves; these are what they are by virtue of objective, external control irrespective of subjective activities. The only way in which the subject affects the nature of the sensa is by limitation of the range of detection. For example, our organs of sight can detect, let us say, only seven colors in a rainbow, whereas conceivably there may be many more there to be detected if our sense organs were more powerful; hence there is a limitation of extent exercised by the subject's capacity. But this is a different type of "making"; the seven colors which are detected are externally forced upon the subject from without. In this we find the duality-theory swinging over to the realistic pole in such a way as to avoid any denial of an independent world, or agnosticism as to its structural order of relations. The relations and structure of independent reality stand in the unique relation of appearing to the subject, a type of theory which in the speculation of Dawes Hicks would mean monistic realism.

(2) Criticisms of the Positivist's Conception of Scientific Knowledge Based upon a Psychogenetic Analysis of the Stages of the Knowledge Process

Without continuing this statement of the results of the duality-theory further, it is pertinent to follow through his psychogenetic analysis of the various stages of knowledge: (a) an unsocialized individual's acquaintance with perceptible private objects (designated by the symbol, small o); (b) a socialized individual's "conceptual" perception of public Objects; i.e., the common things and facts of everyday common sense and empirical science (designated by the symbol, capital O); and (c) a socialized individual's speculative knowledge of the metaphysical reality independent of any subjective activity, the noumenal or ontal object (designated by the symbol, ω). It will be well to state these relations in symbolical form:

Final knowledge situation:

S (a perceiving subject involving a noumenal or pure ego and developing into a socialized mind Σ)—o (private psychological object produced in connection with the sense organs of body)—O (= ϕ phenomenal object of public science drawing its matter or primitive relations from o and its explicit conceptual form from Σ)—ω (noumenal reality).

The stages:

(a)

$$(x) \quad S—o$$
$$(y)^{50} \quad S_1—S_2—o \quad or \quad S_1—oS_2$$
$$S_1—oS_3$$
$$S_1—oS_4$$

50. This is not Tennant's diagram, but the writer's.

(b)

Σ—ϕ or O

(c)

Σ—$\phi\omega$ or O—ω

NOTE: One other symbol is used by Tennant, σ, to designate an object interpreted by subjectivists as a state of the subject.

(a) The Unsocialized Individual's Acquaintance with Perceptible Private Objects

(x) S—o. The beginning of all knowledge is "consciousness" which involves an experient or existent being undergoing consciousness and an object of which this existent being or subject is conscious. In the subject there are three distinguishable general processes: attention, feeling, conation. When sensation occurs the subject attends to a continuous field of vague presentations. Certain minor processes of attention, retention of impression, assimilation, fusion, comparison, differentiation, directed upon the continuum of presentations, result in the sensing of a definite sense-quality or group of qualities. The subject attending to a field of presentation comes by virtue of its exerted activity to distinguish a patch of yellow in some crude sort of relation to other sense-qualities. As previously pointed out,[51] Tennant is careful to state that sensa have relations of their own, such as resemblance, difference, crude time-and-place arrangement, out of which at a higher socialized level the explicit formal categories develop. Detection of these elementary relations involves a bit higher activity of the subject than bare sensing of sensa; i.e., germinal thought activity or sense-transcendence.

Perception does not occur, however, until sensa are interpreted as appearances of persistent things; that is to say, perception involves not only sensation but implicit conceiving as well. Such interpretation arises in this fashion. One peculiarly persistent group of sensa are the somatic presentations of one's own body. From this experience of persistence, of solidarity, and of resistance to touch, a slightly higher activity of the subject derives a vague notion of persisting, abiding thing, which it "reads in" to other groups of nonsomatic sensa occurring in its

51. Cf. above, p. 39.

field of presentation. In this manner the category of substance is born, though it does not come to explicit self-consciousness until after the stage of social intercourse is reached. The category of causality is born in the same manner; namely, by a notion derived from the sensing of effortful activity on the part of the body, and the ejection of this notion into nonsomatic groups of sensa. Thought, though a higher and distinguishably different activity from sense, nevertheless is continuous with sense and originates in conjunction with elementary experience-situations, a fact which causes Tennant to pour scorn upon the rationalists who think of thought categories as disparate and independent of sense. Furthermore, all thought involves a leap of faith, as does also memory. The subject ventures beyond elementary belief in persisting and active material things. In other words, the subject believes where he does not sense; but sensa and their relations are the subject's sole original touch with independent actuality.

Turning from the subjective side of the S—o relation, we may focus on the objective side. Though o is called the private psychological object, Tennant does not allow a subjective interpretation of it. It is not a state of the subject but rather what is over against the subject. At this stage in the evolution of knowledge the individual—a child, for example—does not know anything about the issues of idealism and realism. He does not know that his bodily sense organs have determined the appearance of the presentation. What he perceives is over against him. Such questions as "Are sensa mental?" are irrelevant. He simply perceives something over against himself and this is his private unshared object of experience.

$$(y) \quad S_1 \text{—} S_2 \text{—o or } S_1 \text{—o} S_2$$
$$S_1 \text{—o} S_3$$
$$S_1 \text{—o} S_4$$

The statement of how the subject comes to know himself and other selves we shall reserve for a later part of this chapter. It suffices to say here that the subject perceives material objects, some of which are the bodies of other selves. When he comes to interpret these bodies as having minds and experiences of objects in his field of presentations, he is at the level of an evolving socialized mind. He is coming to the point when he conceives himself as a universal—as it were, disembodied—subject of all the respective private experiences of each separately embodied individual. This is the real place, Tennant says, where the line between perception and conception must be drawn. What common sense and science mistakenly call perception; namely, the perceiving of public things, is in reality conception. The common Object is thought to exist where the private object is perceived, because the individual can by conception put himself into the place of many other subjects, and this involves more intellectual supposition than is usually suspected by unreflective people. This mental enlargement and its conception are verified by overwhelmingly impressive evidence, but it is supposition pragmatically verified and never has the certainty of sense certification. Knowledge at the social level has more interpretative elements in it from the angle of the subject, and from the side of the object it becomes a *tertium quid*. Tennant says that not o but O is the *tertium quid* between the subject and the noumenal reality.[52] O is the object of Σ (universalized mind). Let us look at this more carefully.

(b) *The Socialized Individual's Conceptual Perception of Public Objects. The Facts of Common Sense and Science*

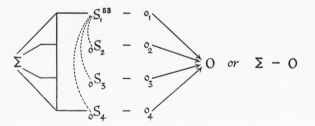

To illustrate what is meant by the above diagram Tennant uses the illustration of several men[54] looking at the sun. Each

52. *Philosophical Theology,* I, 220 n.
53. The lines of the "S-side" of this diagram are not Tennant's, but the writer's.
54. In reviewing Stout's *Mind and Matter,* Tennant points out that Ward's use of this illustration is pressed to yield difficulties which are avoided if instead of ten men, ten infants were used in the illustration. See *The Journal of Theological Studies,* XXXIV, 97.

subject perceives his private object (o) which is numerically and qualitatively distinct from the others' private object. Each subject, however, can communicate to the other a sign, or gesture, or word which suggests that he is having a certain perceptual experience. He can point out that the yellow patch of color he perceives is like the color of a sunflower, for example, and thus communicate common relations. When all the subjects mutually understand the occurrence of respective experiences in each, the mind of the one individual is enlarged in such a way that he becomes the mind of all the others and he then conceives himself as having the common Object of all the others. This common Object is not the socialized individual's own unique percept; it is rather what the socialized individual "reads in" to his private percept by an act of conception. His great mistake occurs in his thinking that this conceptual object, this *tertium quid*, is the real object which exists independently of all perception, when it is a conceptual construction of the qualities which occur in private perception. Such qualities are partially mind-dependent, and must not be attributed to what it takes mind to constitute.

That is to say, Tennant, like Ward, maintains that the presentation-continuum or field of consciousness over against the subject is determined by the range and tempo of the modifications of the sense organs of the body. The bodily mechanisms determine the range of colors to be seen as well as the range of vibrations to be heard. Though there are no subjective modifications of the real objects of consciousness, nevertheless there are bodily modifications which partially constitute the nature of what is presented to the subject. Consciousness of these modifications is possible only for the socialized mind which by virtue of its conceptual entrance into other minds discovers the private idiosyncrasies and common characteristics of the percepts of various individuals and ascribes the idiosyncrasies to bodily mechanisms. When, for example, a person learns that S_2 in looking at the sun does not see a color like a sunflower (yellow), and that other subjects perceive the yellow, he may look for the cause of the color blindness of S_2 in a bodily mechanism. The private unsocialized individual as an experient would not be aware of these mechanisms, but at the social level such matters sometimes become obvious.

Furthermore, the socialized mind may come to realize that the real world might appear differently to it if it had some other sort of body. The real world might well appear differently to a rat. This is not Tennant's illustration, but it represents essentially his position. A real independent world stimulates our bodily mechanism and psychologically a continuous field of presentations results. The distinction between appearance and reality breaks out quite naturally but the presentation is still the appearance of the independent reality. Between the world and the subject stands the body which is man's physiological inheritance coming to him through biological evolution. Man's sense experience as well as his categories of thought are what they are by virtue of his embodiment, and there is no blinking this fact.

The conceptual object, however, is not the private percept, not the primary presentation of independent reality, but a constructed object which the socialized subject attends to or thinks of. Objects of different sorts can be before the mind: conceptual objects, imaginal objects, as well as perceptual appearances of the noumenal. It is in this sense that objects are a *tertium quid*, for in case of objects other than the primary sense contacts and elementary relations, it is necessary to find some evidence for believing that there are counterparts to them in the real world. In case of public facts, there is sufficient evidence of a cumulative nature to substantiate the conviction that there are ontal objects in the actual world which are causing the experiences in the various experients, but this is supposition practically certified and not immediate clairvoyance.

The Faith-Element in Scientific Knowledge

That there is a reality which corresponds to the concept of it is a venture of faith just as the supposition that there is a real God which corresponds to the idea of God is a venture of faith, and the verification of the one is pragmatic coercion as it is in the case of the other, but the common reality is not perceived as sensa are perceived. Furthermore, the common independent reality is neither perceived nor conceived as it is in itself apart from perception. Conception is still a humanly subjective process and not photography of the independent reality. For the realistic scientist to suppose that he is immediately acquainted with public

physical reality independent of the knowing experience is to
entertain a position which is belied by the facts of psychogenetic
analysis. A public reality must be there to account for the rise of
various comparable percepts in various percipients, and it may
well exist whether there be any perceivers or conceivers at all,
but it is not known to exist independently as it is known to appear in the knowing relation. Public science does not describe the
thing per se.[55] The concept of a common thing does not refer to
a common Object which is perceived to exist independently of
human knowledge; the common Object is still a phenomenon even
if the subjective phase of phenomenon-making is conceptual and
intercommunicable as a private perception is not.

The Case Against Scientific Realism

Out of this emerges Tennant's case against realism in any
form. He is concerned to expose the falsity of certain fundamental tenets which are common to all realism: viz., that object is
independent of subject; that knowing sets up no difference between ultimate reality as unknown and as known; that there is
no distinction between appearance and reality.[56] The central
point of his attack is the instrumental theory of perception; i.e.,
that sense organs are instruments or mechanisms by means of
which perception of external world is made possible, but the instruments make no difference to the apprehended external world;
and the external world is known as it is in itself quite apart from
the process.

He first examines the "extremist type of realism"[57] which
holds that things per se are sensa, that independent reality is appearance, that perceiving makes no difference to the thing itself.
He suggests that this type of theory must face the following implications. (1) If sense organs and the body make no difference
to the object perceived and if all perceived objects are real and
independent of the perceiving process, then the real world becomes a more complicated affair than science and common sense
believe it to be. It would then contain multitudes of positions,
shapes, colors, sounds, and all the objects of delirium, dreams,
and drugs. (2) This theory would abolish any distinction be-

55. *Philosophical Theology*, I, 227–228, 235.
56. *Ibid.*, pp. 239–240.   57. *Ibid.*, p. 231.

tween actuality and illusion.[58] (3) On this theory psychology could not account for (a) similarity of percepts when several people are looking at the same object; nor for (b) the grouping of percepts with rhyme and reason. (4) Common sense and science would have no common world to conceive nor any support for discrimination between reality and nonreality.

With these implications in view Tennant points out that common sense and science abandon the extreme theory and resort to the causal theory of perception, the theory that the common Object causes percepts in various observers. In the form of naïve realism it is held that in normal perception the perceived object or *idion* "resembles"[59] the independent reality; in abnormal perception it does not. Science, Tennant points out, soon gives up this point of view by drawing a distinction between primary and secondary qualities. Ascribing only a few characters, such as extension, to independent reality, it relegates secondary qualities to the perceiver. The common Object which common sense takes to be independent reality, science takes to be phenomenal, and frequently science identifies the independent reality with the nonsensorily conceived atoms or electrons of physics. Both naïve and scientific realism maintain that sensa are caused by independent reality and that the sensa are conditioned to some extent by the body and its organs. In this respect both are tending toward a distinction between appearance and reality, but science attempts to save itself by the instrumental theory of primary qualities, and this, Tennant holds, breaks down when con-

---

58. ". . . we should have to believe in the existence, when unperceived, of all the indefinite number of elliptical shapes, e.g., presented when a coin is looked at by a plurality of percipients from an indefinite number of positions; of all the different shades of colour when a flower is seen in different lights; of all the different pitches, loudnesses, etc., apprehended when a sounding body, moving relatively to hearers, is heard; of all the sensa of 'subjective sensation,' those seen when the eye-ball is pressed, and so forth; of all that is apprehended in delirium, dreams, and after taking drugs, which become thereby means of extending our acquaintance with the Real world. A world may be of infinite complexity; it may be endowed with the six dimensions that have been assigned to it, in order to allow this indefinite tale of 'reals' to expatiate. But there is such a thing as external control to be reckoned with by the pure speculator; and when confronted with it, the instrumental theory does not fare well. It needs to abolish the distinction between actuality and illusion, for which psychology, no less than common sense, assigns grounds." *Ibid.*, p. 232.

59. *Ibid.*, p. 233. This term is Tennant's, who uses it with the comment that naïve realism "embodies, in fact, the copy-theory of perceptual cognition."

fronted with the implications of "illusion, the imaginal, and hallucination." These are admittedly not caused by independent reality, and science recognizes that primary qualities are in some cases as unreal and illusory as secondary qualities. Shapes and sizes are often as unreal as colors. From the standpoint of psychology there is no basis for assigning any difference as to ontological status. If extension or matter is appearance of some more fundamental reality—electrons, for instance—Tennant maintains that it would make no difference to science as science if the ultimate entities were unextended monads. Science itself, according to Tennant,[60] can throw no light upon the ontal world per se. Science is always interpretation, human phenomenalizing of the Real.

(c) A Socialized Individual's Speculative Knowledge of Metaphysical Reality

Tennant's account of metaphysical "knowledge" and the metaphysical "object" may now be indicated: Σ—ϕO—ω. The ontal object (ω) cannot be identified with the private perceptual object (o) nor with the common conceptual object (ϕO) of common sense and science, for these latter objects are in part the production of mind, hence not independent of mind or true ontal objects. The ontal object can be "known" through the phenomenal appearance, through the modifications of mind and the resulting symbols or, as Tennant puts it, "through a glass darkly."[61] The phenomenon bears the same relation to the noumenon as a map to the countryside; as stage scenery to realities represented; and as a musical score to a performance of a symphony. The map is relevant and guides the traveler about the countryside; the stage scenery is likewise relevant and conveys real meaning to the audience.[62] It does not matter if the map is rough or the stage mechanism is poor as long as guidance and meaning are given. No warrant is given to philosophy to argue agnosticism simply because knowledge is impure. The mind does not make phenomena out of its own states nor yet out of nothing. There is inescapable stimulation from the outside; a stimulation which has rhyme, and results in similar experiences on part of various observers. The subject reacts to this external stimulation and phenomena are

60. *Philosophical Theology*, I, 235.   61. *Ibid.*, p. 251.
62. *Ibid.*, p. 252.

born. The causation of phenomena is a unique type of productive process in that its total cause is active-subject-*en-rapport*-with-independent-reality. The cause of a phenomenon is not exactly comparable to a situation in which one phenomenon is cause of another phenomenon, because in this latter case the result and the cause are both phenomenal in status whereas in the former case the unknown object proceeds from the status of unknown object into the status of known object, a transposition of status which is unique,[63] and the cause must also be unique.

If, therefore, the subject is to make phenomena, it must be *en rapport* with noumena which are as rich in structural detail as the phenomena which the mind produces out of the noumenal stimulation. There must be a one-to-one correspondence between the Real and phenomena; "the Real and the phenomenal must have more in common or be more alike than is commonly supposed by those who observe distinction between them";[64] otherwise our knowledge falls into subjectivism or the domain of miracles (stimulation *ex nihilo*). Kant was wrong in supposing that we know nothing about the noumenal except its existence. We know it as causally active in stimulating the mind to produce phenomena (percepts and concepts) within itself which reflect the Real but are not pure photographs. Metaphysically we have a phenomenal knowledge of the noumenal object, an impure interpretation which is distinct and relative but relevant. Phenomena are not noumena. Phenomena are in part mind-produced whereas noumena are independent of mind, but inasmuch as the mind-produced is also noumenally stimulated, there is close resemblance as there is close *rapport*, but no numerical, existential identity.

If, then, all that we may be said to suppose to be true of the metaphysically Real is that it is causally active in coöperating with the subject in the knowledge relation and hence must have some structural correspondence to our well-founded common phenomenal knowledge, it is obvious that either a realistic or an idealistic metaphysical interpretation of the causally active Reals, structurally patterned, may be forthcoming. Needless to say, empirical science is not robbed of its public facts, whatever ultimate metaphysical interpretation may prove most reason-

63. *Ibid.*, pp. 235, 247.   64. *Ibid.*, p. 247 n.

able, but materialistic mechanism masquerading as science must come before the bar of cognition and metaphysics. The psychology of cognition shows that the "atoms," "electrons," "quanta," "ethers," etc., of theoretical physical science are not immediately experienced facts but highly conceptualized, abstractive symbols or shorthand formulae, the applicability of which to the metaphysically real world is not coercive but tentative and suppositional. Tennant is willing to concede that some real entity must be there corresponding to some conception of this nature; i.e., to some real entities which are quantitative in character; but he does not think that science can deny the possibility of their being self-active living monads any more than it can state dogmatically that they are microscopic units characterized by inertia and operating according to impressed forces. The entire operating ground-plan of metaphysical nature may be quite as well conceived as moved in process by a supreme end held in view by a world-mind as by a conception of mechanical action. These matters are settled by the nature of the evidence to be considered and will be reviewed later.

The Activity of the Subject in Cognition; the Categories of Reason

At this point, it is necessary to redirect our attention to the activity of the subject in the socialized stage of its knowing; i.e., to the cognitive faculty of the understanding and reason. We have pointed out that along with certain sense-activities of the unsocialized individual, what Tennant calls "implicit" thought-activities emerge by means of which the notions of substance and cause are derived from experiences of bodily self and "read into" (associated with) the nonsomatic sensa to synthesize material objects. In this way the "implicit categories" of substance and cause are born along with the directly intuited formal relations of sensa. Explicit and developed thing-supposition does not appear until intersubjective intercourse and language lay foundations upon the basis of which space-time relations, and formal and dynamic categories, become possible processes in the socialized mind. When the individual transfers his point of view from his private position to a social position, he synthesizes or builds "things" which are spaced, timed, numbered, compared, and substantized into public Objects which are known to be common (instead of universal) and necessary (dictated by actual preconditions) to all socialized minds.

Tennant thus offers psychological preconditions for the synthesis of common facts in contrast to Kant's "logomorphic"—the term is admittedly Ward's—preconditions. He follows Kant's division of the categories of the understanding into "formal" and "dynamic" associated with the prior "intuitions" of space and time. To construct an object in public space and time, to build up out of communicated relations the resemblances and differences in qualities (formal categories) and the dynamic factors of persistent active tendency or cause—this is the synthetic work of the socialized mind as it psychologically constructs various factors into public things. Where Kant thought out the logical preconceptions involved in public facts and asserted the "constitutiveness" of both formal and dynamic categories, Tennant pursuing the psychological "deduction" of categories does not find the supposed constitutiveness of causality to be in accord with the psychogenetic fact. In Tennant's judgment, causality is a regulative category whereby the embodied subject interprets sensa and formal relations in terms of his own enduring, active self. Formal categories are immediately "read off" sensa as causality is not. Hume showed forever that causality, the inner bond of necessitation, is not perceived directly by sense; neither is it intuitively "read off" as the resemblance, difference, and temporal sequence of qualities are "read off." Causality is first derived from direct experience of the embodied subject and then "read in" to the other relations. It is "regulative" as teleology was said by Kant to be regulative, and Kant's distinction between understanding and reason needs revision.

The Nature of Reason

The understanding itself is "reason" insofar as the line is drawn between the "formal" and the "dynamic" categories. It is an "interpretative ejection of ego qualities into things,"[65] a "psychologically conditioned excursus along lines of association of ideas,"[66] and not a logical synthesis independent of all relation to the psychophysical subject. The categories of the understand-

65. *Ibid.*, p. 185.　　　　　66. *Ibid.*, p. 184.

ing modify the utterance of the noumenal world according to human notions, notions derived from the fact that the human ego is embodied. They are not innate, a priori, perfect forms of logical thought; hence a less restricted meaning for reason must be employed in defining the understanding. Reason to Tennant is an alogical faculty; i.e., not rigidly logical but, on the other hand, not nonsensical; a faculty relative to human conditions as well as to ontological requirements of the external world.

Critique of the Rationalistic Conception of Reason and Nature

This conception of Reason he contrasts with the restricted view of Reason held by the pre-Kantian rationalists (Leibniz excepted), the Deists, Kant (in part), and Coleridge. His own he associates "with the principle of sufficient reason, with induction and 'probable' belief, and with satisfaction of conation; the other solely with coercive and deductive logic, with the principle of contradiction, with the requirements of pure cognition."[67] Not pure cognition but impure human beliefful cognition is what we actually have. The rationalists have stood for reason as a unique faculty independent of sense, often independent of body and animal soul, and capable of direct vision of timeless truth. Reason to the rationalists, because of their lack of genetic and social psychology, is said to be either

a special creation, or an original faculty or a divine substance in man. Psychology finds that there is no such faculty. Reason is made not born: an outgrowth of the understanding which has a common root with sense. There are no pure sensa, nor any sense-perception that is not implicitly conceptual; no pure forms of intuition devoid of matter, no matter of thought without form; no understanding in the formal sense, i.e. no intuitive induction [the only "rational" apprehension that is immediate as sense] without impressional data, in the first instance; nor any understanding in the sense of use of "real" categories, apart from conation and ejection; no pure and ideal science that does not arise by abstraction from, and idealization of, the originally in sensu, nor any knowledge of Actuality that is not interpretative or anthropic; no

67. *Ibid.*, p. 189.

deductive physics that is not at bottom suppositional and grounded on induction, and induction that does not transcend logical computation by assuming the indemonstrable, the hoped for and the unseen.[68]

The rationalist conception of the nature of knowledge and of the validity of knowledge is defined by Tennant as follows:

Both in the ancient and the early modern periods it was thought that knowledge, characterised by self-evidence and demonstrable certainty, was forthcoming, valid of the Actual world. The name Knowledge was indeed bestowed only on what was deemed thus certain; no room was found, within science proper, for the presumptive knowledge or probable belief which, as a matter of fact, is all-important for the conduct of life. With rationalism, as with its opposite extreme, sensationalism, the attitude was "all or none." Universal and necessary knowledge, being underivable from sense or empirical observation, was said to be a priori, supplied by the unique faculty of the reason or *lumen naturale*, which was regarded as both genetically and functionally independent of sense. Knowledge, it was held, is thus spun out of the mind itself, originating as innate ideas and truths, or as the result of operation of innate, if not perfected, functionings of the rational soul . . .

What he [the rationalist] would bestow the name knowledge upon is not mediated by sense or by discursive thought thereon, but by immediate apprehension of the self-evident, and consequently indemonstrable yet necessary axioms. From these, by use of logical principles, which are quite distinct from premises or original axioms, theorems are derived that are characterised by necessity and by demonstrable certainty.[69] Instances of this doctrine may be cited. Descartes regarded all knowledge as of one and the same nature, and held the knowing process to consist in combining self-evident truths with other propositions, by steps each of which is self-evident. His model was coordinate geometry. Spinoza presented his system in the form of theorems successively deduced from definitions of concepts taken, by himself, to be the pre-suppositions of all thought, and at the same time to be Real or existent. His model was Euclid. Leibniz had discretion enough to lack, in part, the rationalistic valour evinced by his predecessors. He is

68. *Ibid.*, p. 193.   69. *Ibid.*, p. 194.

not so typical a representative of the school as his audacious disciple Wolff: he was a rationalist with reservations. In so far as he was rationalistic, his model was algebra. One may pass from him to Kant, who remained predominantly the rationalist, for all his contact with empiricism, and observe that he taught, in a work of so late date as 1786, the *Metaph. Anfangsgründe der Naturwissenschaft*, that only a rational or a priori theory of Nature deserves to be called science, so that empirical knowledge is only to be called so "in a figure." Again, in his first *Critique* he insisted that, whereas particular instances of physical law are gotten empirically, yet law, in Nature as known by us, is necessitated by our minds which put it into the data.[70]

. . . .

. . . Commonly associated with these tenets, was the assumption that ideas, in the old comprehensive sense of the word, are subjective states. Brought to the Objective, to the external (phenomenal) world supposed to be in no degree constituted by the human mind, ideas were held to be valid of it. Indeed one of the fundamental presuppositions of rationalism is, that the logical order and connexion of ideas is of the same kind as the Actual order and connexion of things. So the world was assumed to be wholly rational in the formally logical sense. The mind and the world are each a closed system, and they run parallel. The duality in unity of experience not yet being discovered, a dualism of worlds and minds was set up, verbally resolved by Spinoza into a monism of two aspects. The ultimate ground of this parallelism, and consequently of the validity of thought was God; though how it was mediated by God was conceived differently by Descartes, Leibniz, and Spinoza. Indeed validity sometimes came to be identified with consistency of ideas, etc., with one another. In the science of the Actual no less than in pure mathematics, the sole arbiter of certainty was the principle of contradiction, or of the incompatibility of the opposite.[71]

This rationalistic conception of knowledge, Tennant says, was given the deathblow by Hume who made it plain for all time that there is no a priori necessity about the happening of any brute fact. *Causa* is not *ratio*; the order and connectedness of things is

70. *Ibid.*, pp. 199–200.   71. *Ibid.*, pp. 194–195.

not the order and connectedness of ideas and propositions. No matter how clear, self-evident, and immediate the contemplation of such an "intelligible world" of ideas may be, it is not the noumenal world of reality.

The chief error of all rationalistic thinkers is that they confuse validity with existence, coherent ideas with the order of nature; and having made this mistake, they come to regard a system of ideas or laws, physical and ethical, as existing or subsisting independently of things, a prius of law which it becomes fitting for God, Himself, to observe. The Deists, Toland and Tindal, held this conception of natural law,[72] but Tennant is one with Lotze who rejected the "eternal prius" of law for the actual determination of laws by causally interacting things. It is the real things whose actions suggest laws, not laws which coerce real things. That nature is actually ordered and related in such a way that it corresponds in some measure to the logical order of propositions and mathematics, we have reason to believe, insofar as our scientific predictions are sustained, but that nature must correspond to a system of logical ideas is simply not fact. Such science as we have is based upon problematic concepts which it is hoped will be sustained. Such is the outcome of a logical study of inductive logic. But the ground of nature's order is either in the existent entities of nature herself or else in one entity behind these; it is not in the prius of propositions. Such knowledge of ontal nature as we have, and not as rationalists think we have, is of the noumenal through the phenomenal. It is not a direct contemplation of archetypal ideas.

The rationalistic conception held sway when Newtonian physics was regarded as universal, necessary, and absolutely certified knowledge. But physicists have long been denying this a priori type of science, and thinkers such as K. Pearson, Poynting, J. Ward, and Hobson have developed a descriptionist view of science; i.e., that the conceptual entities of physics possess no ontological significance whatsoever.[73] This has eliminated the certainty of materialistic mechanism, Tennant is quite ready to admit. In fact, in his earlier thinking[74] he was an adherent to the descriptionist view of science, but he is not now prepared to ad-

72. See *The Modern Churchman,* XIV, 310 ff.

73. *Ibid.,* pp. 313 ff.

74. See Essay: "The Being of God . . .," *Cambridge Theological Essays,* p. 61.

mit that science has no ontological significance. If the public facts of science are constructed, as the psychology of cognition shows them to be, out of the interaction of the embodied subject and the noumenal world, then even though the subject assimilates the utterance of ontal nature to itself and interprets it in terms of its own sense organs and human (anthropic) categories, it nonetheless does not create conceptual nature *ex nihilo* nor out of its own states. It cannot read just anything whatsoever into ontal nature; there is persistent control from the outside. The position that science has no ontological significance is unacceptable. Tennant finds it quite necessary to press the fact of human subjectivity and of modification by human limitations whenever an extreme positivistic attitude is taken toward scientific knowledge and knowledge is supposed to be plate-glass photography of independent reality, but he does not thereby find it reasonable to carry this attitude through to an extreme subjectivity of the Berkeleyan type or of the dualistic, Cartesian type, in which conceptual nature and ontal nature are two closed systems coordinated by an act of God. Conceptual nature (mind in Cartesian sense) and ontal nature (matter in Cartesian sense) are held together in the unity of human experience by means of which the noumenal is phenomenalized. For this reason, he finds it necessary to reject Kant's view that the mind contributes relatedness to atomistic sense deliverances of the ontal, and Eddington's view that relativity metrics can be attached to any point in ontal nature, it being nature's part to supply the point and mind's part to supply relations and metrical uniformity.[75] Ontal nature suggests its own relatedness and uniform activity to be translated into the language of human knowledge, but knowledge is not the cause of nature's regularity and relatedness. *Ratio* is not *causa*. The cause or ground of such order as nature seems to manifest to human subjects must be sought in the ontal realm itself rather than in human mentality.

The Theological Bearings of Scientific Knowledge

It is this need for an ontal ground of the regularity of nature-in-itself which leads Tennant to consider the metaphysical probabilities of pluralism and theism. Scientific knowledge gives the metaphysician the well-substantiated probability that ontal

75. Cf. *Philosophical Theology*, Vol. II, chap. i.

nature is a relatively—not an absolutely—stable nexus of secondary causes. Psychology of cognition indicates that theoretical science is not in a position to say that this regularity is a mechanism of material entities characterized by inertia and by uniformity. Such a verdict, if cast at all, is human hope motivated by the human desire to reduce the complexities of ontal nature to a scope wherein it can be handled by human minds. In light of the actual discoveries of physicists themselves, there is no necessary reason to believe that these entities are characterized by inertia and by uniformity.[76] As far as the ultimate entities of the universe in itself are concerned, the concepts employed by science to describe them are what Tennant calls "fictions" or concepts which have some relevance to ontal nature but which because of their continual fluctuation and annihilation by new concepts cannot be taken as valid of actuality in any absolute sense. Science is here projecting its concepts upon a mystery about which it may speculate but of which it never may claim to have face-to-face vision. No more than it reveals the ultimate metaphysical entities of the universe does it reveal the ground of the regularity of these entities, and when the movement of the world entities toward the development of life, mind, and the values of truth, beauty, and moral goodness are taken into account, facts to which sciences other than the physical give testimony, it is plain that the ground to which the sciences point for explanation of a more final type is there awaiting explanation by philosophy.

Science as science can pursue its course of tracing the connections between such facts as it selects from the fullness of perceptual nature which is synthesized at the common-sense level of factual data, without any reference to the ground of the whole universe of which it is a part. As such, science is always methodologically "atheous" or exclusive of metaphysical explanation of the theistic type, but this does not mean that it is "atheistic" or exclusive of theistic explanation for other than methodological purposes. It would be fair to Tennant's position to say that each phenomenon is a scientific fact insofar as it is related to some aspect of nature as a uniform system of secondary causes, and that it is a supernatural fact insofar as it may point to, and be related to the ground of nature-as-a-whole, conceived as a value-realizing Being. Science cannot rule out theistic explanation nor

76. Cf. *ibid.*, chap. ii.

any sort of metaphysical explanation, but it can give facts and point out aspects which cry out for a sufficient ground.

Science leads up to a Beyond at several points:[77] (1) the mystery of the fundamental common denominator of matter and energy; (2) the mystery of the origin of this common denominator, and of the epigenetic entities of life and mind, which cannot be accounted for by the mechanical synthesis of inert particles; (3) the sufficient ground of the uniformity of nature which science assumes as the foundation-hope upon which induction is laid; and finally, (4) the sufficient ground of the world's tendency toward the realization of the values of truth, beauty, and goodness. It is these facts and factors which science suggests, but the explanation of which it leaves open, that theism attempts to explain on "probabilities" of a philosophical and theological type.

So far we have been concerned to show that science is not in a position to close out the possibilities of theistic explanation, that it does not of itself give metaphysical explanation, but only appears to do so, when it serves as a masquerade for dogmatic or unconscious materialism; and, finally, that such knowledge to which it really has a right to lay claim is not absolute, certain knowledge of the metaphysically Real but a human version of the noumenal shot through with human supposition and probability. It is now time to indicate how, more positively, the faith which is involved in science is continuous with the faith of theology, and how the ego, other selves, ontal nature, and God stand in a continuous curve of suppositional knowledge.

B. POSITIVE DEMONSTRATION OF THE FAITH-ELEMENT IN KNOWLEDGE OF THE PURE EGO, OTHER SELVES, AND SUBSTANCE-CAUSES[78]

A major part of the reasonable support for the actuality of God is derived from the positive demonstration that, from the

77. Cf. "The Theological Bearings of Empirical Science," *The Constructive Quarterly*, IX, for excellent presentation of the mystery and the Beyond to which empirical science points for philosophical explanation, but of which it is unable by virtue of its methodology to give any account.
78. See above, p. 29.

standpoint of psychogenetic epistemology, God, the world, the soul, and other selves all stand in a similar noetic relation; i.e., all are "mediate" inferences drawn, except in the case of pure ego, on the basis of analogies, to account for the deliverances of immediate experience; and all are concepts which are reasonably probable in an alogical sense rather than rationally certain in a logical sense. To this constructive phase of the epistemological enquiry the attention of this chapter may be directed.

(1) Knowledge of the Pure Ego as Mediate Inference of Faith

First, knowledge of the pure ego is "mediate" inference but there is no use of analogy involved. The pure ego is not known with "immediacy." The conception of the pure ego proves upon analysis to be a cognitive construction which is thought to exist in order to account for immediate experiences of elements of consciousness which are known "by acquaintance," and which point to a ground more fundamental and enduring as their intrinsic base. Psychogenetic analysis of consciousness, Tennant points out, must take as its starting point the ordinary consciousness of consciousness, or self-consciousness, of common-sense experience, and then try to analyze the meaning of consciousness in its earliest, most primitive, and nonself-conscious stage.

Consciousness in its primitive meaning is a term which refers to the existence of that which constitutes the difference between the reactions of a stone to an impact upon it, or the nervous irritability of a plant to the thing which touches it, and the response of an organism to an object which it knows to be touching it. Consciousness can only be recognized as and when it is experienced or *erlebt*. It is an ultimate fact insofar as we have no experience of its being derived from anything else. It is that which must be distinguished from physical and vital occurrences on the one hand and from the wider term, "mental," as inclusive of unconscious psychic traces on the other. It is the difference which is logically discernible in such propositions as "there-is-consciousness-of-red" and "red-exists," or "there-is-awareness-of-a-thunderstorm" and "a-thunderstorm-is." To equate the two is to say "to-hear-a-thunderstorm" is "to-be-a-thunderstorm"—a logical absurdity.

Consciousness Involves Subject

Whenever consciousness is taking place, it involves an experient or subject which is conscious of an object, and no meaning of consciousness is attributable to actuality unless the term means "awareness of something by something." Attempts to analyze consciousness into "pure experience," "conscious states," "contents of experience" are all doomed to the failure of abstraction and of logical absurdity. From a "subject-conscious-of-an-object" it is possible to abstract for purposes of attention such aspects of that total situation as "experiencing process" and the "objective datum" or "pure datum," but from these abstractions as basic premises there is no way to make the analytical statement that "something-is-conscious-of-an-object." A being which is undergoing consciousness is an implication of the existence of consciousness and cannot be avoided by any theory which would take into account the actual facts.

To say that consciousness implies a subject when it occurs is not in this first stage of analysis to assert a permanent enduring ego or a *res cogitans*, but simply to say that whenever consciousness exists a subject is implied. The enduring ego may or may not be needed as a principle of explanation, but if it is needed at all, this must follow later as a sufficient ground for the facts. The enduring ego does not shine forth as an immediately perceived *quale;* neither is it a self-evident and necessary principle as the rationalists insist that it must be. All that Descartes is warranted in asserting is that whenever, momentarily, there is doubting, a doubter is implied for that experience; to imply that the doubter is the thinker or perduring subject is to assert more than can really be inferred from the doubting experience apart from the presupposition of memory and reflection. The existence of the momentary subject, however, is established logically by Tennant as the enduring subject is established by Descartes; i.e., by appeal to the logical principle of contradiction and the absurdity of overlooking it.

Upon further analysis of consciousness, three elements are recognizable with immediacy—feeling, conation, and cognition—all of which are states of the subject or experient. Feeling and conation are the passive and active phases of interest; feeling being the *erleben* of pleasure and pain, and conation being the *erleben* of want and unrest. Cognition is the *erleben* of such activity as is necessary to retain, fuse, compare, and differentiate the presented sense-continuum in such a way that perception of an object occurs. Were it not for the fact that the subject retains the sense-impressions made upon it and thus is able to compare and to differentiate specific features in the presentation continuum, there would be no recognition of a patch of color as distinct from anything else. Perception, imagination, memory, and ideation are progressively advanced stages in the unifying, retaining, and constructive activity of the conscious subject as it works upon the data of experience.

The Genesis of the Concept of the Pure Ego

Without reviewing the psychological analysis of these processes at this point, it is important to note the way by which, according to Tennant, the pure ego becomes known. One of an individual's constantly recurring percepts is his body. In the course of his experience he comes to distinguish his body from other objects of his cognition by virtue of its being a unique center of organic sensation. Action upon the body from without is accompanied by changes in feeling and in conative striving within the body. Distinction is drawn between an outer and an inner zone in which trains of ideas and of memories occur along with feelings and organic sensations, and compete with external impressions made upon the body. The external body often becomes an alien to the inward area which seems to persist at least in part unchanged through changes. The notion of an inner self is formed and consciousness of an inward self arises, which is enlarged and expanded indefinitely through social intercourse with other people.

Social intercourse is founded upon the perception on the part of one individual of the bodies of other individuals, and an implicit process of analogical inference by means of which other bodies are believed to be inhabited by inward selves analogous to one's own. Such ejection by analogical inference is not to be confused with explicit rational inference. It is rather an implicit unreflective process beginning in the child's response to the behavior of the mother, which it perceives as different from that of other things, and continuing by rudimentary introspections, retrospections, and interpretations of sensible signs to more conscious and rational inferences. By means of analogical interpretation and the higher processes of communication, a person observes, imitates, and establishes sympathetic relations with other people. He becomes able to judge his own behavior and valuations from the standpoint of others and thus comes to distinguish himself, as spectator, from himself, as actor. In like manner he becomes conscious of himself as perceiving objects and making judgments, and in this way he distinguishes between thinker and thoughts. The notion of a perduring, thinking, judging agent is a refinement of the notion he has constructed of his self out of varied experience. The pure ego is the concept of an active bond or agent which gives unity and continuity to the empirical self, which is the pure ego plus its objects, states, and relations. As a concept it is the last idea to arise in conjunction with reflection upon conscious experience. Psychologically the I knowing and the pure ego as known are distinguishable; logically they are two terms; but ontologically they are two aspects of one entity. One entity in two roles.

The Pure Ego Mediately Known

Tennant is concerned to point out that the pure ego is not immediately known. Immediate knowledge is knowledge "by acquaintance," or direct experience of a unique *quale* which marks off one object from other. Beyond acquaintance or direct experience of specific *quale* there is indirect knowledge or "knowledge about" an object which is constructed by the mind to account for the data of direct experience. It is this latter type of knowledge which we have of the pure ego; the processes of attention, feeling, and desire, we know by acquaintance. Such acquaintance with these elements of consciousness is not phenomenal knowledge. We do not know these inward processes which compose our empirical selves as we know external objects with whose being we are not identical. It is in knowing sense phenomena, however, that we become directly aware of the subjective activities of cognition and interest. With respect to this situation, we find that Kant is correct in stating that we know inward experience only through external experience, and that Descartes and Locke are also right in saying that we have a clearer and more certain knowledge of ourselves than of external objects. Cognition and especially feeling and conation are only recognizable by each individual experient; we thus know ourselves noumenally and hence more intimately than external objects. Nonetheless our immediate acquaintance with ourselves is with the attending, feeling, and conative activities, not with the involved, underlying existent, or that which undergoes and synthesizes these activities. The isolation of the underlying experient from these activities is a task of abstraction and construction of an idea, which refers to something which can be known indirectly but which does not have concrete quality. The pure ego is a concept rather than a "percept"; it is quality-less[79] and transparent as an idea instead of specific and qualified like an immediate datum. This is the reason why it is not obvious to children and to those who deny its existence.

The Pure Ego Indispensable to Psychology

The fact, however, that it is not immediate and obvious but mediate and conceptual does not mean that it is a concept which has no counterpart in reality, nor that it is superfluous and dispensable to psychology. While it transcends immediate data, Tennant contends that it is a concept necessary to psychology. Psychology may ignore it for various purposes of description and scientific analysis, but methodology does not give sanction to denial of its existence. To analyze mind into a series of "events" in forgetfulness of the fact that events transpire in a peculiar experience which is aware that these events are "my events," to analyze mind into "presentations" without acknowledgment of that to which these analytica are presented, or into discrete "phenomena" without admission of that to which phenomena appear, is to hypostatize pure abstractions and to interpret mind after the pattern of atomistic analogies which cannot

79. There is a confusion which may involve a contradiction in Tennant's discussion of the "qualitylessness" of the pure ego. He maintains that it is qualityless (pp. 77–78) and in the footnote on p. 79 he states that the pure ego is pure "only in the sense of having fewer empirical qualities." The matter is further complicated by such questions as may arise out of the following points: How do we know that "consciousness involves a subject" as stated on pp. 17 and 77, and yet not know the subject directly; and how can the "empirical" self be defined as "pure ego plus its objects, states, and relations" (p. 76) and it also be said that we know the latter immediately but not the former. Also, if the pure ego is qualityless, in what sense is it known to be characterized by the quality of idiosyncrasy (p. 96). These references are to *Philosophical Theology*, I.

account for the unity of mind. The burden of Tennant's argument is that true explanation in the realm of psychology is never adequately guided by the principle—*entia non multiplicanda praeter necessitatem*—if application of this principle means simplification of the actual situation to such an extent that mind becomes a string of beads or worse still, beads without a string. The atomic conception of mind to which abstract simplification leads is utterly impossible. Psychology needs the conception of a subject to account for the continuity, unity, and individuality of mental life; such a unifying agent or synthesizing bond is presupposed by psychology even though it may focus its analyses upon distinguishable elements.

Critique of Psychological Theories Which Reject the Pure Ego

Tennant proceeds to give reasons for his belief that theories which reject the actuality of the pure ego are inadequate and to substantiate his conviction that the pure ego is the indispensable ground of the continuity, unity, and individuality of conscious experience. Any theory which attempts to describe momentary experience in terms of discrete instants or to divide the momentary ego-life after the manner of spatial divisions of matter or of separate pictures in a cinema is utterly false. Actual mental experience is a continuous present, an experience of change in which consciousness includes successive events. In a moment of awareness there is always a residuum of the past and an anticipation of the future combined into a present which is psychically instantaneous and unified. From this specious present, it is possible to distinguish discrete portions or separate units, but if you start with discrete parts, it is impossible to add separate entities into a continuing conscious experience. The separate pictures of a cinema are only possible because there is an actor whose behavior is continuous first; there is no way from discrete pictures back to the actor. In any moment of conscious experience it is necessary to admit a momentary subject of experience, a unifying bond of consciousness, which continuously synthesizes a range of distinguishable elements. Those who dispense with it and substitute discrete instants are discussing mathematics not psychology.

Theories which attempt to dispense with the abiding ego are not successful in accounting for the fact of memory or the retention of experiences involving a wide range of time. The series-theory is put forth as an alternative to that of any abiding ego. A series of psychoses is aware of itself as a series; no ego is necessary. This is one theory. But Tennant points out that in order for a series to be conscious of itself as a series, the whole series must somehow constitute and run through each part, a situation for which we have no analogy and which becomes more complicated when it is necessary to suppose that in any series of thoughts all the past presentations must be in some way presented to the last thought of the series in order for it to have unity which is found in retention. To save the series-theory from such absurdity, James introduced the theory that each term is a subject which absorbs its predecessor and thus accumulates past mental inheritance. Instead of a series of subjectless events or thoughts the last of which contains all the preceding, James introduces a series of subjects each of which has its object and then becomes the object of another subject in the series itself. Tennant finds that this introduces more difficulties than it can explain. If each subject is discrete, and if admittedly the object which one subject experiences can never be the same object as that which another subject experiences, how is it possible for one subject in a series to recognize an object as one which a former subject has experienced? Either we have a miracle or else there is one abiding subject which persists throughout the lifetime of one individual, which undergoes, or *erlebt*, various experiences of objects and is able to recognize and compare former objects with later objects as those which have passed through his unique center of experience. Tennant believes that Hume was far wiser than his modern successors when he offered no substitute for the ego about which he had become skeptical. Hume attempted to analyze consciousness into discrete impressions, but without success. Hume may never have found himself without an impression, but Tennant points out that had he been more discerning, he would have realized that he never found an impression which was not "my impression" and that this peculiar fact of ownership of impressions needs to be accounted for.

In like manner, the pure ego is able to account for the facts of the unity and individuality of conscious life whereas the serial theory is not. It is a fact that a person lives a more or less ordered and purposeful life. On a series-theory it must be assumed that each successive discrete ego takes up the purpose and the control

of the former and devotes itself to the furtherance of the causes
of its predecessors. Why should this be so? Why should not the
purposes of disparate egos be different and conflicting; why
should not the orderly character of one ego resolve itself into a
chaos in the next? There must be a sufficient ground for the unity
of purpose and character which exists in personal life. This sufficient ground Tennant finds in the actuality of the abiding ego.
One ego binds various psychoses into one unity so that there is
no absolute disparateness; in so unifying, however, it separates
this stream of experience which I call "my life" from that stream
of experience which is uniquely "your life." My feelings are my
feelings, not yours; my strivings and sensations are mine in a
way that they can never be yours; this is what Tennant means by
saying that the abiding ego is "individual." Individuality, unity
of psychoses, and continuity of experience all find sufficient
ground in the actuality of an abiding, unifying, synthesizing
cause or agent. Though the concept of the pure ego is a concept
and not a percept, it is nonetheless a concept which reflection
finds to be the only explanation for such facts as require explanation. It is thus known to refer to an actual existent, an actual
substance-cause or continuing efficient agency without which the
introspected facts of conscious life are unaccountable.

The Pure Ego an Actuality

That the pure ego refers to an actual existent it is basically
important to establish, for, in Tennant's system, "unless there
be a soul in man, it is idle to talk of a God in the world."[80] The
argument for God is an argument based upon analogy: we know
noumenally one active efficient agent—the pure ego; we know
each other by analogical inference or suppositious ejection; we
know God by wider analogical inference from the evidences of
purposive behavior in the world. It is not to be inferred that the
theistic argument determines the inference of the pure ego; the
ego is a concept drawn to account for the facts of conscious experience and stands upon its own claim to validity. What is important is to note the way it fits into the wider argument.

In order to show that the pure ego is an actuality, Tennant
finds it necessary to examine Kant's position; i.e., that the pure

80. *Philosophical Theology,* I, 94.

ego is a logical construction. If we examine the first *Critique* we shall find that in one section Kant asserted that the thinking ego is "a mere form of consciousness." This causes some interpreters of Kant to affirm that the result of the *Critique* is that the ego is pure form or regulative idea. But Tennant does not believe that this is the real outcome of Kantian thought for two reasons. (1) The occasion of the statement that the ego is a "mere form" is one in which Kant is combating the ontological fallacy of the rationalists who extract from the logical proposition, "I think," the actual fact, "I exist," or make the *cogito ergo sum* an a priori proposition solely without reference to empirical data. (2) But underlying the entire constructive part of the *Critique* is the belief that underlying all the categories is the synthesizing activity of a unifier. The thinking I "does not know itself through the categories but knows the categories only, and through them all objects, in the absolute unity of apperception, that is, through itself"[81] and this represents the actual position of Kant. From an a priori concept of the "I think" it is impossible to affirm the existence of an actual self; but from a noumenal knowledge of the ego as active unifier of the categories and of the entire range of conscious synthesis, it is possible to assert the reality of the pure ego.

The pure ego, then, is an actual, existent ground of conscious experience, involved in all its empirical states of cognition, feeling, and conation as active bond of unity but not as identical with any of these distinguishable elements. By isolating this unifying bond from its presence in any actual moment of conscious experience of which we can have immediate acquaintance, we can reflectively infer what it is from what it does. We can have "knowledge about" the ego if not knowledge in the form of "direct acquaintance"; i.e., the manner of knowing is mediate inference; the knower knows the known by reflective inference, but the knower and the known are metaphysically one though playing two distinguishable roles in the knowing process.

The Nature of the Pure Ego

We can correctly believe that the pure ego is (1) numerically singular, simple, monadic; (2) individual in the sense that its

81. *Ibid.,* I, 93.

states and objects (*idia*) belong to its life alone and to no other conscious being; (3) individual in the sense of idiosyncrasy: i.e., a person's peculiar type of feelings, etc., are what they are because the pure ego is what it is; this is the source of genius; (4) an active agent with powers to cognize, feel, and strive, not a *tabula rasa;* (5) an essence as well as an existence—its essence being to function not in isolation from objects but *en rapport* with objects; (6) noumenal or ontal and not phenomenal; the pure ego does not appear. From the standpoint of metaphysics, we can infer that the ego is a substance (logical substance) in the sense that it is not an attribute or an adjective of any other thing; that it is relatively permanent, and finally, that it is an efficient cause. It is not a substance in the sense of self-subsistent, underived, indestructible, indiscerptible, static, changeless substratum such as the essence of substantiality was conceived to be before Leibniz. It cannot be conceived in terms of spatiality, inertia, and quasi-materiality but rather in terms of the *conatus* of Leibniz; i.e., as active continuent-cause of the unity of conscious experience. Such a ground of conscious facts philosophy cannot dispense with and science cannot deny even though it ignore it for departmental purposes. It is not a logically certified concept; it is not self-evident and a priori; it is rather an alogical interpretation of the facts judged or believed valid of the actual by its pragmatic usefulness in accounting for the facts whereas other theories do not. It is grounded in reasonableness, not in rationality.[82]

(2) Knowledge of Other Selves as Mediate Analogical Inference of Faith

The establishment of a soul in man is connected with and leads to a further discussion of the self's knowledge of other selves. It is Tennant's contention that we know other selves only "mediately" or through "analogical supposition," justified not by logical certainty but by culminative pragmatic reasonableness. His analysis of this "analogical inference" and "intersubjective

82. Tennant's account of possible theories of the metaphysical origin of the pure ego, and his discussion of the empirical self, its inheritance, and development into personality (*Philosophical Theology,* Vol. I, chap. vi) are omitted in this discussion at this point as being irrelevant to the trend of the argument as here presented.

communication" is not treated in any single chapter of *Philosophical Theology* in its entirety but in portions of several chapters dealing with the pure ego, valuation, thought categories, and divine purpose, respectively.[83] The importance of this analysis for theology cannot be underemphasized, for Tennant's final argument for God rests in a vital way upon the analogy between the manner in which a hypothetical Robinson Crusoe would infer the presence of another self in a body which he had not seen before and the manner in which we infer the existence of God from certain behavior of the world.[84] Other selves, ontal causes, and God stand in the same epistemological relation to the self; no one of them is known immediately; only mediately by analogy and then pragmatically justified.

The Genesis of Knowledge of Other Selves

A self's rudimentary knowledge of itself awaits interaction and recognition of other selves like its own. The process of analogical interpretation does not begin as a reflective, consciously drawn inference. Tennant's psychogenetic account of this analogy refers to the whole process of implicit and explicit awareness of another self from the baby's vague, unreflective awareness of his mother's bodily behavior in its action upon him to the gradually increasing explication of intercommunication with other people as well. If the account of this process in *Philosophical Theology*[85] emphasizes the intellectual factor more than the conative and feeling aspects, it is no warrant for the criticism that Tennant invokes an "innate, yet fully developed capacity for reasoning by analogy."[86] In fact, Tennant's whole system of metaphysics is based upon the basic fact of interaction, the interplay of efficient ontal causes in a relatively stable network of *rapport*. Selves are ontal causes of one identifiable type, the presence of which in bodily behavior is recognized by analogous inference.

At first, communication is by gestures and more elementary signals, but when language supervenes, a world of common concepts can be developed and referred to a world of ontal activities.

83. *Philosophical Theology*, I, 72–74, 145–146, 163–165; II, 115–117.
84. *Ibid.*, II, 88.   85. *Ibid.*, I, 72–74.
86. *Mind*, XL, 241–246: Tennant's review of "The World and God" by H. H. Farmer.

In this larger world, one self transcends its own narrow boundaries; becomes able to take an overindividual point of view; and by virtue of its native sympathies with others, develops the characteristics of personality—reason and conscience, which are capable of indefinite extension. The communication of reason and conscience, means and purposes is accomplished by intersubjective intercourse in which words convey or point to concepts which another self can grasp and respond to. But there is no sharing or mutual interchange of private experience. Ten men look at the sun; each has his own unique sense-experience which is absolutely unsharable by any other; but by his gestures and language each mutually informs the other of the position and character of his experience; thus a common concept is built and referred to the actual sun which acts upon all ten experiencers in more or less comparable ways. Another's experience is transcendent to me, but from his bodily behavior I infer by the analogy of my own experience and socially acquired concepts a comparable experience in him. That he is truly such a conscious being with such a comparable experience I can verify, never by self-evidence or logical coerciveness, but solely by culminative pragmatic inference or alogical reasonableness. The person who would deny the existence of God on the grounds that God's existence is not self-evident would have to abandon belief in other selves for a more or less comparable lack of self-evidence if he were to be consistent.

(3) Knowledge of Substance-Causes as Mediate Analogical Inference of Faith

Other selves are not the only metaphysical existents which we know mediately and by analogy. Interacting with the pure ego is an external system of efficient causes, the nature of which is not immediately self-evident but can only be inferred. That something coöperates with the self to produce experience, we know; that that something is intelligible and increasingly sustains intelligible interpretation, we know; what this is in itself we can but infer. Inasmuch as mind is the only existent we know to be intelligent and causally efficient, we may infer by analogy (if no other alternative is available) that these ontal causes must either be spiritual monads or, if dualism be true, have mind behind them. The whole concept of causality assumes a place of utmost importance for science and for theology, and Tennant analyzes it with the utmost care.[87]

The Causal Category

His discussion proceeds by a threefold distinction in the meaning of causality: the causal category—function of the ego in its conceptualizing work; the causal principle—every effect must have a cause; and the causal law or principle of uniformity—like causes produce like effects. First, the causal category. There are two important elements in the causal category—effectuation and necessitation—both of which are derived from inward experience and projected on to things external. From our observable psychical experience of acting and being acted upon, we build the notion of productive agency or effectuation; from our observable experience of effort by means of which we make a thing take a certain shape we derive the notion of necessitation or constraint. Whenever we observe a sequence of phenomena, as for example lightning and thunder, we may interpret the sequence by the notions of effectuation and necessitation although neither of these is directly observed or experienced (*erleben*) in the sequence. We see the flash of the lightning; we hear the sound of the thunder: but the productive efficiency and constraint exercised by the first member of the sequence relative to the second we do not directly observe as we observe the color and sound. Temporal succession is a formal category, not a real or dynamic category; formal categories such as likeness, difference, number, and temporal succession are directly "read off" the data; but the dynamic categories of substance, cause, and teleology are not directly "read off" but "read in" to the data by analogy with the conative self.

In this situation the causal category is not a logical category but an alogical category; it is regulative and not constitutive as Kant, who interpreted the understanding in cognitive terms rather than conative-cognitive terms, falsely suggested. It is not a function of the mind prior to experience nor in abstraction

---

87. Important discussions: *Philosophical Theology*, I, 180–183, and pp. 386–402 append.; "Causality," *Encyclopaedia of Religion and Ethics*, III, 261; *The Journal of Theological Studies*: Review of Stout's "Mind and Matter," XXXIV, 93–94.

from the objects of experience, but rather a function which originates in the interaction of subject and object as a matter of analogical supposition and is thus sufficient to the practical business of living and getting about the world. Beginning in the crude anthropomorphism of the primitive who projects his entire human experience into nonhuman sequences, the causal category becomes refined into the anthropic[88] notion of effectuation and necessity without which it is impossible to interpret the world of nature with any degree of sufficiency. The notion of effort is equivalent to the idea of determination necessary to interpret a relation of temporal sequence in which one event does not emerge without a certain predecessor and in which the sequence of the two is constant or relatively constant. Constancy of sequence together with the indispensable conditioning of a second event by a first demands a notion of determination or causal connection as the sufficient ground of the evidence. Such a conception of cause is not gross anthropomorphic interpretation of the ground of such data; it is not a matter of ascribing to this connection human will or complete anthropic determination; it is, however, an interpretation of the data upon an analogy denuded of all the gross anthropomorphism possible, an attempt "to find some concept intermediate between cause as force or effectuation of the anthropic kind and cause as logical *ratio* which is not cause at all."[89]

Tennant objects both to the attempt of descriptive science to conceive causality in terms of temporal sequence alone and to the attempt of the logician to regard the causal relation as that of logical ground to consequent. Temporal sequence—either variable or invariable—does not logically imply efficiency or determination; hence the conditioning of actual events is not touched by the experience of sequence alone. Logical *ratio* may have nothing whatever to do with actual relations in the world per se;

88. In *Philosophical Theology,* I, 175 n., Tennant makes the distinction between "anthropomorphism" (likeness of man; i.e., "of God as with body and passions, of the sun as rejoicing to run his course") and "anthropic" interpretation (conceiving other beings without personifying them; i.e., without full "anthropomorphic vestiture," but still in terms of those aspects of the human being which are appropriate to the other beings, the signs of whose existence are given; i.e., in the case of physical objects, interpreting them in terms of the efficient activity of the embodied self. The term "anthropic" does not refer to the psychological as distinct from the material aspect of the human being).

89. *Ibid.,* p. 388.

whole systems of logical implications might be developed with perfect logical validity, but whether or not any of these implications hold true of actual interactions in the real world must be decided by inductive and pragmatic verification. The necessity involved in logical *ratio* is not the same sort of necessity as is involved in the efficient necessity of events in the realm of reality. As long as efficiency is the essential element in causality, and as long as the only substance-causes we noumenally know are living subjects, we are forced to eject in some degree our own life and individuality into things; always careful to read into things no more lifelike activity than their behavior suggests. On the common-sense and scientific level of knowledge, inanimate things do not appear to exhibit that spontaneous behavior which is characteristic of life. But if we pass from science to metaphysics, Tennant points out that this verdict may be reversed and inertia may be translated into terms of conation. Here at least we stand on rock bottom, for our interpretation of efficiency is in terms which we know most adequately. Science has been unable to give us a real interpretation of causality; it shifts from one definition of cause to another—from attempts to construe cause in terms of temporal sequence alone, to the principle of uniformity, and to the relation of logical implication—and finally it has become silent about the inward working of efficiency altogether.

It is this confusion of meanings which leads Tennant to distinguish between cause as efficient agency, the causal principle, and the causal law; to point out the implications of these distinctions; and to show how these implications debar intermixtures of meaning. The conception of efficient agency is already before us; it remains to indicate the distinctions between the causal principle—the principle that every effect has a cause and the causal law—the law that like causes produce like effects.

The Causal Principle and the Causal Law

Obviously, the causal principle that every effect has a cause cannot be confused either with the notion of efficient agency or with the principle of uniformity. The causal principle does not denote what the nature of the cause is that produces an effect; it is perfectly possible to interpret the nature of the cause in terms of occasionalism, preëstablished harmony, or some other theory.

Prior to observation and careful analysis of the situation, any sort of productive agency is an open possibility, and the causal principle is perfectly consistent with any one of them. As long as actual efficiency is behind an event to make it determinative of an effect, and as long as there are indications that the cause-effect relation is occurring, the causal principle is a convenient supposition which designates a real relation.

But this principle in itself is distinguishable from the causal law or the principle of uniformity. There is nothing in the principle that "every effect has a cause" to imply that "like causes produce like effects." The notion of likeness is a further matter to be denoted under another principle; namely, the uniformity of causes. There is nothing in the definition of the causal principle which implies that "like causes produce like effects," that the effects resemble their causes, or that the causes are equal to their effects. The causal principle is capable of a variety of interpretations which are largely relative to the purpose of the investigator. Under no circumstances, however, does the principle give one the right to reduce the concept of an actual efficient ground to temporal succession, regularity of sequence, or of logical *ratio*. All attempts to construe causality in terms of certain designated states, attributes, or portions of a process are necessarily abstractive because a complete account of the causal ground of any effect might involve the whole process of nature and this situation would be impossible of useful manipulation in science. By thus cutting the comprehensiveness of the actual causal ground, science is necessarily abstractive and the denotation of a cause is simplified.

It is in conjunction with the uniformity of nature, however, that additional difficulties are encountered and additional abstractiveness is involved for science. Not only is it necessary to specify what part of the process of nature is to be designated as the cause of a particular effect, but it is necessary to denote what parts of the process are like other parts in relation to the recurrence of the effect. This purpose of discovering likeness between antecedent conditions is responsible for the attempt to denude the antecedents of a causal sequence of all quality and to state the likeness in terms of quantities and motion; in other words, to state the causal law or the principle of uniformity in terms of the principle of the conservation of energy. By this method we have passed from an interpretation of nature in its actual quantitative and qualitative fullness to a statement of an aspect of the historical flow in terms of an abstract conceptual diagram. We are enabled by this method to do very important work of a necessary nature, but we have still to remember that the ground for the efficiency of the sequence is unexplained by the quantitative momentum of the sequence, and that there is no way to derive the qualitative fullness of nature from an abstract diagram of motions if all we have in the beginning is this diagram.

Tennant points out that the attempt to substitute regularity of sequence for the notion of efficiency is abortive even in science. Day regularly follows night, but day is not thereby assumed to be the cause of night, as it ought to be if regular antecedents are the causes of consequences. On the other hand, if the sun and the motions of the earth are the causes of day and night, there is some actual necessitation which cannot be avoided. Science must work with a *conditio sine qua non* if it is to do its work. Things in nature have determinate potencies which constitute the actual ground of specific regularities; this science believes even though these potencies are not empirically self-evident. Underlying all inductive science is the postulate of the uniformity of efficient causes, a postulate which is supposition verifiable only by empirical experience up to the present moment and supported by the expectation that nature will behave with similar uniformity in the future. There is no a priori reason why nature must behave uniformly. That nature behaves with relative uniformity seems to be a practically certain probability; that there must be a sufficient causal ground for this uniformity in the actual world is demanded by the fact. What this causal ground of uniformity is, science cannot say without passing over into the realm of metaphysics and here it is no longer science. But in any case, the causal ground is not *ratio* or logical ground.

Efficient Causes and the Cosmic Ground

We are not now concerned to analyze possible conceptions of the actual ground of uniformity of nature as a whole. The question of proximate, efficient causation is before us, and the outcome is that if the element of efficiency in the conception of causation cannot be replaced by regular sequence, temporal sequence, and logical implication, and if the actual efficient ground of an

effect is not immediately perceived as it is in itself, then the only
actual interpretation of the effectuation-element in causality is
in terms of analogy with the self or a cause of which we do have
noumenal experience. In this event, a conception based upon
analogy is supposed to exist to account for the observable temporal and regular sequence in which the activity of nature manifests itself to human minds. Caution must be taken to restrict all
attempts to anthropomorphize the effectuation in inorganic
things at the scientific level of experience-organization. What
the inorganic is in itself when metaphysical speculation is in
order is another matter and here anthropic analogies may be permitted. Efficient causes in nature stand in the same epistemological relationship to the self as other selves; neither type of agents
is known immediately, but mediately by supposition and analogy
practically necessary in accounting for the "immediacies" of
sensation. It is not otherwise when our knowledge of the cosmic
ground is examined. The conception of God is a postulate derived by analogy from the self to account for the ground of a
vast, cosmic complex of interrelated facts. Before this epistemological "demonstration" can be adequately completed,[90] it is necessary to proceed to the second general channel of argument
mentioned on page 28 of this chapter; namely, the attempt to
establish the theistic world-view as the most probable of the various possible world-explanations. When this is done we can return to point out the epistemological similarity between the concept of God and the concepts of the ego, other selves and other
causes.

II. DEMONSTRATION THAT THEISM IS THE MOST PROBABLE OF POSSIBLE WORLD-EXPLANATIONS

It is the second general part of Tennant's argument that
theism is the most probable of the possible world-explanations
from the standpoint of objective reasonableness rather than subjective certitude. A thoroughgoing critique of materialistic
mechanism makes it impossible to say that we know that ontal
nature is a plurality of entities characterized by inertia and
qualitative likeness and moved by impressed forces in rigid uni-

90. Cf. p. 83, below.

formities. On the other hand, psychogenetic analysis makes it impossible for Tennant to accept a subjective interpretation of nature's uniformity. A realistic theory of knowledge of the type indicated above rules out the probability that the subject introduces order into nature. Mind produces conceptual nature in reciprocal interaction with the exacting requirements of an ontal nature which has a uniformity of its own. Thus the important problem to Tennant is how to account for ontal nature's being what it is and not something else. Pluralism, whether dualistic or spiritualistic, is incapable of giving sufficient reason for the world's being what it is and not otherwise. It is incapable of accounting for the characteristics of the ontal world which we believe on substantial probability to exist.

A. FEATURES OF THE REAL WORLD WHICH CALL FOR COSMIC EXPLANATION

(1) An Order Amenable to Thought

The real world as revealed by common sense and science manifests a certain definite general character. First it is an order which is stable and sufficiently related so as to be amenable to human thought. Descartes divided the world of thought from the world of things and then argued that God is necessary to insure correspondence between the two orders of thought and being. Tennant does not find this argument valid because he has grounds for denying the Cartesian epistemology. In Tennant's theory thought arises from things in a duality of experience; hence there is no mystery in the fact that the order of being corresponds to the order of thought. What demands explanation in Tennant's mind is that the order of being is an order and not a chaos. If it were a chaos of unstable entities it could not be known at all. The ground of the stability of its relations and qualities is independent of the human minds which know them, and it is this ground which must be conceived if it is to be understood at all.

(2) An Order of Progressive Organic Changes

A second feature of the world known to science is the progressiveness and direction of changes in the organic world. Unlike Paley, Tennant is not concerned to argue from particular adap-

tations of particular organs for particular purposes to a designer. He is quite willing to accept the Darwinian theory of
natural selection and gradual change. A nexus of proximate
causes offers no insuperable difficulty to theism. What demands
explanation is not the selection of the fit but the arrival of the fit.
Darwin accepted the existence of variations as a given fact and
made no attempt to account for their origin. Such a fact demands a sufficient ground, and if general direction of a process
of proximate causes is demanded, it may be that along with the
general guidance of a plurality of causes toward an end, it is
necessary to assert an original plan manifested in the primary
collocations out of which the relatively independent nexus of
proximate causes arises. Whatever the explanation of the fact
of organic variation, the fact itself is a character of the real
world to be explained.

(3) An Order of Inorganic Adaptations

The third aspect of the world which demands a sufficient
ground is the adaptation of inorganic nature to living organisms. If scientists such as Henderson are to be trusted, it is clear
that a host of factors—astronomical, thermal, chemical, etc.—not
causally related have conspired to constitute an environment
which is fitted for living organisms to evolve. The wonder of this
fact is not lessened by the comment that if some other kind of
environment evolved, some other type of organism might have
emerged. The important fact is that any environment suited to
any sort of life should have appeared at all. It is logically possible that all this happened as a result of the ungrounded coincidence of material particles but that such is the case is humanly
incredible. Inasmuch as the inorganic environment is not known
to have life or mind, and inasmuch as mind is the only force we
know which can control and meet the crises caused by blind
forces running counter to the main objective of the process, Tennant concludes that another feature of the known world points
toward theistic explanation.

(4) An Order Which Evokes Beauty

The fourth characteristic of the real world which requires explanation is its capacity to evoke the experience of beauty in
man's consciousness. Man's psychophysical organism may be

responsible for a large part of the generation of the experience of beauty out of the *rapport* which exists between man and ontal nature. Color, for example, may not be an intrinsic property of ontal nature apart from its relation to man's psychophysical constitution, but man no more generates beauty *ex nihilo* than ideas. In both cases, ontal nature is possessed of a certain intrinsic formal structure which saturates every phase of nature awaiting, as it were, the discovery of man. Ugliness, in Tennant's estimation, is largely the result of man's artistry; nature herself is unspoiled and infinitely capable of evoking the esthetic sentiment in man. Here too it is not argued that design is present in each particular experience of beauty any more than it is discoverable in each particular organic adaptation. Beauty is not solely discoverable in things which are products of purposive art. But judging from the wide range of nature's esthetic potency together with the fact that nature seems to come to herself in man—without man nature's esthetic potency would be meaningless—it is more probable that this situation is due to design than to groundless coincidence. The universality of nature's intrinsic capacity to evoke beauty is as great as its uniformity of natural law. Both point toward an intelligent ground as sufficient reason for existence.

(5) *An Order Instrumental to Morality*

The fifth characteristic of the real world is its instrumentality to the moral experience of persons. Phenomenal man, as distinct from the pure ego, is an organic part of nature. Man is not a freak or sport in the course of nature. His body and the bodily conditioning of his mentality are genetically continuous with humbler organisms. We cannot say that nature suddenly stumbled upon man; man is the culmination of the known history of nature and may be thought of as nature's goal. If it be true that man is organic to nature, then it is not true that nature is indifferent to moral ideals. In the first place, the precondition of morality is intelligence and intelligence is dependent upon nature's uniformity. The uniformity of nature and the hardships involved in a progressive order of nature make nature instrumental in the production of moral life. Secondly, while it is true that the appetites of man are the sources of immoral choices on the part of enslaved wills, it is also true that such impulses are necessary raw materials upon which the human will can function. Nature is not indifferent to virtue; nature herself puts a premium upon health, vigor, temperance, and self-control. Third, Tennant is not impressed with the assertion that the future breakup of the solar system constitutes the final evidence of nature's indifference to the moral struggle. The wider universe may possess the power to make all things new on earth, for all the scientist knows,[91] to say nothing of personal immortality. The knowledge upon the basis of which the scientists advance these predictions is too fragmentary to be conclusive. Hence the fact that man is organic to nature means that nature is instrumental to the occurrence of moral life. It is this adaptation of nature to morality which requires a sufficient reason and points toward the theistic explanation.

(6) An Order of Interconnected Causes

The need for theistic explanation becomes more exacting when these five separate lines of fact are taken in their interconnectedness. The dovetailing of several fields of fact which are not directly connected by proximate causation suggests design on a cosmic scale. There is no intrinsic necessity why the world should not be a chaotic assemblage of disparate parts. Nontheistic philosophy can assign no reason for the world's not being an indeterminate chaos. If it insists upon a self-subsistent plurality, it leaves the intelligibility of the world out of account. The mystery is minimized if the explanation of the world is an intelligent creator who designs the world to be a theater of the moral life. This is less unintelligible than the attractive theory of chance-coincidence. Intricate interadaptation appears to common sense to be the outcome of intelligent design rather than of blind co-incidence. The conception of "unconscious purpose" does not appear to be an impressive alternative to common sense. Some philosophers argue quite vigorously that the known world is the outcome of a formative tendency which moves things toward a goal or goals of which there is no foresight. Just as striving men sometimes accomplish results which work out more advantageously than they had planned, so an unconscious teleology is at work in nature. Tennant rejects this conception upon two

91. See below, p. 135.

grounds. First, the "unconscious wisdom" which nature must manifest in order to deal with the catastrophes involved in evolution is vastly superior to the wisdom and foresight of humanity. When men and societies follow blind urges, they may run amuck as well as achieve unintended advantages. At such times it is conscious correction which saves the day. In the larger world, however, we are asked to believe that many days are saved by unconscious wisdom and this seems to Tennant improbable. Second, insofar as the course of organic evolution has been largely determined by a selective process exercised by the inorganic environment, it must be assumed that the inorganic order possesses a formative tendency about which the physical sciences know nothing. It is this difficulty which forces the conception of unconscious purpose over into the conception of blind coincidence and this, though logically possible, is alogically improbable. If we are to account for the suggestiveness of cosmic design, we had best resort to the conception of a cosmic intelligence who creates and designs the world to be a theater for moral values. This is the most intelligible ground to account for the world's being what it is and not otherwise. No logical proof is possible, but a wide alogical explanation of the world's uniformity and its instrumentality to values is possible on grounds of a probability which is theoretically but different in degree from the probability available in inductive science. From the standpoint of values, the explanation is morally certain if considerations of worth are sound at all. Consequently it may be said that theism is the most reasonable explanation of the world as we know it.

Knowledge of God as Mediate Analogical Inference of Faith

From the standpoint of psychology of cognition[92] the idea of an efficient, intelligent, ethical ground is a complex synthesis of analogical discovery and ejective inference built up out of the *rapport* of a socialized self and the ontal world and used by the self to interpret the world before it. The being of God is not self-evident. It is discovered by an effort of consciousness to form an idea of ground of experiences which are partially determined by stimulation of ontal reality. Epistemologically, the validity of

92. Cf. p. 78, above.

the idea is a venture of faith which is supported by the superiority of its explanation-value when compared to other possible theories. Just as one person's idea of a foreign self is built up by "reading into" sense-experiences the presence of design and of intelligent mind on the basis of analogy to one's self, so in a much broader way the idea of God is "read into" a vaster range of interpreted sense-experience to account for the marks of complex, cosmic adaptation. The former recognition of a foreign human self may have more concrete evidence of a more obviously designated area of experience to base itself upon, but the difference between this and the theistic concept is solely a matter of degree. Thus we draw together Tennant's two central "demonstrations" of the truth of theism: (1) the greater probability of it when compared with the other possible interpretations of the facts; and (2) the essential continuity and likeness of the theistic interpretation to the ideas of other self and other cause.

B. THE NATURE AND ACTIVITY OF GOD

It remains now to state briefly Tennant's exposition of the nature and activity of God and his justification of God's goodness in the face of evil. God is conceived first as creator whose being is transcendent to the world, the primary ontal constituents of which He posits. The act of positing is ultimate and mysterious beyond the power of any analogy from human experience. We do not need to conceive God as existing prior to, and without, a world. God and the world, knower and the known in an ultimate duality of experienced unity—this is the limit of our power of conception. Creation is to be conceived in terms of responsible volition rather than in terms of nonvolitional emanation, but here we are admittedly faced with an ultimate mystery.

God is secondly conceived as designer or being who acts in such a way as to constrain His partially wayward creatures into the general direction of an evolutionary progress toward the existence and maintenance of intelligent creatures in an environment suited for the achievement of goodness, beauty, and truth. Such general guidance of the world toward this end is to be conceived differently in the respective realms of being. If we hold a dualistic metaphysics and conceive the realm of matter to be a lifeless mechanism; (i.e., characterized by inertia and moved by impressed forces), the immanent active guidance of the Supreme Intelligence may be conceived in terms of a change in the direction of the material entities without any change in the physical energy involved. If, on the other hand, we hold a spiritualistic or monistic metaphysics and conceive the realm of matter in terms of rudimentary spirits, the immanent guidance of the Supreme Mind may be conceived in terms of spiritual *rapport*. Such guidance as is exerted in either case is continuous general constraint over and beyond the primary determination of creation. At times, it is theoretically permissible to suppose that the divine will may act specifically and miraculously to devote some natural process to a higher end, but such activity can never be adequately isolated from the natural potentialities of the process, the nature and extent of which we do not know to the full. Miraculous action is possible but not knowable with substantial probability at this stage of the game.

In the realm of personality the immanent action of God upon man can be conceived only in the light of the freedom of man and the moral nature of God. If God is moral personality, whose aim is to develop finite moral personalities in His world, then God must respect the freedom of men. No conception of "infused grace" or "infused light" is reconcilable with human freedom or the morality of God. If inward insight and ability to achieve the good come as the result of the coercive pressure of divine consciousness and power without an achievement of these gifts on the part of man, then man is not free, his morality is not his achievement, and God is not a respecter of personality. The revelation of God's existence and purpose resides in the natural world itself awaiting the effort of man to read the meaning which is engraven upon the world. Man's love of God and the spiritual consequences of this devotion is a natural love which follows a natural insight into the theistic ground of the world.

Again, God is conceived as intelligent being. From the conception of God's intelligence certain limitations of human intelligences must be eliminated. Human intelligences are restricted by sense organs and physiological functions which God is not thought to have. Man knows appearances of the Real; God knows the Real in itself. God being creator, He knows the noumenal world in all its potentialities. No processes of analogous ejection are necessary to God's knowing. By virtue of His posi-

tion as creator, we may conceive his mind as present to all sections of His creation and throughout all the time. Knowledge of
past and present will be His; knowledge of the future must be
His also, insofar as it is predictable from the preformed natures
and uniformities of creatures; but wherever creaturely spontaneity enters in, there we may surmise God's foreknowledge is
limited. He does not know what free creatures will do until they
actually perform.

This limitation with respect to God as intelligence is corre-
spondingly evident in our conception of God's power or will. If
God's purpose is to create free agents who will voluntarily
choose the good, God relinquishes the power to act arbitrarily
and absolutely throughout His creation. If evil arises because
of the presence of free agents in the world, it is an accompaniment of a situation which God intended for the good involved.
In the lower orders of nature, God's power is likewise limited
by the determinateness of His character and of His work.
God cannot work out one plan and a contradictory one at the
same time. If God wills a world in which growth and creaturely
spontaneity are present, He cannot enact a complete and static
world at the same time. If God gives specific properties to the
characters of His creatures, whether high or low, the very determinateness of their natures involves the possibility of evil. If
water is given certain properties which are beneficial to the life
of organisms, it will drown people whenever they do not adjust
themselves to these properties. Determination of creatures involves the possibility of natural evil as a by-product just as
spontaneity and free will involve the possibility of moral evil.
These accompaniments even God cannot set aside without violat-
ing His purpose which on the whole works for good.

Tennant appeals to the general trend of the evolving world as
being rightfully judged to be good. Men feel that moral evil is
not too great a price to pay for moral freedom. Men know that
in general evil tends to destroy itself whereas goodness goes from
strength to strength. Tennant thinks that evil does not come
out of good though good may come out of evil. The crux of the
problem of evil comes in what Tennant calls the "trial of faith."
God has not chosen to reveal Himself and His goodness in such a
way that man can be coercively certain of His character. This involves a venture of faith beyond the evidence. No attempt to

reconcile the goodness of God with the reality of evil is possible in Tennant's judgment if particular evils are thought to imply some hidden intention of Providence. A wide theodicy is the only alternative open to a theist in his attempt to substantiate his hope in God's goodness, as a wide teleology is the only course open to the theist in his attempt to substantiate his faith in God's existence.

With this brief and inadequate statement of Tennant's exposition of the nature of God and the reconciliation of His goodness with the presence of evil in the world, we conclude our statement of His answer to the central problem of faith.

CHAPTER II

A CRITIQUE OF TENNANT'S EMPIRICAL VALIDATION OF THEISM

The Purpose of This Chapter

IT is the purpose of this chapter to substantiate the following conviction: That Tennant's general position; namely, that the truth of religious belief can *only* be established by philosophical arguments which exclude the data of religious experience, is untenable because the implied conception of the origin and nature of religious apprehension (as conceptual construction of "atheous" data by way of analogical inference from secular data) is untenable. The conception of religious experience which underlies this conception of validation is false largely because the inferences are not validated. The only way the truth of religious belief can be supported is first and primarily to point men to those experiences which make the belief possible, and then to build a philosophical argument from a wide range of data which includes the specifically religious experiences. The first step is to denote direct experiences. Religion does not arise in indirect reasoning; neither is it entirely validated by indirect reasoning. It is validated primarily by repeated direct experience and secondarily by indirect conscious reasoning.

A Summary of Tennant's Position

In setting out to accomplish the task which is thus defined, it is necessary to recall that the exposition of Tennant's position has brought out the following points:

1. The truth of religious belief can *only* be established by philosophical argument.

2. Reason is the sole judge of truth in religion as elsewhere.

3. Reason is the sole judge of truth in religion because Reason constructs the idea of God by a complex process of synthesizing inferences from empirical facts of the natural world. The inferences are drawn on the basis of analogy. They are at first crude and implicit; but later they are made explicit. The explicit process by means of which intelligent man rises to his idea of God is

illustrative of the crude process of "un-self-conscious" reasoning by means of which man first reached his notion of God or gods. The idea of God originates in a process of ideational construction and inference from facts perceived originally by the senses —facts, it should be noted, which originally do not contain any suggestion of the divine presence but which finally by projective in-reading acquire a conceptual accretion which stands for God.

4. Though man begins his career without any notion of God, he acquires it by reflection. His emotional and practical response to this idea is his religious experience. The feeling and practical responses do not apprehend the religious object; they follow it and derive their character as religious feelings and behavior from the idea of God.

To summarize this statement in reverse order, science is first. Religion arises by reflection upon the facts ascertained by science. If the resulting conclusion of this reflection is "demonstrated" to be valid on the grounds of "probability" which is not different in kind but only in degree from that underlying the concepts of scientific fact and theory, then the central object of religion is validated. If this reflective construction is invalid, then religion is illusion.

Testimonies of Various Authors with Respect to the Weaknesses of an Empirical Philosophical Theology Which Rules Out Religious Experience at Its Base

To introduce a discussion of the weaknesses of this position, it is illuminating to present the testimony of other thinkers in the field of religion and theology for whom these statements are untrue. To these thinkers theism cannot be established by rational argument alone; an appeal to religious experience is necessary.

A. *Professor N. K. Smith.* After disclosing the logical weaknesses of the design argument and the impossibility of deriving the concepts of omnipotence, omniscience, eternity, and omnipresence from primary finite apprehension, Professor N. K. Smith writes:

If, without any antecedent or independent apprehension of the Divine, we have to start from the creaturely, as exhibited in Nature and in man, and by way of inference and of analogy—on the pattern of what is found in the creaturely—through enlargement or other processes of ideal completion, to construct for ourselves concepts of the Divine, then the sceptics have been in the right; the attempt is an impossible one, condemned to failure from the start. We cannot reach the Divine merely by way of inference, not even if the inference be analogical in character. By no idealization of the creaturely can we transcend the creaturely.[1]

Setting aside the assertion of eighteenth-century thinkers, notably Hume and Kant, that nature gave them an irresistible impression of design as a misinterpretation of the actual facts, Professor Smith continues:

When we turn to the spontaneous utterances of the religious mind, we find quite a different response to the impression made by Nature. We may take as typical the Old Testament writers. As A. B. Davidson has made so convincingly clear in his *Theology of the Old Testament*, "it never occurred to any prophet or writer of the Old Testament to prove the existence of God." For them that was quite needless. They moved among ideas that presuppose God's existence—a Being with whom they stood in relations of religious fellowship. This conception of God already possessed is used by them to explain the world. In Davidson's own words: "The Hebrew thinker came down from his thought of God upon the world; he did not rise from the world up to his thought of God. . . . There seems no passage in the Old Testament which represents men as reaching the knowledge of the existence of God through nature or the events of providence, although there are some passages which imply that false ideas of what God is may be corrected by the observation of nature and life."[2]

Summarizing this section, he says:

The position, then, as regards the convictions of religious writers, whether in the Old Testament or elsewhere, is this. In and through their religious experience of fellowship with God, they have belief in God, and coming to Nature and history with this belief in their minds, they interpret Nature and history freely in accordance therewith. They do not observe order and design, and therefore in-

1. "Is Divine Existence Credible?" *Proceedings of the British Academy*, XVII, 220.
2. *Ibid.*, p. 224.

fer a Designer: they argue that order and design must be present even where they are not apparent, because all existences other than God have their source in him. They start, that is to say, from an immediate experience of the Divine; and only so are their methods of argument and modes of expression possible at all.[3]

Finally, he concludes:

I come now to my last point, which is also my main point; it can be quite briefly stated. Though religion of any high type thus comes late, and is made possible only through and in connexion with our specifically human modes of activity, none the less the initial experiences in which religion takes its rise continue to be the source from which we can still best learn, and from which indeed we can alone learn, one all-important side of Divine Existence. It is, we may still maintain, through and in connexion with the cosmic setting of our human life, that we can alone experience that aspect of the Divine which is so essential to its credibility, because so essential to its possibility, and which is also required in order to give proper perspective to all our other assertions in regard to the Divine—the otherness, the non-creatureliness, of the Divine, as a Being whose throne is the heavens and whose footstool is the earth.[4]

B. *Rees Griffiths*. In a vigorous attempt to defend the a priori character of the religious apprehension, Rees Griffiths reveals the weaknesses of the "ideal construction" hypothesis as follows:

. . . the ideal construction theory proceeds on the assumption that religion is strictly a posteriori, and therefore is built upon non-religious material by a process of inference. The tree of experience, it is surmised, can be made to yield religious fruit although the tree itself must give no hint of its fruit-bearing properties. Even were the theistic proofs valid, the theistic position thus reached would not bear the weight of religious faith unless the proofs themselves were constituted of religious judgments and valuations. But this latter condition the ideal construction theory will not allow, for it must start with a world where no direct acquaintance with God is given, where there is no immediate aware-

3. *Ibid.*, p. 226.   4. *Ibid.*, pp. 232–233.

ness of God until a long process of reflection and bitter struggle has been passed through. Let me repeat that the God who is an hypothesis to explain the world can gather into Himself only the elements of the world to explain which He is postulated. God must be somewhere in experience before He is requisitioned to explain it. And He must be in experience in His character as He is known to the religious consciousness. We shall be avoiding the crucial issue as between the a priori and the a posteriori factors in religious faith unless we are willing to make clear to ourselves this important consideration. If God can be regarded as an hypothesis formed to explain facts of experience, then the facts to be explained must in some sense be already religious facts. The function of hypothesis in science is not the creation of facts but the explaining of them, by the discovery of the law of their behaviour. When the hypothesis works, it may lead to new facts, but these are always facts of the same order as those already experienced. Thus, a physical law never leads to moral facts, nor a moral discovery to new physical facts. If God be an hypothesis, experience must yield as a precondition some a priori element where God is already intuitively apprehended. If, however, we speak of God as an hypothesis, framed to explain not religious facts but the facts of secular experience, then we are using the word hypothesis in an illegitimate sense, and by so doing we confuse the epistemological issue.[5]

.   .   .   .

But if the apprehension of the divine quality of the world is not given within that world, as it presents itself in "natural experience," we cannot bring that quality into experience via a God who is nothing more than an hypothesis consciously framed to supply a mere uniting or completing function which speculative reflection demands.[6]

With reference to the appeal of theologians to rational proofs of God's existence, Griffiths says:

The ideal construction theory of religion makes much use of the theistic proofs. Time was when the philosophy of religion was comprised in an examination of such proofs. The certitude of faith was taken to depend, in the last resort, on rational arguments that

5. Rees Griffiths, *God in Idea and Experience*, pp. 66–67.
6. *Ibid.*, p. 76.

could be considered valid on philosophical grounds. This natural inclination to resort to such proofs is evidence that underlying this view of religion there lurks an implied belief that the nature of religious faith is governed by the same logic as that employed in the proofs themselves. The proofs are taken and used as if they were a more explicit application of the categories that are involved in the religious attitude to the world and life. This, I would urge, is a perfectly unwarranted assumption. Though the arguments which produce the proofs may all be legitimate and helpful, constituting an effective defence of faith's citadel, they certainly do not provide a complete and satisfactory vindication of faith. Few indeed would claim perfect cogency for any of them. At the same time it is equally certain that the nature of religious experience and practice reveals an inner assurance such as the proofs cannot produce. At best they are but supports of a truth which is already, for religion, above all misgiving. For faith is always "the assurance of things hoped for, the proving of things not seen."[7]

C. C. C. J. Webb. Professor Webb is certain that it is impossible to "demonstrate" the existence of God by "proofs" which set aside specific and direct religious experience. He writes:

It is true to say that only in and through a religious experience have we any knowledge of God; what are called "arguments for the existence of God" will never prove to those who lack such an experience the existence of God, but only at most the need of assuming, in order to account for our experiences other than religious, a designing Mind, or a Necessary Being, or an Absolute Reality. But the religious experience is ever an experience of a Reality distinct from and unexhausted in the experience as mine. And where there is religious experience present, the arguments which apart from it prove the existence of something which is yet not God are informed with a new significance.[8]

. . . .

. . . it is vain to suppose that, apart from some specifically religious experience in our hearer, we can, so to say, force religion upon a reluctant mind by means of such reasonings. It would be as idle to expect to do this as to expect to create by arguments of a

7. *Ibid.,* pp. 62–63.
8. Webb, *God and Personality,* p. 152.

quite general sort an appreciation of music or of poetry in a soul unsusceptible of aesthetic emotion. Kant himself, we must here remember, did not rest content with his destructive criticism of the old "rational theology." By appealing to the inexpugnable sense of moral obligation, the existence of which would be, he held, unintelligible unless the ultimate nature of the universe were other than without it we could have suspected it to be, he opened a way to those who have since appealed in support of the claims of Religion to elements in our consciousness of ourselves in relation to the world around us—such as the sense of reverence—which we may subsequently discover to underlie even the activity of scientific investigation, which ever pre-supposes what it can never prove, namely the ultimate rationality of the universe which it sets itself to explore. . . . The new defence of Religion which arose in the 19th century, and of which the German philosopher and theologian Schleiermacher is perhaps the most celebrated pioneer, did not aim at compelling men to admit the existence of a God quite apart from any direct consciousness of standing already in the presence of an Object of religious awe and reverence; but rather at calling upon them to recognize such a consciousness in themselves where they had neglected to attend to it and had therefore failed to cultivate and develop it.[9]

*   *   *   *   *   *   *

The attempt to deduce the reasonableness of Religion from a belief in God's existence based on other than religious grounds is bound to fail; for the non-religious arguments alleged in support of the belief can only help to establish a genuinely religious faith when they are themselves interpreted in the light of that religious experience which alone originally makes us aware of God at all. Apart from this they cannot reveal God to us; they can at the most remove obstacles to the reception by our minds of a revelation mediated by that capacity for communion with the divine which is, as I said above, a normal feature of our humanity.[10]

*   *   *   *   *   *   *

. . . the ultimate appeal of Theism is not to arguments, however strong when brought forward in support or defence of a be-

9. Webb, *Religion and the Thought of Today*, p. 38.
10. Webb, *Religion and Theism*, pp. 25–26.

lief natural from the first to the human mind, but to the actual experience of the normal excitation in our souls by the Reality by which we find ourselves confronted and environed, of perceptions and sentiments which, apart from such an object as Theism assigns to them, must be regarded as essentially illusory and incapable of satisfaction.[11]

D. *C. D. Broad.* In his critical review of Tennant's *Philosophical Theology,*[12] Broad contends that Tennant does not establish a "probability" for the validity of the theistic idea by teleological argument. In another passage,[13] he states that Tennant "does not do so well" to ignore the mystics' experience, especially when such testimony comes from intellectually respectable sources. Through such experiences Broad is willing to believe it likely that men are coming into contact with a Reality which they do not apprehend in any other way. In other words, the testimony of religious experience is more convincing to Broad than the teleological argument, which he regards as failing to establish a "probability" for Divine Reality. From written sources we derive an explicit statement of his position. In the preface of a recent book he writes:

Dr. Tennant, in his *Philosophical Theology,* after quoting a characteristic passage from Jacob Boehme, as characteristically remarks that "the critic does well to call nonsense by its name." No doubt he does. But he does not do so well if he ignores the problem presented by so much similar nonsense from so many and intellectually respectable sources. To me, for one, this fact strongly suggests that there is a genuine and important aspect of reality, which is either ineffable, or if it is not, is extremely hard to express coherently in language which was, no doubt, constructed with other aspects of experience.[14]

Elsewhere Broad writes:

Finally I come to the argument for the existence of God which is based on the occurrence of specifically mystical and religious experiences. I am prepared to admit that such experiences occur among people of different races and social traditions, and that

11. *Ibid.,* p. 134.   12. *Mind,* XXXIX, 476 ff.
13. Cf. below.
14. C. D. Broad, *Examination of McTaggart's Philosophy,* preface, pp. li–lii.

they have occurred at all periods of history. I am prepared to admit that, although the experiences have differed considerably at different times and places, and although the interpretations which have been put upon them have differed still more, there are probably certain characteristics which are common to all of them and will suffice to distinguish them from all other kinds of experience. In view of this I think it more likely than not that in religious and mystical experience men come into contact with some Reality or aspect of Reality which they do not come into contact with in any other way.[15]

E. *Alban G. Widgery*. The testimony of Widgery is worth citation because of its special reference to Ward, Tennant's philosophical master. Though Tennant does not believe that Idealism as a metaphysical theory must be established before theism is justified he does, as Widgery charges Ward, tend to make religion predominantly a response to an idea or hypothesis rather than more directly to a living reality. Widgery writes:

Religious Realism charges most of the Idealist descriptions of religion with being occupied too predominantly with the ideas of religion. In contrast with this it presents religion as a complex of ideas, feelings, practical attitudes and actions, having their roots in distinctive immediacies.[16]

. . . .

Ward's treatment of religion is even more unsatisfactory than his treatment of physical nature. What he does in the main in this direction is to show that certain traditional ideas of religion fit very well into his general scheme of thought. In taking over these ideas he fails to make the necessary acknowledgements that he has

15. C. D. Broad, "Belief in a Personal God," *Hibbert Journal*, XXIV, 47. In fairness to Broad, lest the above gives a false impression of his position, it is important to quote his commentary upon this: "But I do not think that this Reality which manifests itself to certain men in religious and mystical experiences is personal. I think that we are inclined to believe this because we are most familiar with the religious experiences of Western Europeans and of Jews most of whom have put this interpretation upon them. We do not know, or we forget, that the mystics and religious teachers of the Far East on the whole reject this interpretation. And we are inclined to forget that certain Europeans, such as Plotinus and Spinoza, who have had these experiences also reject this interpretation of them."

16. D. C. Macintosh, ed., *Religious Realism*, p. 113.

obtained them from the realm of religion in which they have their bases. Having to his own satisfaction shown the difficulties of Naturalistic Monism, Pluralism, and Singularistic Idealism, he turns to theism as the one remaining plausible alternative view. After all has been said, the idea of God remains for Ward an hypothesis. It is required to round off his spiritualistic system. He does not show how he arrives at the content which the idea has for him. Thus, both as regards the spiritualistic character of nature and the theistic view of the whole, he really gives us no more than speculative hypotheses.[17]

Under the same general charge of "intellectual hypostatizing," Widgery places Hastings Rashdall and W. R. Sorley.

For both Rashdall and Sorley God is primarily a speculative, conceptual implication of ethics. Yet both insist that ethics itself is to be based on moral experience as sui generis. Unless it is to be asserted that religion is nothing more than morality, it is reasonable to maintain that the concepts associated with religion are likewise first to be understood with reference to religious experience as sui generis, whatever application may be made of these concepts thereafter with relation to morals.[18]

Widgery states that historically religion has been concerned with a reality and not with hypothesis,[19] that each area of reality has its own distinctive "immediacies"[20] in which the concepts of that area have rootage, that religion has its own "immediacies"[21] and its own particular methods and training for acquiring experience comparable to the requirements of obtaining experience in other fields.[22]

F. The testimony of other theologians who believe that religious experience occupies an important part in validating the truth-claim of religion might be continued at length.[23] The im-

---

17. *Ibid.*, pp. 102–103. 18. *Ibid.*, pp. 105–106.
19. *Ibid.*, p. 115.
20. Cf. Widgery, *The Comparative Study of Religions*, pp. 142 ff., for indication of the "immediacies" in which the higher concepts have their roots.
21. *Religious Realism*, p. 113. 22. *Ibid.*, p. 114.
23. Reference might be made to writers in the field of religious psychology: James, Pratt, Thouless, Hughes; to theologians who defend religious experience by pointing to its rootage in the nature of man: Inge, Paterson, and Matthews compare it to an instinctive movement of the self; Griffiths and Knudson, developing the thought of Troeltsch, Otto, Kalweit, compare it to a priori condi-

portance of this testimony is that there is a widely held conviction that religious experience cannot be set aside in attempts to substantiate the validity of the idea of God. Notwithstanding the variations in the concept of "religious experience," there is no evidence that any of these thinkers believe with Tennant that religion can be "established" by rational argument alone.

The Central Difficulty: The Conception of the Nature of Religious Apprehension as Analogical Inference from Nonreligious Data

The central difficulty with Tennant is that his implied and underlying conception of the origin and nature of religious experience is false. Given originally purely secular, "atheous" data, it is impossible to rise to valid thought and experience of God by way of inferences from such data. Given an original apprehension of God, it is possible to argue from God and the world to God with some larger measure of plausibility. It is the purpose of this chapter to show that Tennant means to hold that man "creates" his idea of God by an implicit teleological argument of the type that he justifies explicitly, and that the explicit attempt to substantiate a consciously controlled inference from secular data to theistically interpreted data is not legitimate apart from a prior direct apprehension of God.

The Idea of God Derived from Implicit Analogical Inference

The first part of the above purpose can be accomplished rather quickly. In an unpublished lecture,[24] Tennant states that "analogical interpretation of other selves and of natural causes is as old as humanity" and that this same analogical interpretation is involved in man's most primitive theological analogizing. Such a process is involved in the crude natural religion which ever precedes revealed religion. Man, whether primitive or civilized, never comes to God until he first believes that God is. Tennant's entire psychogenetic analysis is aimed to reveal the actual psychological process by which the cognitive results of man's knowing are obtained. This is the whole point in his insistence that

tions of mind; or to those who emphasize the objective reference of religious experience: D. C. Macintosh, K. Edward, W. Spens, C. E. Raven, H. H. Farmer, John Oman, R. L. Calhoun.

24. Class lectures given at Cambridge on "Philosophy of Religion."

"implicit" analogizing occurs before it is possible to make this process "explicit" in psychology. It follows that religious knowledge arises in the way psychogenetic psychology describes. Man found the world without any direct experience of the divine involved in the facts of the world. Then by analogical construction, he developed the concept which when "read into" the experienced world gave him religious data. Man derives his religious idea at the end of "implicit" analogical reasoning.

The Implicit Inference Is Fallacious if the Explicit Teleological Inference Is Fallacious

This, it will be necessary to show, is essentially fallacious. To do this an examination of his explicit theory is in order. His theory stated in extremely brief fashion is that certain generally accepted facts demand a certain type of sufficient ground for their being what they are instead of something else. These facts are as follows: (1) the primary collocations of environmental materials such as are necessary for the support of organisms; (2) the progressive variations of organisms from lower to higher forms; (3) the presence of minds which know an environment orderly enough to be known when it might have been otherwise; (4) esthetic form and structure of an environment which evokes the experience of beauty in minds; (5) the contributions of nature to the materials and possibilities of moral experience in human selves; (6) the complex, intricate dovetailing and interconnection of these various factors with one another; i.e., the subservience of natural processes to the experience of Values. These six demand a sufficient ground as the causal explanation of the working unity and contribution of diverse elements to the achievement of value experience. This sufficient ground, Tennant believes, is the coördinating purpose of a Supreme Mind. Not every determinate system needs to be interpreted in terms of rigid materialistic mechanism. The diverse entities of the universe can be held into a mechanicalness or uniformity by a purpose which coördinates the facts into creative achievement. It is only in viewing the cosmos as a whole that we perceive an interlocking system comparable to Paley's watch, a mechanism subserving the end for which it was designed.

Reviewing the facts enumerated above, it may be noted that

Tennant maintains that the primary collocations of environmental materials could not have been informed by a purpose unless those materials were first existent and potential with the
properties necessary to such a change. The foundational elements out of which the collocations emerged in accordance with
design were not formless material entities, but entities sufficiently determinate to permit collocation. Thus the foundational
elements demand a ground upon which they depend, and this
ground is creator not designer. Creator means ground-of-the-
dependent-many. The many are dependent upon a more fundamental ground in a way in which the ground itself is not dependent upon the many. Yet the ground does not exist without
the world; neither can we conceive it as existing prior to the
world in time. The many and the ground are coeternal. Of the
creative relation between ground and the many we have no possible analogy or insight, but pushing the fundamental analysis
of human consciousness to an ideational limit, we note that conscious experience is always a duality-in-unity; i.e., a subject-
object relation in the unity of awareness—and applying this
concept to the ultimate mystery, Tennant says that we may suppose that ground and the world (foundational entities) are also
bound into a subject-object relation in the unity of experience.
Creation then might be likened to creative intuition in which the
mind posits its Objects, subject and object being coexistent and
apparently mutually determinate if the objects are metaphysical entities with causal power of their own and not merely ideas
in the mind of God. The whole *modus operandi* of creation Tennant readily concedes is an ultimate mystery. It is a mystery
which confronts all world-views alike, however, and its plausibility (probability) rests in its superior power to suggest a reason for the world's being what it is and not otherwise.

Hume's Objections to the Teleological Inference Applied to Tennant's Argument

The objections to this argument will be stated with direct reference to Hume's criticisms of the teleological argument. A
major part of Hume's criticism of the teleological argument
turns upon the inadequacy of the argument by analogy from
human workmanship and the product of human artistry to the

world and its author. In the world of our experience when we see a house, we can infer that the house has had a builder because we have had previous experience of both houses and builders; i.e., we have a prior basis in experience for applying an analogy to both the effect and the cause of the effect. Given similar or analogous effects and given previous experience of causes which produce such effects, the inference that a house has a builder is strongly substantiated.[25] But in the case of the universe, we are confronted with certain great difficulties. (a) First it is not clear that the universe is an artificial product such as a house or ship; it may be like an animal; i.e., a self-originated, self-maintained order, or it may be an order due to chance arrangement as the Epicureans held.[26] (b) Second, it is not true that the only cause of order which we know in experience is mind. "Instinct, generation, vegetation"[27] are known causes of order. Hume thinks that it is illegitimate to take one of the several springs of order, namely, thought,[28] and apply it to the source of the order of the world. Logically there are several possible inferences, the analogies of which we find within experience, which may be applied to the source of the universe as a whole. Therefore, there is no final demonstration of the teleological argument. (c) The third point which is made by Hume is that even if the inference were legitimate, the experience of finite effects does not justify the inference of a Being who is Infinite,[29] Perfect, and One. Hume points out that the world may be a very inferior product created by finite deities who have "botched" and "bungled" their job.[30] The world as we know it is defective;[31] hence you cannot possibly infer that its cause is perfect.

A fourth point which Hume brings out in his *Enquiry Concerning the Human Understanding*[32] and is relevant to the above is this: religion not only infers a cause far greater than is necessary to account for the present data, but magnifying the glories of the God thus inferred, it then proceeds to broaden the data so

25. Cf. Hume, *Dialogues of Natural Religion* (N. K. Smith's ed.), pp. 178 ff.
26. *Ibid.*, pp. 224–225.   27. *Ibid.*, p. 220.
28. *Ibid.*, p. 183.   29. *Ibid.*, Pt. V, pp. 205 ff.
30. *Ibid.*, p. 207.
31. Cf. *ibid.*, pp. 237 ff., in which Hume gives a list of the miseries of finite existence to illustrate the unsubstantial factual basis for inferences to a deity possessed of moral qualities.
32. Cf. N. Kemp Smith, *Hume's Dialogues*, pp. 66–67.

as to gain a true basis for its inference. The effects which God has produced are said to be only a minor part of those which He will produce. The present data is part of a greater whole which is yet to come. Thus the order of the argument is reversed—the cause gives the effect which is to validate the cause.

I. WEAKNESSES OF THE EMPIRICAL ANALOGIES

These criticisms must now be applied to Tennant. First, the "analogy" weaknesses: Tennant is thoroughly aware of the fact that we have no analogies in experience which are applicable to the act of creation which he states is implied by a designer of the world. Plan and deed are accomplished simultaneously and eternally by the Creator-designer. We are never to conceive God as existing without a world. We are not to conceive of an original matter existing independent of formal properties or as independent of the Creator. The Creator eternally posits the finite members of His creation somewhat after the manner of a creative artist who forms his masterpiece in thought and in deed simultaneously. The closest analogy which we have to world-positing is creative intuition in which mind puts forth its ideas. Even this example is imperfect because the world entities are not ideas, but semiindependent active causes.

The Contractor, Architect, and Creative Artist

Obviously, Hume's exposure of the cruder analogies, such as the contractor and the architect, do not apply to Tennant's theory. But there are still difficult half-true analogies which are suggested to cast light upon the ultimate unexplicabilities. The world as a whole is still regarded as an eternal artificial product, a gigantic mechanism like Paley's watch, which is "planted out" and designed to produce semiindependent beings capable of struggle for spiritual values. It is in connection with these suggestions and the admitted lack of suggestions that Tennant's empirical theism loses its probability. In human experience we have knowledge of certain types of designers. One is the contractor who constructs a building according to a completely drawn plan. Manifestly, if we apply this analogy to the designer of the world, we must suppose that he is possessed with a completely drawn plan of the entire world-structure and process, that he is confronted with already existing materials, and that his task consists of informing the materials with his design. This means either that the materials are independent, uncreated entities or that they are dependent, created entities. If the former be true, God is not God, a supreme and final source of all; if the latter be true, God is Creator not Designer, the analogy is inapplicable, and we have no analogies in the experienced human realm which fits creation from eternity or creation *ex nihilo*. If the former be held and the materials are independent, where did the plan come from? A contractor does not create his plan, he executes a design already drawn. From whence comes the plan by which a world contractor guides the formation of his materials? Plans are either created or repetitive ideas. That is to say, if a person has done something once, he remembers what he has done and can plan to repeat the order of his activities a second time. If we apply this to the designer of the world, can we say that God designs this world on the basis of former creative acts? Manifestly we do not know of the creation of former universes from experience.

On the other hand, if we say that plans are created by the contractor, we are saying that the contractor is the architect also. The architect may not have in mind a completely thought-out plan of what is to be built, but he begins his plan only when a demand for a building is made upon him by another person. Knowing in general what is wanted, and knowing the compositions of the materials with which he has to consider, he proceeds to create a plan which the contractor can execute. The creator of the plan will be guided by the reference to the general purpose, to the materials involved, and to intercommunication with other individuals as the plan is made, and changed, and remade according to emerging considerations of need and expense and labor. Obviously, if we are to apply this analogy to the designer of a world-plan we face the same type of situation; namely, the existence of a general idea or wish, and the existence of materials of definite structure. Manifestly, we are far removed from monotheistic creation.

If we cease using the analogy of the architect creating a plan and employ the analogy of the genius in the fine arts, the analogy becomes more subtle but not entirely different. The genius may not have a notion of what he wants to create nor any other mind to inform him; the moment of creation may mean that thought and deed occur simultaneously as when a musician plays off his new masterpiece as he creates it in his mind, but even here we realize that his psychophysiological organism, the energy he employs, the instruments he uses, and his audience are all there in his environment. He creates music but does not posit his environment. We have no analogies for this. It is sheer mystery.

God, the Creator-Designer

God the Designer is God the Creator, by implication, we are told. The Creator does not precede his creation in time; creator and the world or some entities of the world are coeternal. Purposive idea and creative deed occur in simultaneous "togetherness" and elementary world-materials are the result. These elementary world-materials are of such a nature that they can be further molded into an environment which is fitted for organic life, and thence into organic structures which are instruments into which life and eventually the pure ego come by later acts of pure creation. Thus we are presented with two types or instances of purposive action on the part of God: (1) creation before which neither design nor deed exists; and (2) formation before which designed materials and incompleted plans do exist and are expressed subsequently in formative activity.[33]

Now it is possible that the analogy of design may have some

33. Pringle-Pattison (*The Idea of God in the Light of Recent Philosophy,* p. 325) writes this concerning the traditional design argument: "In truth the traditional forming agent seems to represent the Creator as originating a material which has no relation to his purposes—which has no formative nisus in itself and which has therefore to be moulded into accordance with his ends, and directed in its course, by a supplementary exhibition of divine wisdom. It is as if the existence of material were referred simply to the divine power— treated as a result of a fiat of omnipotence—the introduction of order and plan being a subsequent operation of the divine wisdom, specially calculated to serve as a proof of the divine existence. But apart from the criticism that this comes perilously near to creating difficulties in order to solve them with credit, it is obviously inadvisable to treat matter and form in this way as initially unrelated to one another." Tennant avoids this last criticism but surrenders the design argument for creation in doing so and comes "perilously near to creating difficulties in order to solve them with credit" by intermingling design with creation.

relevance to the second instance of designing activity, if an ultimate dualism were maintained and God were thought of as introducing order into uncreated materials. But this is not Tennant's
theory; consequently when the analogy is applied to the first
type, it breaks down. There is nothing in human experience
analogous to the creative activity of God.

The Fatal Admission

In admitting that our empirical analogies break down before
this ultimate mystery, Tennant throws away the case for an
empirical theism of the type he has erected. For it is his contention that his theory is more probable than any other theory, that
his theory accounts for the world's being what it is in a way in
which other theories do not, and that the greater adequacy of
his theory will bring conviction to those outside the community
of believers. If the "outsider" approaches the problem of world-
explanation without any immediate sense of the presence of a
world-ground, it is hard to see how he regards an analogy, which
he does not find in experience, as establishing a greater probability for one world-explanation than another. If this conviction is already there or taken as fact, then the exposition of the
points at which the analogy fails will help to make explicit the
fact of the mystery and thereby bring some satisfaction to some
minds.

II. WEAKNESSES OF THE COGNITIVE ANALO-
GIES TO RELIGIOUS APPREHENSION

At this point, however, it is extremely important to note that
the empirical analogy which Tennant depends upon to give
"probability" to his argument for God is taken from the realm
of knowing or of psychological genesis. The psychological process of coming to believe that God exists is comparable to the way
in which we come to believe that other selves and other things
(substance-causes) exist. Knowledge of God is psychologically
generated "in much the same way"[34] as new-born belief in another self. It is necessary to examine the nature of this analogy
somewhat at length, for Tennant's whole case is believed to gain
its "probability" here.

34. See reference to Robinson Crusoe, *Philosophical Theology*, II, 88.

A. SUBSTANCE-CAUSES NOT APPREHENDED BY A PROCESS OF MEDIATE ANALOGICAL INFERENCE

We learn from Tennant that a psychological analysis of the genesis and evolution of consciousness results in the deliverance of the commonly accepted fact that a rudimentary consciousness first becomes aware of sensa in a sense continuum. Sensa at this stage are not regarded as permanent active things. Consciousness of thinghood or of substance-cause is due to a process of "implicit analogizing" in which a subject becomes aware of the persistence and activation of his own body and by analogous ejection throws out the primitive postulatory idea of enduring thing. This process is accomplished in two steps: first, consciousness of bodily self and sensa, and second, an "in reading" of a notion derived from the bodily self into the sensa. None of this process, it is to be noted, is explicit or introspectible by the observer. It all evolves prior to the observer's consciousness of his mental activities. We assume the process to be the actual process because we arrive at it by a critical and analogical regress from what we introspect in deliberate and self-conscious processes. What is to be thought of this analysis?

(1) No Way to Check the Theory by Direct Experience

In the first place, it does not appear that Tennant is warranted in his insistence that this analysis is fact. Admittedly there is no direct introspection of it, and consequently there is no way to check the theory by appeal to direct experience.

(2) The Theory Not Reconcilable with Subhuman Apprehension

Secondly, the existence of any such primitive consciousness which is shut in to sensa alone prior to an implicit thought-intuition of the persistence and activity of its own body and a projective association of this notion with the occurrence of sensa, if it really is taken as a fact, is not easily reconciled with instinctive consciousness of subhuman beings. Are we to assume that the consciousness of human infants and, in the subhuman order, that the consciousness of dogs and of fishes, insofar as they are conscious of the presence of other material objects which act upon them, evolves in this manner? Even if this were a correct interpretation of the evolution of awareness of external material things in the subhuman realm, there is no possible way of verifying the conjecture. The least that we are entitled to say is that sense-experience is the occasion of an immediate response to external active objects which in itself assumes the causal reality of the object which confronts it. The "thing-notion" is inseparable from the experience of sensa.

(3) Consciousness of the Body's Substantiality Is Not Prior to Consciousness of Interacting Substance-Causes

Third, the assertion that a primitive consciousness becomes aware of the substantiality of its own body before it is aware of the persistence of another nonbodily object, or that it derives primitive notions of the substance and activity of the body prior to its derivation of primitive notions of a nonbody-substance-cause, is a distinction which is fallacious at the higher human level. Consciousness of the body is not given prior to things reacting upon the body. Veridical consciousness is always consciousness of some external object simultaneously with consciousness of the body; the two are given together not successively. There is no reason why the primitive notion of substance and of cause should not be derived from external objects and then by reverse analogy applied to body. In developed consciousness there is analogical introjection as well as analogical projection, and a critical regress from developed consciousness might conceivably involve the one as it does the other. For this reason it is difficult to accept this theory of the genesis of categories of substance and of cause. It may well be, as Tennant says, that the categories of thought are what they are because of the embodiment of a psychological individual in a physical organism, but there seems to be no reason for giving the body a place prior to the physical world in the evolution of consciousness, or in making it alone peculiarly responsible for the origin of primitive thought-forms. Certainly both are involved in the birth of these powers.

(4) The Facts Do Not Sustain the Disjunction
of Formal and Dynamic Categories

Fourth, underlying Tennant's distinction between the formal
and dynamic categories, there is an implicit subjectivism which
does not do justice to the facts of the case. It is his conviction
that sensa are experienced in such a way that their relations are
given to intuition whenever they are experienced in the process
of sensation. The formal categories of qualitative likeness and
difference and number are "read off" the sensa with "immediacy," whereas the dynamic categories of cause and active substance are "read in" to sensa by analogical derivation from the
active self. The facts do not sustain this distinction. The judgment of Professor Stout is important at this point:

It is not true, as Mill supposes, that we are far more familiar or
even that we are at all more familiar with the sequence of volition
and fulfilment, than with other regular sequences. I do not merely
mean that we are spectators of a routine in nature (e.g. the succession of day and night) which is in no way dependent on us. The
important point is that even in our own practical activity we can
only set going trains of events which then take their own course.
We may push a stone over the edge of a precipice, but its consequent career is beyond our control. To gain our ends we have to
anticipate such occurrences, as they vary under variable circumstances, and to adjust our own initiative accordingly. Even our
command of the appropriate motions of our own bodies, so far as
it is not instinctive, is originally attained through trial and failure
and adaptive variation. We have incessantly to accommodate ourselves to a regular course of events, which is determined for us and
not by us. Familiarity with this order and familiarity with our
own voluntary initiative both develop pari passu in inseparable
unity.[35]

Stout's thesis is that our will-to-realize certain objectives is so
closely linked with active processes in nature that we have immediate insight into the causal process of nature as well as into
the efficiency of the self. This insight or intuition is not the psychological process of sensing; it is a more complex form of appre-

35. G. F. Stout, *Mind and Matter*, pp. 34–35.

hension, but it is nonetheless immediate. Immediate experience cannot be limited to the experience of sensa without dire implications. If experience does not give some objective basis for the rise and application of the categories, there is no possible basis for imputing the categories to a real world. Tennant clearly sees this point with respect to the formal categories. In deriving the causal category from the embodied self, he is struggling to give this category a real ground in our experience of the objective world, but this implies that there is no equal ground for imputing this category to causes other than the self. The sensa which give us ground for "reading off" formal categories do not give us ground for apprehending dynamic centers of activity. The result is that there is no basis for applying the causal category to anything beyond the embodied self. Tennant is in the same predicament as the subjectivists who derive the categories of substance and cause from the psychological self as distinct from the embodied self and then impute them to the objects signified by sensa, even though he maintains that sensa are not purely subjective states. Of this position Professor Smith writes:

If we grant the subjectivist thesis that, as data for determining the nature of independent existences, only sensa can be experienced, this view of the origin of these two concepts[36] will doubtless, for lack of any conceivable alternative, have to be adopted. Sensa, which as such are alleged to be merely private, purely subjective, and constantly changing,[37] could certainly never suggest them. But this surely is to prove overmuch. For if such be the character of our other experiences, what clues can they afford sufficient to justify us in imputing to them the categories, even if otherwise obtained? If the sensa be in unceasing change, what ground is there for asserting that they represent something substantial and abiding? If they be mind-dependent, what ground is there for asserting that they causally determine one another or stand for objects which so behave?[38]

The truth appears to be that the data of experience is not correctly interpreted by the process of deriving categories first

36. I.e., the subjective derivation of the categories of substance and of cause from the psychological self.
37. In Tennant's case, sensa are private but not "purely subjective."
38. N. K. Smith, *Prolegomena to an Idealist Theory of Knowledge,* p. 129.

from the embodied self and secondly, by projecting them analogically upon something which does not evoke them. The fact
is rather that our experience of physical data is the outcome of a
process of sensing and conceiving which is immediately directed
as a whole toward the apprehended object.

(5) The Transition from Private Psychological Objects to Metaphysical Objects by Way of Intersubjective Intercourse Impossible

Fifth, another serious difficulty which breaks out in connection
with Tennant's theory of thing-perception is his conception of
the psychological process by means of which "public" things or
objects are apprehended. The implicit inferences of this process
cannot be legitimately said to give rise to a public Object, or to a
public Object which appears to the individual. It will be well to
orient the discussion at this point by reference to the difficulties
felt by two reviewers of Tennant's book, and by two writers who
have criticized James Ward. Reference is made to Hicks's and
De Burgh's reviews of Tennant,[39] and to Hicks and Stout on
Ward.[40]

The criticism of the Tennant-Wardian psychological method
and analysis centers about the status of the private psychological
object (o) of the private individual, and the statement that the
only way a private individual can arrive at the concept of a
public metaphysical or ontal object (ω) is by way of intersubjective intercourse and a resulting common-public Object (O)
which is often mistaken for a metaphysical object. The object
(o) of the individual subject is called by both Tennant and
Ward "psychological" and "private." Both Ward and Tennant
—at least Tennant interprets Ward thus—it ought to be remembered, start their enquiry from a certain standpoint;
namely, the denial of Cartesian dualism and the supposition that
a subject is shut up within the closed system of its own ideas and
states. The psychological object then for Ward and Tennant
means that-which-is-over-against-the-subject not as its state but
as an object-appearing. They insist, however, that this object

39. *The Hibbert Journal*, XXVIII, 174 ff.; *The Journal of Philosophical Studies*, III, 537 ff.
40. Hicks, "Prof. Ward's Psychological Principles," *Mind*, XXX, 1–24. Stout, *Mind and Matter*, pp. 290–293; also cf. pp. 171–173.

(o) is strictly private and also, both in the earlier and later stages of their analysis, that determinations of sensa and the presentation-continuum by bodily mechanisms make it impossible to identify phenomena with noumena.

On the basis of this situation all the critics mentioned above interpret "o" as a psychological object or *tertium quid* in the subjective sense.[41] What an individual who looks at a rose sees is not the rose but private presentations of sensa which stand between it and the real rose. Obviously, if sensa be interpreted in this fashion, the way to a real object (ω) by that of intersubjective intercourse and a conceptual common Object is full of difficulties. In the first place, other minds and sensa of other minds must be known to exist independently of the private individual before he can know that material objects exist independently of him. In this case the private individual transcends his private sensa in case of other selves, and, though these critics have not pointed it out in this connection, the argument of analogy to other selves is impossible on the theory that sensa are private and not public Objects or signs of public Objects. The only possible basis for an argument by analogy to other minds is on the presupposition that either some sensa are public and known by other minds, or that sensa are private but directly indicate material objects.[42] Inasmuch as Tennant uses an argument by analogy to justify our belief in other selves, a subjective interpretation would be devastating.

In the second place, to resume the position of the critics, the inference that is drawn from the existence of subjective private sensa in several individuals to the existence of a public independent object is logically invalid. The most that an individual could logically infer from his knowledge that several individuals are having sensa is that there are certain common characteristics existing among various groups of sensa. These are only characteristic of immanent psychological objects and cannot be thought of as characteristics of independent noumenal existents. No addition of the common elements of psychological states will ever constitute an independent reality. This being the case, all

41. This is particularly true of Hicks who opposes any disjunction of sensa from object, and challenges the propriety of Ward's calling sensa "psychological objects."
42. Cf. Broad, *Mind and Its Place in Nature*, pp. 346–348.

the critics conclude that there is no way from the private psychological objects of an individual to a public independent reality by way of intersubjective intercourse.

Tennant's reply to this criticism, however, is that neither he nor Ward are solipsist at any stage of the game.[43] The private o is from the epistemological standpoint an appearance of an independent reality; it is only from the rudimentary psychological standpoint that it is not explicitly and consciously realized to be so. There is an implicit projection or ejection of a rough idea of substance-cause into the sense data so that there is implicit awareness of "material thing" before the explicit awareness is brought about by intersubjective intercourse. What Tennant does not admit is that this "implicit" awareness is awareness of a public object, a matter which turns largely on the definition of "public," and the attempt to follow the *ordo cognoscendi*. To Tennant an object is made "public" by intercommunication of common relations through gestures, signs, and symbols. A private individual is a closed monad toward material world until he is opened by *rapport* with other human monads. After the individual adopts the standpoint of a socialized subject he has a concept before his mind, a communicable object or *tertium quid*, which he confuses with his sensa.

This definition contains the root of our difficulties; namely, if the independent object which appears to the private individual is not in some sense implicitly known not only to be independent (i.e., a reality appearing) but "public" in the sense of being available to the experience of others, all the difficulties which the critics have advanced against the Tennant-Wardian position hold true. There is no way from private objects to public metaphysical objects by intersubjective intercourse; a "public" world must be there from the first in order for the knower to arrive at a "public" world. Undoubtedly Tennant is correct in holding that a rudimentary consciousness, such as the private unsocialized individual is supposed to be, does not possess the mental equipment of either language or reflection to carry on a discussion of epistemology, but it seems to be true that the indi-

43. Cf. Tennant's review of Stout's *Mind and Matter* in *The Journal of Theological Studies,* XXXIV, 97. Tennant says Stout may give a wrong impression of Ward's teaching; namely, that Ward taught solipsism prior to intersubjective intercourse. Tennant says this is not true.

vidual in practice acts as if the objects of his consciousness were real and independent existents. Along with this strictly sensing experience, there is an instantaneous leap or thinking transcendence to material things which are in a public position in the system of moving reality. The categories are already socially universal in their outer reference and derivation. There is no way to derive the categories of public things from intersubjective experience and thence to project them into sensa without falling into social subjectivism.

If the charge of subjectivism is implicit in the derivation of the categories of substance and cause from the self, as it has been argued in the former objection, then the extraprivate objectivity which is implied in social subjectivism is unfounded. The problem which is involved here is the problem of the origin of an individual's knowledge of another self. Is such knowledge based upon analogous inferences derived from the self and read into the sensa which signify another person's body? If this is the nature of the process, and if this proves to be an impossible analysis of that process, our "public Objects" gained in intersubjective intercourse are profoundly dislocated from independent reality. An examination of the analogical process of inference in our knowledge of one and other is important.

B. OTHER SELVES NOT APPREHENDED BY A PROCESS OF MEDIATE ANALOGICAL INFERENCE

Tennant's theory is that knowledge of another self arises in the following way. A child first experiences a continuum of presentations out of which he discriminates his body and other sense objects. His body is not only perceived through the regular five senses, but also by an inner awareness composed of organic sensations; i.e., coenesthesis and its constituent factors. He gradually derives the notion of substance and of causal activity from his experience of his body and then, by a process of rudimentary analogy, he projects this notion into his sense-percepts. Having achieved the complex perception of material things, he comes to distinguish a perceptible difference between the bodily behavior of his mother and that of other things. Upon the basis of this perceptible difference, he analogically infers, not explicitly and rationally, but implicitly and rudimentarily, a self analogous to himself. The self which he ejects into the bodily behavior of his mother must always be conceived to be a self of the sort which he is analytically capable of knowing at any stage in his development. At first this self is simply a vaguely felt active body; later it is more conscious of itself as an inner center of experience. The self ejected into the sense-perception of another's body must be equivalent to the self as known. Tennant insists upon this latter point in order to refute the suggestions of those who hold an opposing theory and charge: (1) that the inference assumes too great a capacity for rational inference on the part of children, and (2) that the inferences are based on a child's knowledge of his own facial expressions before he interprets those of others.

In order to show that his theory is the only possible theory of the origin and development of our knowledge of other selves, he refutes what is called by other thinkers the intuitional theory of our knowledge of other minds. Tennant understands that this theory attempts to support the conviction that we apprehend the mental states of another immediately and directly. It does not assert that one person lives through (*erleben*) another's states; i.e., one person does not existentially become another, but it does assert that one person can have as an object of his immediate acquaintance the thoughts and feelings of another. Admitting this as a theoretical possibility, Tennant says it is refuted by the following facts. (1) One person cannot detect what is going on in another person's mind apart from a perception of his body. We do not know what is going on in another person's mind in the dark. (2) One person never apprehends another "thinker" or pure ego. (3) Perception of another mind is always "interpretative-perception" from the standpoint of reflective analysis. That the interpretative element is accomplished instantaneously is no reason to suppose that the perception actually is noninterpretative when put under analysis. The intuitionalist theory confuses the psychic with the "psychological," i.e., the psychological with the epistemological, standpoints.

Preliminary Difficulties

Before it is possible to give reasons for rejecting Tennant's theory, certain preliminary difficulties must be brought to light.

First, Tennant's statement of this problem is exceedingly brief and inadequate. It is given two pages in *Philosophical Theology;*[44] the position of the intuitionalists is not accurately presented, and the meanings of phrases in his own analysis are not clear and explicit. Representative intuitionalists do not hold, for example, that a mental state can be apprehended apart from bodily manifestations; nor do they claim that the "deeper self" or the whole self is revealed in the content of any direct apprehension; nor do they fail to realize that the apprehension of another is complex with elements of interpretation sooner or later involved.[45] Tennant ought to have examined this position more carefully.

Furthermore, explicit meanings of his own terminology are greatly needed. What, for example, does Tennant mean when he says that "a mother's behaviour is, to the young child, *perceptibly different* from that of other things";[46] that "the initial reading in is not to be confounded with rational inference";[47] that it proceeds from "humblest beginnings" by "incipient introspection and retrospection"? A vague appeal to inferences which are not "rational," to *incipient* introspection and retrospection, and to "*implicit* analogical inference" cannot inspire high regard for the factual character of this analysis. The interpretation of what transpires in the mind of the child is actually determined by the assumptions of the analyst at the beginning of his analysis. If it were not already held that we cannot apprehend another's mental states directly, the reference to the child's knowing-processes would have to be construed in a different manner. The working presupposition which controls Tennant's entire psychology is that our sole, firsthand contact with the ex-

44. Cf. I, 72–73.
45. For example, cf. Broad, *Mind and Its Place in Nature,* chap. vii; N. A. Duddington, "Our Knowledge of Other Minds," *The Proceedings of Aristotelian Society,* XIX, 147; H. H. Price, "Our Knowledge of Other Minds," *The Proceedings of Aristotelian Society,* XXXII, 53 ff. (Price refutes intuitionalist theory but, unlike Tennant, he refutes it in detail and supports the teleological theory rather than an analogical theory of the type which Tennant argues); C. C. J. Webb, "Our Knowledge of One Another," *The Proceedings of British Academy,* XVI, 281 ff.; also *Divine Personality and Human Life,* chap. vii; John Laird, *Problems of the Self,* pp. 24–28; C. Delisle Burns, "The Contact of Minds," *The Proceedings of Aristotelian Society,* XXIII, 215 ff.; H. H. Farmer, *The World and God,* pp. 13–17; S. Alexander, *Space, Time, and Deity,* II, 31 ff.
46. *Philosophical Theology,* p. 72.   47. *Ibid.,* p. 72.

ternal world is sense-perception. Sense-perception yields our
external touch with reality; introspection yields our internal
touch with ourselves. These two are the only sources of immediate
acquaintance. Therefore, what Broad calls "extraspection" or
direct acquaintance with other minds is ruled out at once. Analogical inference is the only alternative.

(1) The Basic Presupposition Is Fallacious

The first criticism of Tennant's theory must, therefore, be
directed toward his basic presupposition; namely, that an object
must present sense-qualities in order to be directly and immediately apprehended. It has already been argued that Tennant's
failure to admit that the categories of cause and substance are
immediately derived from external causes introduces a subjectivism into the apprehension of material things which is disastrous to the realism of his duality-theory in epistemology. The
only alternative is to admit that we have direct acquaintance with
causes which are intimately connected with sensory manifestations but not sensed as sensa. If external causes are brought
within the realm of direct acquaintance, and if their presence in
a complex sensory experience is not detected by sense but in conjunction with sense processes, then it is evident that not all aspects of reality need to give sensory manifestation in order to
come within the area of direct acquaintance. The principle implied in this situation is that an object or an aspect of an object
gives evidence of its existence and presence if it exerts some constraining power or influence upon the apprehending mind. Such
a constraining influence can be detected in conjunction with sensory signs in a complex experience. The primary requirement is
simply that this constraining influence gives some evidence of its
nature and character. It is difficult to ascribe an exact nature or
character to a mental element which is thus directly apprehended, but the difficulty does not allow it to be denied. In the
case of the existence or nonexistence of a characteristic, it need
only be asked if the presence and absence of it makes a difference
to the situation. If a body is not characterized by living mind,
there is something plainly and severely lacking; if it is so characterized, we plainly stand in the presence of a new aspect of
reality. Suffering, pain, anger, love, are powerful constraining
influences. Whenever these mental states are apprehended as

characterizing another person, there is more given to the apprehending mind than the sensory elements.

This, of course, is the central point at issue in the controversy between the intuitionalists and the analogical theorists. The arguments for the intuitional theory are largely the central arguments against the analogical theory, and vice versa, the arguments against the intuitional theory are arguments for the analogical theory. It is necessary, therefore, to examine the arguments against the analogical theory as represented by Tennant.

(2) *Major Obstacles to the Body-Basis of the Analogical Inference Theory*

Accepting Tennant's precaution not to interpret his theory of analogical inference as implying that a child ejects its mind into another's body upon the basis of observed likeness between another's face and its own, there are still major obstacles to the bodily basis of the inference.

(a) *The Expressive Behavior of Other People Presents No Primary Analogy to the Percipient's Own*

In the first place, a child knows another person's body through the outer senses, largely by means of visual pictures; he knows his own mental states primarily through internal sensations. When the child is angry, he feels his anger from within; he does not see his own exterior expressions. The physical signs which indicate anger in another person are not the same kind of signs which signify anger in the child. If he associates the anger of another person with physical signs to which he has no analogy in his own experience, he is certainly doing that which the analogical theory gives him no right to do. Duddington expresses this objection as follows:

Another objection against the orthodox psychological theory is this. If our knowledge of the existence of other selves depended on the analogy which their behaviour presents to our own, we should either not even suspect that they exist, or at best possess only a very problematic knowledge of it. This objection has been urged by more than one Russian writer, and it is also elaborated by Lipps in his article Das Wissen von fremden Ichen. [*Psychologische Untersuchungen*, I, 4.] Put briefly, Lipps' argument is that, from the point of view of the percipient, expressive behaviour of other people presents no analogy to the percipient's own. Through the observation of other people's behaviour we become aware of facts of an order totally different from those revealed to us through the observation of our own behaviour. The bodily changes and attitudes of others present us with a visual picture, while our own bodily changes are felt as a series of kinaesthetic, visceral and organic sensations. Take, for instance, the expressive behaviour accompanying anger—redness of the face, a certain characteristic setting of the features, stamping with the feet, and so on. In the case of another person being angry, we see all these changes, but we do not see them in our own case. If I turn red when I am angry, I cannot possibly know that I do, for as Lipps observes, we do not gaze into a looking glass while in a fit of rage. What I am aware of is a hot sensation in my cheeks, a catch in the breath, violent beating of the heart, etc.—and these sensations present no analogy whatever to what I observe in the case of other people's anger.[48]

(b) Observed Behavior Analogies Lead to Memory of the Percipient's Own Past Experience Not to the Inference of Other Self

It might be suggested that objection (a) is not conclusive because the child associates the expression of his anger with other aspects of his own bodily behavior such as sounds, cries, and blows. To this, however, there is another real objection. Why should the child leap to the assumption that another's anger is associated with a cry which is comparable to one which he remembers himself to have made in the past? Why should not the cry of another simply remind him of his own past utterances?[49] The cry may lead a child to think of his own past experiences, not to the inference that the cry is a present expression of another's mental state of anger. Duddington restates the further thought of Lipps and Lossky as follows:

Another criticism which Lipps brings against the inference theory is that even if we could observe any analogy between our own be-

48. N. A. Duddington, "Our Knowledge of Other Minds," *The Proceedings of Aristotelian Society*, XIX, 160–161.
49. Cf. Broad, *Mind and Its Place in Nature*, pp. 325–326.

haviour and that of others, it would lead us merely to remember our own past experiences, and not to infer the existence of other mental lives. If I perceived the symptoms of another person's anger it would lead me to think of my own anger and not of somebody else's. This consideration has been previously urged by Professor Lossky. [*The Intuitive Basis of Knowledge.* Introduction.] Lossky points out that analogical arguments can never lead to the discovery of any new reality, such as the presence of selves distinct from our own. He also emphasizes the fact that the conclusion of an inference from analogy is never certain, but only more or less probable. If he is right in this—and I think he is—it follows that, on the accepted view, an element of doubt would necessarily attach to the judgment that there are in the world minds other than our own. We ought logically to be less confident of the existence of our friends than of the existence of tables and chairs; and the obvious circumstance that we are not less confident would have to be regarded as a fresh instance of the way in which human affections lead us astray. But the point is that human affections would not be there to frustrate the demands of logic if it were true that other minds were for us merely inferred entities. How could one love or hate "an uncertain supposition of we know not what"?[50]

(c) "*Analogical Arguments Never Lead to the Discovery of Any New Reality Such as the Presence of Selves Distinct from Our Own*"

The point referred to above; namely, that "analogical arguments never lead to the discovery of any new reality such as the presence of selves distinct from our own," is an important one, for, as Griffiths says in another connection: "The function of hypothesis in science is not the creation of facts but the explaining of them, by the discovery of the law of their behavior. When the hypothesis works, it may lead to new facts, but these are always facts of the same order as those already experienced. Thus, a physical law never leads to moral facts, nor a moral discovery to new physical facts."[51] Essentially the same principle applies here. If you assume that analogical inference can give appre-

50. N. A. Duddington, "Our Knowledge of Other Minds," *The Proceedings of Aristotelian Society*, XIX, 162.
51. See above, p. 92.

hension of a new and qualitatively different reality, you are actually saying that the new reality is *created* by the inferring mind out of nothing new at all. If the idea of "other mind" is created out of elements which are not controlled by the constraining presence of an objective reality, which is the mental reality itself, then there is actually only pure subjective creation in the process. It is extremely difficult to believe that the only realities which call forth profound responses of love and hate and anger are hypothetical conjectures "read into" sense-data upon the basis of analogies which do not really exist.

Again it cannot be too greatly emphasized that this mental reality or aspect of reality, the presence of which is necessary to our apprehension of other people, does not give evidence of itself entirely disconnected from bodily behavior. It is given with the bodily behavior in a psychophysical whole, and the presence of this whole before the apprehending mind results in the experience of another self.

Furthermore, this experience or datum may be interpreted as a third term in the process of representative perception, but if it is, then the coaction of both sides of the subject and object relationship must be required in the generation of the "datum" or *"tertium quid"* of experience. The respective merits of direct realism and duality-theory do not need to be drawn out further at this time. It is sufficient to show that the process of analogical inference results in ungrounded subjectivism unless there is a mental factor in the objective reality which gives and controls the experience of other selves. Neither analogical inferences from bodily behavior nor direct associations of mental states with bodily behavior can account for the origin of belief in other minds. Broad says in this connection: "It seems to me to be absolutely certain that belief in other human minds, and the belief that a certain mind is having a certain experience on a certain occasion, are not reached by inference, even if they can be afterwards justified up to the hilt by inference."[52]

If it is true that the apprehension of other minds could not have arisen by analogical inference from the observed similarities of bodies, then it follows that developed interpretative perception of other minds is not completely a matter of acquired

52. *Op. cit.,* p. 324.

inferences associated spontaneously with the sensory appearances of other bodies. That there are in adult experiences complex associations of the spontaneous, subconscious type aroused by the most limited sensory signs no one needs to deny. The term "experiences of redintegration"[53] means that the whole of a former experience can be stimulated by a relatively simple sign or token of that experience. It does not mean, however, that such experience could have originally come into being without an original and fundamental awareness or recognition of the presence of other minds in coöperation with which the experience arises. The fact that the analogical theory fails to give us our apprehension of other selves means that Tennant's criticism of "confusion of standpoints" is broken. The point is that, from the reflective standpoint, it is shown that such inferences as we may unreflectively perform and acquire are unwarranted. We have to assume that there is direct acquaintance in the beginning, and that in this direct acquaintance there resides the original recognition of responsive as distinct from unresponsive behavior.

It is against the background of the above discussion that the question is raised concerning Tennant's meaning in saying that there are "perceptible differences" between the behavior of a mother and that of other physical things. From Tennant's standpoint, these differences can only be taken to mean sense-differences. Neither is it possible for him to escape the difficulties of the analogical theory by an appeal to "rudimentary implicit analogizing," which arises and develops step by step with "knowledge of one's self and knowledge of other selves 'proceeding' *pari passu* from the humblest beginnings."[54] In order for the analogical inference to exist at all, knowledge of one's self must always precede knowledge of other minds. To say that we know both simultaneously is to surrender the theory altogether. Thus even a rudimentary process must be interpreted as preserving this original order of procedure. If the order of procedure and the sensory-differences are traced into rudimentary stages, there is no basis for the inference to arise legitimately. Thus it may be said that Tennant's resort to "implicit processes" ends in irrational mythology.

53. Cf. H. L. Hollingworth, *Psychology: Its Facts and Principles.*
54. *Philosophical Theology*, I, 72.

(3) Two Important Defenses of the Inference Theory Reject the Analogical Form of the Argument

(a) To G. F. Stout the Analogical Form of the Argument Is Psychologically and Logically Improbable

Two important attempts to sustain the inferential theory of our knowledge of other minds are made by Stout and Price.[55] Professor Stout is convinced that we do not know other minds immediately but by inferences from responsive behavior. "Behaviour is responsive," he writes, "when it is in a distinctive and spontaneous way relevant to the individual's own interests, his emotions, and practical needs." But this is given a curious twist by virtue of his theory of general animism. The inference is not based upon the special resemblance between the external appearance and behavior of other bodies and the external appearance and behavior of our own. This constitutes a part of the basis, but not all of it, as the opponents of the inferential theory fallaciously maintain. In fact, this part of the basis is "not even in principle essential.[56] . . . What is really essential is what I have called responsive behaviour. If when the baby was hungry, his bottle spontaneously approached his lips in the right position, and spontaneously went away again when his hunger was appeased, the bottle would be for him an embodied self, in spite of want of resemblance between him and it."[57]

This position is obviously quite different from Tennant's which insists upon the necessity of a bodily resemblance and which neglects to mention the relevance of behavior to the furtherance or hindrance of purposes, emotions, and practical needs. It becomes manifestly more distinctive when, after revealing the impossibilities of the theory of analogical inference from bodies, Stout states that his own position is free from these difficulties because it accepts the double kinship of all objects in nature; i.e., all objects are composed of matter animated by mind. The inferences from responsive behavior do not yield an apprehension of animation, but they yield rather a recognition of higher and of lower types of animation. Inferences from respon-

---

55. G. F. Stout, *Mind and Matter,* pp. 303–307; cf. also 286 ff. and H. H. Price, "Our Knowledge of Other Minds," *The Proceedings of the Aristotelian Society,* XXXII, 53 ff.

56. *Op. cit.,* p. 304.   57. *Ibid.*

sive behavior lead to a recognition of the presence of self-consciousness in another. They do not give you an original idea that this physical object is qualified by something living and mental. This original apprehension of animistic-quality in nature is immediate knowledge. The recognition of self-consciousness is inferential.

It is not relevant to a criticism of the analogical theory to subject this animistic amendment to minute criticism. It is rather important to quote Stout's analysis of the defectiveness of inferences based upon analogies. This is developed in the following paragraph:

. . . there is a fundamental assumption underlying the special arguments of those who hold that experiencing individuals do not know each other by inference. They assume that, if this were so, all knowledge of anything in nature akin to and continuous with mind in the individual would be inferential. Prior to the inference, the individual would know his own body as fundamentally of the same nature as, and continuous in existence with, other bodies, as parts of one purely material world. But his mind, they assume, would be a unique and isolated fact. It may well be doubted whether, starting from this initial position, the individual could have even the thought of a mind other than his own. If we set aside this difficulty, it is still hard to see how any inferential process could account for the intimacy and certainty of such knowledge, as we actually possess it. Inference by mere analogy is clearly precarious; for it would be generalising from the single instance in which a body is initially known to be connected with a mind, to an indefinite multitude of cases in which this is not initially known. Inference from responsive behaviour would hardly be more secure. It would indeed be only a subtler form of the argument from the analogy of the single instance. The individual may indeed reach a position in which he can say with certainty that if this external body were his own, its behaviour would express will and intelligence. But the point is that it is not his own. On the contrary, so far as he initially knows it, it is supposed to be for him merely a material object with nothing in its constitution akin to mind in himself. Hence there is nothing left but the analogical argument: "This external body behaves in a way which in my own case would imply the presence of a mind; therefore it is in fact actuated by a mind."

Psychologically, this is a most improbable account of the process by which, e.g., a baby comes to know its mother or nurse. Logically, the inference is precarious because it does not sufficiently exclude the alternative possibility that the responsive behaviour of bodies other than our own may be determined by purely material conditions.[58]

Stout has stated here the central difficulties of the analogical argument. It is an inference which first involves the transcendence of a position which is initially solipsistic, and, second, it involves a wide generalization upon the basis of a single instance. It is psychologically and logically improbable.

(b) To H. H. Price Reference to Body-Analogy
Is Unnecessary

Price,[59] on the other hand, maintains that arguments by means of which the analogical theory is refuted are inadequate to support the intuitional theory. The first argument for the intuitional theory is that our developed knowledge of one another is not consciously reached by any process of analogical reasoning. We jump straight to the conclusion that a friend is angry or afraid when he appears before us. There is no prior consideration of evidence and no doubt about the matter. Price rejects the claim that we are having "immediate knowledge" at this point. He suggests that the fact that we do not reason is no reason why we should say that we are having "immediate knowledge." We may be just "guessing" or "taking it for granted," hence we ought to doubt, to reason, and to prove.

It is difficult to weigh this criticism; namely, that even if we do not arrive at our knowledge of other selves by reasoning yet "we ought to." Perhaps an adult ought to reason his way to such knowledge of another as he may attain, but this does not indicate what he does do. Price realizes this and brings forward another consideration; namely, that the adult is drawing upon acquired associations which were formerly acquired by reasoning. A rapid apprehension of another person's mental status represents the rapid application of two strata of reasoning: an earlier one in

58. Stout, *Mind and Matter*, pp. 304–305.
59. H. H. Price, "Our Knowledge of Other Minds," *The Proceedings of the Aristotelian Society*, XXXII, 53 ff.

which the ideas about the relationship between bodily movements and mental processes were laboriously acquired, and a present one in which the idea is applied to a specific case. That there is an application of acquired ideas in adult experience no one will dispute. The question is whether or not the original association of notions of other mind can have arisen in this fashion. Price in discussing what he calls the third argument of the intuitional theory gives his reasons for believing that this is possible.

The so-called third argument of the intuitional theory consists in emphasizing the fact that our knowledge of other people is largely a matter of reading facial expressions. There is no common ground of bodily behavior upon which to base an inference to other mind because the child cannot see his own face. A mother's frown is the "natural sign" or occasion of the child's consciousness of his mother's disapproval. Price rejects this argument first because he believes that the child's knowledge arises inductively, and second because, if this were not true, it would be impossible for him to misread faces. The child first observes that facial expressions are usually preceded and followed by overt actions. He notes that frowns accompany thwarted or aggressive behavior. Comparing his own thwarted or aggressive behavior with those of another, he "reads in" to others his own feelings of anger. The association of anger with the frown on another's face arises by analogous inference from a common basis of thwarted or aggressive action.

It must be noted, however, that this theory has not met the obstacles suggested by opposing theorists such as Broad. Broad points out, for example, that even if frowns were followed by blows or overt actions, so also is fire followed by burning when the child touches it. If you have overt results in cases of inanimate as well as animate objects, upon what basis, if nothing but overt action is involved, can the child come to think of one object as possessing mental characteristics and the other not?[60] Furthermore, this difficulty still remains: why should not the overt action of another body simply remind the child of his own past feelings? If his own feelings are the only feelings he originally knows, other signs would remind him of his own feelings and not give rise to the consciousness of feelings in another. For these two

60. Cf. Broad, *Mind and Its Place in Nature*, pp. 326–327.

reasons, it does not appear that Price has established his case for the analogical and inferential origin of consciousness of other minds.

His second reason for rejecting the third argument of the intuitional theory is that immediate acquaintance would make it impossible to misread faces, an argument which also underlies his onslaught upon what he calls the second major argument of the intuitionalists. It will be appropriate to set forth the rebuttal of this second argument before replying to the basic charge.

The second main argument of the intuitionalists is that animals and children do not reach their beliefs in other animals and in other people by a process of inductive reasoning. They certainly have these apprehensions but they are instinctive rather than reasoned. Price does not take up the problem of animal apprehension of one another but confines his argument to children. The gist of his argument is that at first the child does not necessarily regard his mother as different from inanimate objects either because she responds to his cries of need or because she speaks to him. There need be nothing social about the early transactions between mother and child. The child cries and a bottle is placed in his mouth. This does not mean that the child recognizes his mother as an animate object. She may occupy the same position in his mind as a penny-in-the-slot machine occupies in adult minds. On the other hand, mother's cry, "naughty child," is usually followed by a smack. The cry does not necessarily convey the thought of another person, but the cry and the smack together may simply convey the notion that here is a pain to be avoided, and, therefore, the child will not do what brings it to pass.

In other words, Price believes that a child can live a long time before recognizing that other mental beings exist, and that the idea of other mental beings, when it does arise, probably arises by reasoning from analogy. That the child does actually live for a long time without recognition of other animate and mental beings, Price believes to be the case, because a child will hurt a dog or cat quite mercilessly and not realize that the creature feels pain. If he apprehended the mental state of these playmates directly, he would be a little fiend. That we do not regard him as a fiend is true simply because we know that he does not realize the pain he is causing in another. We know that he is treating his pet as he would treat a thing. This failure to recognize the signs of another's pain as well as errors in reading facial expressions indicate that elaborate inductive generalizations have to be built up in the child's mind between bodily behavior and mental accompaniments before social recognition and social insight result.

It is clear from the above that Price is using an argument which Broad uses to prove the opposite position. To Broad, the fact that overt effects upon a child follow upon the activity of inanimate as well as animate objects means that no basis for interpreting the animate as animate is thereby given to the child for his analogical inference. To Price, the overt effects of his mother's action in meeting his needs and in training him by words and smacks means that she is regarded by him simply as another physical thing. The overt acts which first mean "other thing" in the course of time come to be the basis for inferring "other person" or "other mind." Verily a miracle is performed! Why should the child not continue to interpret his mother's overt activity as that of a purely physical inanimate object? He has no possible basis for reasoning correctly to the other position unless he is able to apprehend directly the animate by some more fundamental process of knowing. Price does not possess Stout's animism upon which to rely. In fact, Price asserts that even if the child as primitive man before him were an animist, animism itself would not give a basis for the distinction between an animated object which is physical and an animated object which is mental. This is undoubtedly true, but the real question is whether or not both children and primitive men have a fundamental consciousness of "kind" which forms the basis of rudimentary inferences based upon analogy. If there is a basic consciousness of "kind," the inferences from bodily behavior can be drawn without assigning to them the miracle of mental creation *ex nihilo*. It is just this fact; namely, that discovery of a totally new reality or quality of reality cannot be simple inferences from realities which do not possess the quality originally, that constitutes the difficulty of the analogical theory. This difficulty Price has not succeeded in overcoming.

The fact that a child misreads faces and fails to recognize mental states which accompany the overt behavior of other bodies does not mean that he has no prior consciousness of other people at all. Before a child could misapply the notion of an-

other person or a mental state connected with the bodily behavior of another person, the child must first have the idea of
other person. Error presupposes a prior first acquaintance with
reality; it is impossible to be in error about nothing. Certainly
error enters into our apprehension of material things; our introspective awareness of our own states is notoriously full of misapprehension; why not assume that there are no material objects
or that there is no empirical self because the child is mistaken in
his judgments with respect to these realities? Price's whole argument is explicitly presented upon the basis that the child does
know directly independent material objects, not by sensation
entirely, but by an intuition which is conjoined with sensation.
If, therefore, the fact of error does not destroy this type of perception, it should not destroy the other.

Furthermore, why is consciousness of a physical object tem-
porally prior to his consciousness of a personal object? It is certainly true in adult life that men know other people often much
better than they know other things or even themselves, and it is
equally true that in the case of the child his mother is quite the
foremost and most conspicuous object of his experience.

It is true, of course, as Price points out, that we could not have
experience of other people without at the same time experiencing
the apperceptive processes which unify and make this experience
of others possible; but this does not give superiority to our
knowledge of independent inanimate things. We do not know
others apart from the experience of participating in the subject-
object relationship. Neither do we know ourselves apart from
this knowing process. Neither do we know other things apart
from such a process. Knowing is not equivalent to being-a-thing.
A person, to be a person, necessarily lives through (*erleben*)
mental states; it is by virtue of this fact that he exists; but still
another and a higher mental process is involved in coming to
perceive the states through which one is living. The introspective
process of knowing one's mental states is something more than
the existence of those states. It is a knowing process directed
toward those states. It might be argued that the process of knowing is first directed toward the outer world; i.e., toward objects
whose existence is not lived-through, before it is directed in-
wardly toward the empirical self which is lived-through. But the

knowing involved in perception and the knowing involved in introspection are the same type of cognitive processes. Likewise, the knowing involved in "extraspection" is the same type of awareness as that found in introspection and perception. The data of these processes arise because of different stimuli, but the cognizing act of the subject which is cast upon the data is one fundamental act in all three cases. No cognitive superiority characterizes one more than the other, and certainly no priority can be assigned to perception of inanimate things. This possibility has not been examined by Price, and it would have to be if he is to reject the position of the intuitionalists[61] that we know others before we know ourselves, "others" being both physical and psychological substance-causes.

The reasons, however, which Price has given for rejecting the central arguments of the intuitionalists against the analogical theory do not overcome the difficulties which the analogical argument from bodily behavior is forced to face. His constructive case for a critical analogical inference theory reveals a tacit recognition of these difficulties, for his whole argument rests upon a basis which has no reference to bodily behavior whatsoever. His argument is based upon the relationship of things in one's environment to one's own purposes. If one finds that his own purposes are repeatedly being furthered or hindered by the presence of certain material objects in his surroundings, he may legitimately argue from the purposive action of his own self upon objects in that environment to the existence of beings which have purposes relative to his own and are manifesting them by producing changes in the same material environment. The other beings or minds may have any kind of bodies whatsoever or perhaps none at all. According to Price, the argument is exactly the same as the teleological argument for the existence of God. When used to argue to the existence of finite minds (not infinite and perfect mind) who have produced effects by altering preëxisting matter upon the basis of the analogy of a person's own ability to effect changes in preëxisting matter, it constitutes a perfect argument for the existence of other minds. All the difficulties which Hume and Kant found with the design argument for God are in this case overcome. Finite minds are proved to exist by the

61. Webb, Burns, Alexander.

respective occurrences of changes in the environment, some of them being produced by the individual, others, when persistently relative to his purposes, by other minds like his own.

Obviously, this theory carries with it great difficulties. If the argument makes no prior reference to the experience of finite minds in finite bodies effecting changes in an environment known to be common to both, it is obviously unable to infer finite minds which are embodied in specific bodies. The argument proves the existence of finite minds; whether they are embodied or not is beyond the scope of the basic factual analogy. Embodied minds are not proved to exist by the argument. If this is intended to be an account of how awareness of other minds arises, it is manifestly impossible.

C. THE RELATION OF THE FOREGOING CRITICISMS TO THE APPREHENSION OF GOD

This extended criticism of the "analogical inference" theory of our knowledge of substance-causes and other minds must now be brought into relationship with the central issue in behalf of which it was undertaken.[62] That issue was this: Knowledge of God is analogous to our knowledge of other selves. The psychological process of coming to believe that God exists is comparable to the way by which we come to believe that other selves and other things exist. It is this analogy which gives "probability" to the theological idea. "Analogical inference," however, has now been shown to be utterly incapable of bringing forth from rudimentary elements in experience an apprehension of the realities or aspects of reality which are not given in or with the elements from which the inferences are drawn. We do not psychologically create ideas of new realities out of inferences from data which are not these realities or direct signs of them. "Analogical arguments can never lead to the discovery of any new reality such as the presence of other selves distinct from our own."[63] A system of inferences and analogies may be used to justify ideas of realities after they have been originally apprehended, but they do not originate those primary ideas. Inferences and hypothetical ejection of ideas may lead to a discovery of new facts, but these new facts

62. See above, p. 105.   63. Cf. above, pp. 119 ff.; also p. 92.

are always of the same general order as those which suggested the hypothesis. Inferences from sensa may lead to a discovery of new sensa, but never to underlying active causes. Inferences from bodies may lead to a discovery of more facts about bodies, but not to discovery of other mind.

God Not Apprehended by a Process of Mediate Analogical Inference from Nonreligious Data

In like manner, inferences from the world of men and of things cannot lead to a discovery of a Creator to whom man can ascribe the name God. The origin of the conception of God must be found, if it is to be found at all, in a direct intuition of God's reality and nature, or of a phenomenalized version of God's reality. Such an immediate experience of God is not at its inception a complete and clear system of theological conceptions.

. . . Since the realization of God's presence is always fitful and difficult [writes Dean Inge], nothing in the least like a scheme of theology is given intuitively. This latter is the creation of the imaginative intelligence, which has to form out of its prior experience, some picture, idea, or history of the world, to which the religious conviction may correspond, and in which its activity may find scope. Parts of the framework may afterwards prove to be unsound and to need reconstruction. In this sense it is permissible to say that illusion has played an important part in the history of religious belief. . . . But when some thinkers go further than this, and assert that religious truth is "poetic" in the sense that its objective correspondence with fact is a matter of indifference, we cannot agree.[64]

Theological interpretation may be partially false, but the important point is that it is evoked by an original experience and thus bears some direct relationship to the reality manifested in this experience. Apart from such prior experience in which the divine reality manifests itself, the interpretative factors are ungrounded in anything other than subjective thought-construction. If God is simply an ideal object constructed out of thought-projections, religious experience becomes a matter of experiencing theological-conceptions, and not a matter of "experiencing-a-living-reality."

64. W. R. Inge, *Personal Idealism and Mysticism* (3d ed. 1924), p. 27.

On Tennant's theory, the only reality which is known to constitute the foundation of the conceptualized and hypothetical object of religious experience is that with which there is sensory and introspective contact. These contacts are insufficient to evoke the original experience of a being such as God. The content of the data from which the idea of God is derived is not rich enough to support and to control and to originate the idea of God. The revelation of reality must be sufficient to evoke the rational concept in a mind which is capable of responding to that demand. The rational is the witness of the Real, not because the rational creates reality but because the Real evokes and controls the rational. The rational involves an intuition of the reality which it conceives whenever there is a direct experience. Without the constraining presence of an actual and vital object, the rational conception and interpretation of it are devoid of supporting content.

Unless we have some experience of reality which is not inferred [asks Waterhouse], in what way can we have ground for inference? The chain of inference cannot hang upon inference. Spinoza's "scientia intuitiva" was the third and highest kind of knowledge. It would, perhaps, be better to regard an immediate grasp of reality as the basis of knowledge. If that is to be so, it is not possible to deny that the religious consciousness may have an immediate sense which forms the basis of its knowledge which can be apprehended as reality without inference.[65]

Dean Inge also tells us that there is a wide agreement among the saints to the fact that the experience of God is immediate and not a matter of inference. He writes:

It will be found that these men of acknowledged and pre-eminent saintliness agree very closely in what they tell us about God. They tell us that they have arrived gradually at an unshakable conviction, not based on inference, but on immediate experience, that God is a spirit with whom the human spirit can hold intercourse: that in Him meet all that they can imagine of goodness, truth and beauty; that they can see His footprints everywhere in Nature and feel His presence within them as the very life of their life, so that in proportion as they come to themselves they come to Him.

65. E. S. Waterhouse, *The Philosophy of Religious Experience*, p. 103.

They tell us that what separates us from Him and from happiness is, first, self-seeking in all its forms, and, secondly, sensuality in all its forms; that these are the ways of darkness and of death, which hide from us the face of God; while the path of the just is like a shining light, which shineth more and more unto the perfect day. As they have toiled up the narrow way, the Spirit has spoken to them of Christ, and has enlightened the eyes of their understandings, till they have at least *begun* to know the love of Christ, which passeth knowledge, and to be filled with all the fullness of God.[66]

The original awareness of the presence of God is forced upon the individual by a peculiar sort of experience; it is not originally the invention of analogy and inference. If this basic recognition of the divine presence is given, then it is both possible and necessary that man should attempt to conceive the nature of the divine by means of analogies and inferences. If it is not given, then there appears to be no way by which the divine can be derived from the finite aspects of experience. This is well illustrated by reference to Tennant.

The world of interrelated entities is compared by Tennant to a complex mechanism such as a watch. The physical world is not, therefore, likened to the body of God. Thus there arises at once the question of the difference between coming to know God and coming to know another self. The other self is known by analogous inferences "read into" the experience of the body of the other self. God is known by inferences drawn by partial analogy from creative artists and "read into" the world-machine. The physical basis of the analogy in the two cases is quite different. Furthermore, as pointed out above,[67] there is no human analogy for the creative power and wisdom of God. God does not have a body, nor sense organs. God's manner of knowing and his manner of "positing" the world's creatures utterly transcend the knowing and creative activity of man. In order to establish a "probability" for the theistic world-explanation some antecedent experience of world-making would appear to be necessary in order to eliminate alternative explanations on the negative side and to establish the one most probable alternative on the

66. W. R. Inge, *Christian Mysticism,* pp. 325–326.
67. *Supra,* p. 105.

positive side. Such experience man does not have; hence it is difficult to understand what evidence certifies its probability. This difficulty becomes particularly acute when it is viewed in connection with the tendency to draw an inference from evidence which is widened in the process of supporting it.[68]

III. THE DIFFICULTIES INVOLVED IN THE EXTRAPOLATIONS OF EMPIRICAL DATA NECESSARY TO GIVE SUPERIOR PROBABILITY TO TENNANT'S ARGUMENT

Tennant's theological argument is based upon the evolutionary trend, beginning with primary collocations and advancing toward embodied minds cognizant of progressively higher values. It is known, however, that the environmental conditions suited for the existence of organisms did not exist in this area of the universe prior to a certain period. There is no sufficient evidence that they exist elsewhere; and there is reason to suppose that they will not continue indefinitely in the future in this section of the universe. In which event, this relatively short, clumsy, perhaps bungling trend toward embodied minds struggling for values will cease to exist. To argue upon the basis of this relatively "trivial"[69] trend in a universe of vast extent in space and time to a ground sufficiently wise, powerful, and good enough to sustain human consciousness in an eternal quest for higher values, when the evidence is to the effect that this trend will not continue in the known universe, when not the slightest attempt is made to seek or to examine evidence for the immortality of minds in cases where the claim is made, and when no direct experience of such a being is admitted, is obviously to go vastly beyond the evidence which we have. This argument is supposed to move from the essentials of a known trend to a ground sufficient to cause this trend, but in order to arrive at a ground which corresponds to the religious idea of God as wise, powerful, and morally perfect, the trend is greatly extended, and a great deal more than is known tends to be included in the data which is needed to support that inference. Extrapolations of the data occur at several points.

68. *Supra,* p. 101 ff. This characteristic was noted by Hume.
69. By "trivial" is meant "limited in space and time."

A. THE PERSISTENCE OF THE KNOWN
UNIVERSE AND THE BENEFICENCE
OF THE UNKNOWN AREAS

Though Tennant does not assert that it is God's purpose that the goal of the world; namely, the achievement of ethical personality, must necessarily be connected with the fulfillment of the evolutionary process on this earth, he does make extrapolatory implications on a basis which reveals inconsistency. He dismisses in a few sentences[70] the scientific prediction that this fragment of our universe will be broken up with the dissolution of the solar system by asserting that predictions as to the ruin of a partial fragment of the universe based on a partial knowledge of a larger fragment are too precarious to be considered. "For all we know," he writes, "the universe may be possessed of a power to make all things new." And so it may, but compare the basis of what is being said here to what was said earlier about the "known chaos."[71] In the earlier part of his case for cosmic teleology, he considers the objection that in a universe of vast extent in time and space, it is not improbable to expect that there might be a pocket in which conditions suitable to the development of organisms arise fortuitously in a vast chaos of physical elements unsuited for life. To this he replies that the possibilities of the unknown do not refute the known facts. In other words, he does not allow suppositions as to the unknown to disturb the argument for theism in any way whatsoever. But above he urges that a supposition concerning the unknown—namely, that "for all we know the universe may be possessed by a power to make all things new"—dissolves the speculation of the dissolution of the solar system and the end of the evolutionary trend. The real implication of this is that the possibilities of the unknown support theism. Here is an example not only of an inconsistent use of "speculation as to the unknown" but of extrapolation as well. A limited trend in the history of the universe is regarded as continuing indefinitely to make life possible and to foster its development. From this expanded factual basis, it is easier to justify the theological inference of a beneficent God, but only to the "faithful." It does not easily convince the "unconverted."

70. *Philosophical Theology*, II, 103; also see above, p. 82.
71. *Ibid.*, II, 80.

B. THE ASSUMPTION OF PERSONAL
IMMORTALITY

In the appendix of *Philosophical Theology*[72] we are told that God cannot be a morally perfect being unless man's life continues after death. This is undoubtedly true, but it obviously means that a valid, inductive, empirical argument, from known facts to a morally perfect God, cannot be drawn until evidence for man's immortal existence is forthcoming. Lacking such evidence at present, the evidence of man's temporal existence is extended to include the anticipated evidence of his eternal existence and the inference of a morally perfect God is thereby justified upon a basis of hope. This is wide extrapolation to say the least. Dr. Broad criticizes Tennant for not attempting to investigate the pretension to direct evidence of personal survival propounded by psychical research,[73] but Tennant does not find these pretensions sufficiently substantiated to take them seriously. Whether or not his attitude is sound at this point, it is certainly true that an argument which claims to have a superior measure of inductive probability on the basis of known facts opens itself to the charge that the known empirical facts have to be reinforced by anticipated facts in order to substantiate the full theistic inference. This, of course, is admitted by Tennant, but it is not easy for "outsiders" to accept the superior probability of its truth.

C. THE RELATIVITY AND EXTRAPOLATION
OF MORAL VALUES

There are serious difficulties involved in Tennant's theory of moral value along with the matter of extrapolation. These concern the nature of value itself. Value tends to be equated with psychological complexity rather than a quality or a demand in the nature of things upon individuals universally.

In Volume I of *Philosophical Theology* the psychological genesis of moral standards is traced in the following manner. A valuable object to the primitive unsocialized individual is an object which is desired. Such an individual might say "X is good," but good in this case is not a quality of an object as blue is the quality of the sky in the proposition: "The sky is blue." The

72. *Ibid.*, II, 272.   73. See *Mind*, XXXIX, 476 ff.

statement "X is good" means "X is desirable to me" or "I find that X is desirable to me." In other words, the linguistic form of the statement incorrectly objectifies the goodness of the object. Good is a statement about my desire, not about the nature of an object.

The second step in the psychological evolution of the un-socialized individual is the discrimination between things which are more desirable because they give more lasting pleasure. Thus when an individual learns that some things are better to eat than others because of the more wholesome after-effects, he can say "this is good," meaning "this is more desirable to me than that." The third step occurs when an individual has learned to discriminate between his outer bodily self and his inner or more ideal self and finds that some objects give greater pleasure to this inner self than others. He judges objects by their approval to this inner self. Desirability to an inner self, a more complicated psychological individual, is the new standard of value used by a person at this stage of the process.

Side by side with this egocentric trend of development is the psychological development of the social individual. No individual is born into the world a pure egoist; he is by nature a sympathetic animal. In the course of his intercommunication with others, he learns the standards and value-judgments of others. As he becomes an ideal spectator, he can apply these standards to himself and to others. By idealization and conceptualization he builds up a sense of the common good. In a conflict between the common good and his own good, the force which obligates him to follow the former rather than the latter is his native altruism. The reason that a prophet towers above his fellows in his judgment of the good is due to his greater idealization of common judgments and to his wider altruism. His nature being more complex, his judgment as to an object's goodness is a statement of its interest to him or to him as a member of society. Higher stages than this are reached by progressive advances of idealization and altruism. In a case where a high idea of personal self-regard and a high ideal of social welfare come into conflict, we are told that there is no ultimate standard by which one course of action or object can be considered better than the other. That is, for example, if in a battle an emergency should arise when a general's orderly is in danger and the general is in a position to

save his subordinate's life and lose his own or to save his own
upon which the success of the battle depends and allow his orderly to be killed, there will be no principle by which he can decide whether to follow a high principle of personal honor or a
high principle of social welfare.

It is here that difficulties begin to break out. Is it true that
there is nothing in the nature of this situation whereby one
course of action ought to be followed rather than another? Is it
impossible to say that social welfare ought to be followed instead
of the individual claim? Is it true to say that the higher of the
two courses is the one which is psychologically more complex
than the other? If so, is psychological complexity a criterion of
the nature of value? If it is said that there is no real higher and
lower course of action to be followed in the above situation, can
it be said that there is a higher and a lower in other cases? Let us
suppose that men who have conceptualized the common standards of their group to a high degree and who also have a measure
of altruism come into conflict with a prophet whose judgments
are entirely different. These men say that the prophet who denies
their judgments of good for his own judgment of good is insane.
Is there nothing in the situation which makes his judgment truly
right against theirs, or is he simply more complex than they? If
he is more complex than they, can we say that they ought to be
more complex and mean anything?

Again, if all moral judgments are simply relative to the complexities of psychological states, can we argue from this to a
morally perfect God? Tennant gives us an analysis of value in
terms of psychological complexity and relative differences; then
in order to draw the inference that there is a moral God, he has
to assume that these standards are somehow ends for God as well
as men. If this be true, he has not only assumed human moral
standards to be the divine purpose, which is extrapolation of
the highest order, but he has shaded the divine purpose with relativity in which case it is difficult to understand how God can be
morally perfect. A morally perfect God ought to be conceived as
demanding through the nature of situations a best course of action which ought to be followed by all men. Men may not perceive
this true best in situations because of the variability of psychological states, but these psychological-colored glasses need not
imply that there is no real good commanding obedience from the

situation. It is one thing to assume that God's purpose for the world is the achievement of the moral vocation, it is another thing to imply that man's relative claims are the claims of God. It is one thing to claim that there is a real objective best course in every situation and it is another matter to claim that the moral pressure of this "best" course is the influence of a supreme personal Spirit or God. Not all people who defend the objectivity of moral value maintain that this objectivity gives immediate evidence of the Holy Spirit of God. To assert this is to the non-religious person either pious error or undue dogmatism. It is to enlarge the moral data into a revelation of designing purpose. But Tennant's theory involves not only extrapolation but the denial of any objective best course in moral situations, a fact which exposes it not only to the charge of extrapolation but to subjectivism (either social or individual or both). Upon such a basis it is difficult to see how a morally perfect God is "proved," or how it can be convincing to "outsiders" who have no conscious religious experience.

Summary

In view of the discussion of this chapter, several considerations of serious importance have emerged to cast doubt upon the possibility and probability of arriving at a valid belief in God. First, a human analogy to divine creation is admittedly not possible for us. Secondly, the genetic analogies, by means of which Tennant claims that things (substance-causes) and other selves are known, stand revealed as false to the subtleties of the process by which these realities are known. Third, the data from which the theistic inference is drawn tend in the course of the drawing of the inference to be supplemented by the hoped-for effects which the inferred God may yet produce and thus substantiate the inference which is not yet warranted by the present data.

CHAPTER III

AN EXAMINATION OF TENNANT'S CRITICISMS OF RELIGIOUS EXPERIENCE

Summary of Tennant's Criticisms

IT is the purpose of this chapter to undertake an examination of Tennant's criticisms of religious experience and to evolve a conception of the nature and validation of religious experience as an intrinsic type of apprehension. His criticisms,[1] it will be remembered, are: (1) The data of sense-experience are our only, original, underived, firsthand, immediate contact with the actual. This original objective nucleus all the profane sciences have in common. (2) *Numina*[2] differ from sensa in lacking specific quality of the intensity of color. They have no immediately perceived, specific quality. (3) *Numina* are so vague and devoid of specific quality that they are connected with all kinds of objects throughout the history of religion. If all the objects which are perceived to be instinct with numinous power are actually thus endowed, then theism is refuted. If the divine power has selectively indwelt various objects, progress in theology has been made by successive denials of its actual presence in these objects. (4) *Numina* are so private, exclusive, and autobiographical that they cannot be constructed into common, conceptualized thought-objects as sensa or *idia* can be. (5) The experience of the numinous may be psychologically immediate but epistemologically it is actually proven to be mediate. This confusion of psychological and epistemological immediacy pervades all mystical and intuitionalist theology, and the majority of discussions of religious experience. (6) The experience of the numinous may be accompanied by a high degree of "certainty," but this may be simply a high degree of subjective psychological certitude and not of objective, reasonable certainty. The confusion of "certitude" and "certainty"—or of "certitude" and "probability," if complete objective certainty is impossible—also pervades most discussions of religious experience. (7) The religious experience

1. Cf. *supra,* pp. 23 ff.
2. The content or data of religious experience. See below, pp. 144 ff.

involves no unique faculty of cognition as certain mystical and intuitionalist writers assert. It is impossible to distinguish this so-called higher faculty of mystical apprehension from certain subliminal functionings of mind, or from anesthetic and hypnotic revelation.

I. SENSA ARE OUR SOLE, ORIGINAL, UNDERIVED, IMMEDIATE CONTACTS WITH INDEPENDENT REALITY

Sensa are our sole, original, underived, immediate contacts with the actual. It is extremely difficult to criticize this statement without bringing into the discussion points which are connected with the other six criticisms that Tennant makes of religious experience. There will be, therefore, a considerable amount of repetition in the following analysis. The statement—"sensa are contacts with the actual"—must be interpreted in the light of Tennant's epistemology. Sensa are given to a subject by way of a process of perceiving. Sensa are therefore relative to a subject which is owner and agent of the act of perceiving. Sensa are, however, not purely subjective states of the knower. They are also relative to the independently actual. We do not know merely phenomena; we know the reality as it appears. Phenomena and independent reality are not two absolutely distinct particulars; they are rather complexly related, semidistinct yet united orders. In other words, the above statement is made in the light of critical realism; absolute realism as well as absolute subjectivism are rejected. This means that what is "given," though relative to both subject and object, is nonetheless "immediate contact with the actual."

From the standpoint of the experiencing process, this statement rests upon the conviction that perception is not a pure process. Sensation is connected with interpretation and thought-construction. The subject is active in transforming what is "given" to it passively into a true perception of what it is that is "given." So that there is no such thing as "pure-data" or "pure sensa" or "pure phenomena," but only "interpreted data," or "constructed sensa," or "recognized phenomena." There is no process of perceiving which is pure sensation or pure perception, but only a mixed process of thinking-sensation and thought-interfused-perception. It is impossible to distinguish what is purely given "from what is impurely given." The "given" is always colored by interpretation, mental comparison with remembered "givens," and thought integration.

Thought-Construction Not in Itself a Negation of Epistemological Immediacy

Now then, if we accept, as Tennant does, that the "interpreted data" or "constructed sensa" are nonetheless definable as "immediate contact with independent actuality," then the term "immediate" is not thereby to be denied to an object which has elements of thought-construction in its recognition. Neither does it appear that the term "immediate" is to be restricted to the subject's contact with sensa as absolutely disconnected from independently existing reality. The term "immediate" at this point is used to cover both psychic (psychological) and epistemological contact between mental process and independently existing reality, between idea and thing-in-itself, between experience and reality. If there is epistemological as well as psychological "immediacy" of contact between subject and reality given through sense, and if "immediacy" does not mean the total absence of thought-synthesis in the case of the perception of a sense-object, then the term "immediacy" cannot be denied to the experience of *numina* (religious objects) solely on the grounds that thought-construction enters into the religious experience or that psychological and epistemological immediacy are mutually exclusive. The denial of the term "immediacy" to religious experience rests upon other differences between religious experience and sense-experience than the general denial of all immediacy in the relationship of experienced object and independent reality. Whereas an absolute dualist[3] is explicit in his denial of the term "immediate" to any object of experience, sensory or non-sensory, Tennant does allow the term to apply to sense-experience.[4] Such "immediacy" is always a qualified or relative "immediacy," but it is

3. A. C. Knudson, *The Philosophy of Personalism*, pp. 100–114; cf. *The Validity of Religious Experience*, pp. 89 ff.
4. Knudson and Tennant do not differ practically from each other at this point. Knudson states that there are "different degrees of relative immediacy." No absolute immediacy exists in any knowledge, but sense-experience, Knudson would urge, has a higher degree of relative immediacy than religious experience.

"immediacy," nonetheless, and an "immediacy" which exists, in spite of error, wherever true perception occurs. "Immediacy" then does not mean absolute infallibility, but relative assurance, whenever it occurs. Certitude and objective "certainty" (relative certainty) coincide in veridical sense-perception or in immediate experience. That we have such immediacy and assurance of truth in the case of sense-perception and not in the case of religious "perception" is a question which cannot be decided a priori, but only after careful probing of the facts.

Greater Thought-Construction Does Not Imply Greater Untrustworthiness

Tennant, of course, does analyze the facts; he does not decide the matter a priori, but his genetic method does betray him into a bias against the admission of religious immediacy. In the evolution of consciousness, both human and subhuman, sense contact with reality is the first, in time, and the most obstinate of all facts. No one wishes to dispute this, but if one starts with this what has to be watched is the tendency to assume that the simpler stage is more immediate and trustworthy, and that the later stages are derived, hence less immediate and relatively more untrustworthy. The implication of Tennant's principle that knowledge involves a progressive manifestation of venturesome faith is that this greater faith is needed to overcome a lurking sense of the untrustworthiness of thought-construction. But this does not necessarily follow if thought-construction arises out of the givenness of each reality or quality of reality which it recognizes.

Thought-Constructed Awareness of Other Selves Epistemologically Immediate

We have already argued that the experiences of other selves are not experiences derived from certain types of sensa without the "givenness" of an other-than-sensory stimulation. The "immediacy" of this contact with personal reality is as original and underived as the contact with sense-objects. Both sense-object and personal reality are presented together whenever apprehended; a subject's contact with personal reality is not exactly the same as the introspection of the other self's own states; but such contact is not to be explained in terms of derived contacts with sense-objects alone or a combination of immediate contacts with one's own mind and other sense-objects. By no manipulation of these two immediate contacts can you derive the third; nor by manipulation of subjective contents derived from the first two can you derive the third. To assume that this is possible is to fail to do justice to the immediately "given." Thought-construction may enter into the recognition of personal reality, but it does not create the reality, nor create the idea of it out of other "givens." Neither does it introduce into other-self perception any greater element of untrustworthiness than thought-construction introduces into sense-perception. If thought-construction does not corrupt the one, it does not corrupt the other. Faith in the trustworthiness of each seems to be equally demanded.

The Possibility that Numina Are Epistemologically Immediate

Sufficient reason has now been given to doubt the statement that sensa are our "only, underived, immediate contact with actuality." "Persona" (to coin a phrase) may also have this character. Whether *numina* are to be deprived of this qualification can only be decided after a discussion of their contrasting differences.

II. *NUMINA* HAVE NO IMMEDIATELY PERCEIVED SPECIFIC QUALITY

Definition of Numina

Numina lack specific quality; they have no immediately perceived specific quality; they are vague like a "thing-in-itself," the pure ego, or an electron. In order to analyze this statement some definition of *numina* must be given. *Numina* is a term corresponding to sensa and as such designates the phenomenal appearance or appearances of deity to a subject. For religious epistemological (monistic) realism all manifestations of God's presence are objectively real; for religious (monistic) subjectivism these manifestations are subjective ideas or experiences of the individual or group mind; for the religious dualist, the manifestation as experience or idea is absolutely distinct from the external reality; for the critical realist some more intimate

relation is invoked to overcome absolute dualism as well as the
disadvantages of extreme realism and of extreme subjectivism.
In comparing *numina* to sensa, a critical realism is assumed;
namely, that the manifestation of God is neither totally or
absolutely real independently of experience, nor totally or absolutely subjective experience or idea of the subject, but a partial combination of idea and reality.

Religious Experience Illustrated and Defined

No definition of *numina* or "manifestation of God" is usable
until it is illustrated by concrete reference to actual experience,
and even here it is necessary to present an analogous instance.
Religious experience like "being in love" is difficult to describe
to those who have not had it; but, as it is possible to describe
"being in love" to those who have not had this experience by
pointing out its likeness to friendship, an experience which most
people possess, so it is possible to describe religious experience
by pointing out its analogies to the patriot's experience of patriotism.[5]

Patriotism or love of country is a dual experience which involves not only love of a man for his country but also the love
of his country for him. In other words, it is reciprocal relation.
Though not always conscious of his country or his love for it, a
patriotic citizen in ordinary times will give his time, his leisure,
and his money to work for, and to contribute to, his country's
good. In extraordinary times of war and crisis, the patriot will
cast aside his most cherished interests; he will leave wife, children, profession; he will sacrifice comfort, health, and even life
itself for the good of his homeland. This is love of country from
the standpoint of the patriot.

But there is also a reverse experience, the love of the country
for the patriot. It is the love of the country for the patriot that
calls forth the love of the patriot for the country. For centuries
the country has through countless representatives prepared for
his appearance. After birth, it has exercised continual care and

5. In this description and its implications, the writer is following very closely
an article on "Religious Experience and Philosophy" by Sir Francis Younghusband in *The Proceedings of the Aristotelian Society* (new ser.), XXVIII,
115–134.

supervision, registering the fact of his birth, looking after his
health, providing education, protecting his life and property,
insuring him against accident, unemployment, and old age.
Upon special occasions when the patriot has rendered some conspicuous service, his country will shower upon him unbounded
honor and love. In a Jubilee celebration, England showered lav-
ish love upon Queen Victoria, who had devoted long years of
service to her people. England pays continual tribute to her unknown soldiers by honoring a tomb which represents them.

The love of the country for the patriot is a continual fact.
The individual may not be conscious of it in his ordinary daily
life, but there may come to some, usually at moments of crisis,
occasions when the individual suddenly becomes aware of his
country's love for him. He responds to his country's call because
she first loved him and acted in his behalf. Sometimes his realization flames to white-heat intensity as he realizes what his
country means to him and he to it. The Englishman understands
that he is sprung from England; that he is a part of her life;
that England's spirit dwells within him and throbs in his heart;
and that England's image is proclaimed in his characteristics.
A transcendent power grips his heart; he feels utterly over-
awed, prostrate before its august presence; yet at the same time
he is melted by the tenderness of this power's devotion to him;
he is exalted, often elated beyond measure, by the spirit which
is coming home to him. The whole country concentrates its love
and existence upon him; its spirit enters him, and he, in turn,
enters into it. He catches a glimpse of its inner motives; he understands what it is driving at; he is eager to give his all to its
welfare. No experience results in a greater desire to give and to
work creatively for a higher good than the experience of a country's love and need focused upon the individual. The response
on the part of the individual leads to unlimited effort and service.

Religious experience may be suggestively compared to patriotism. Setting aside momentarily the question of personality
both in its application to the country and to the world, it may
be said that as patriotism is the reciprocal love of man and country for each other, religion is the reciprocal love of man and the
world (universe)-as-a-whole for each other. The religious per-

son loves sincerely and wholeheartedly the world about him; its glories, its beauties, its goodnesses. He struggles to serve the highest and holiest things of life; this is the love of man for the world-as-a-whole in its heights and depths.

The universe, however, is continually exercising a love toward the individual. The human being is born out of the universe. Science is ever confirming the fact that we are sprung from Mother Earth, the earth from the sun, and the sun from the stellar universe. Nature is an organic whole; men are parts of the universe; the system has produced men; the spirit of the universe is reflected in the product at which it has aimed. Man is the "heir of all the ages"; the object of its creative movement and solicitation. Even higher than does one's country transcend the individual, so does the greater universe transcend and yet encompass the individual.

At times an individual comes to realize that the whole universe is concentrating its love upon him as its "beloved son." The spirit of the universe touches him; he catches a glimpse of what it is aiming at; he understands what is going on in the heart of things. Devoutly prostrated in soul before the majesty, the glory, the authority of the universal spirit, he nonetheless is moved by its tenderness and continual care. The depth of the love of the world-as-a-whole for him calls forth in the religious man a tremendous creative energy making him ready to place his life at the service of the world's need and eager to bring forth the end toward which creation moves, a veritable Kingdom of God, wherein a great society of human cells moves in one universal organism. Some such experience as this resides at the basis of the energy of great religious leaders such as Jesus who, in response to the love of God toward Him, sought to work for a Kingdom or society through which the spirit of the universe might surge. The great moments of religious experience are moments in which experiencing subjects become peculiarly aware of the spirit of the universe, an-unimaginably-greater-than-they, in whom they live and move and have their being. It is from moments of experience such as these that man is able to form conceptions of the transcendent Power whose image he bears.

This brings us to the question of the "personality" of the

universe or world-as-a-whole. The question is likewise relevant to the country as a whole. Is the country a personality?; is the universe a personality? Love, some would say, can be manifested only between man and man or man and woman; it is a sentiment that can be shown only toward individual people; hence we are not warranted in speaking of the love of country toward the individual or the love of the universe toward the individual. There is, however, a relationship of both country and the universe toward the individual which stirs such deep responses in the individual that his love toward these objects becomes more commanding than his love for individuals. The country's goodness to him causes his responding love to take precedence over his love of wife or child or friend; God's love for man may evoke a responding love for God which is more absolute than love of wife, child, friend, or country. Any object which does so much for its offspring and evokes such a response to its sacredness is certainly not less than personal even though it is mysterious and transcendent.

The Unique Characteristics of Ultimacy and Intimacy

According to C. C. J. Webb, religious experience is characterized by two features: (1) ultimacy, and (2) intimacy. It is concerned with ultimacy, "the very heart and inmost reality of things," "the nameless secret of existence," the "Quiet, as the Highest beyond whom is no other," "the innermost secret of ourselves and our environment."[6] It is, however, an experience of the ultimate which is characterized by intimacy. It is:

. . . not as something remote, inferred, indifferent to ourselves, but as something "disturbing" us, not indeed always, as in Wordsworth's poem, with "the joy of elevated thoughts"—at certain levels it disturbs us with thoughts far from joyful and which seem to us far from elevated—but always disturbing us, haunting us, as Job was haunted, on the right hand and on the left, or, as the Psalmist knew, "about our path and about our bed and spying out all our ways": nay more *within* us, and, in the phrase of Tennyson, "closer than breathing and nearer than hands or feet."[7]

6. C. C. J. Webb, "The Nature of Religious Experience," *The Hibbert Journal*, XXXII, 21–23.
7. *Ibid.*, p. 23.

Webb in another lecture says:

. . . by religious experience I understand the consciousness of
Something to which all else that we experience, ourselves included,
totum quod sumus et in quo sumus, is related as to its background,
its meaning, or its cause, and related, since we are thus ourselves
included, not merely remotely and inferentially but directly and
intimately; which therefore excites in us a sentiment of awe and
reverence, which may range from a cowering fear like Caliban's up
to the "perfect love" of St. John, which "casts out fear, because
fear hath torment," but of which this is the peculiar and distinguishing object, not to be confounded with other objects of fear
or love which are not, to use the convenient term lately made current by Professor Rudolf Otto, "numinous."[8]

Religious and Social Experience Distinguished

Webb then proceeds to point out that the language in which
people of Western tradition are accustomed to describe their
religious experience is usually borrowed from social intercourse
and consequently invites critics to misrepresent the experience
as merely fallacious anthropomorphism. The failure to distinguish between social experience and religious experience is responsible for much of this misrepresentation. Religious experience differs from social experience in the following respects: (1)
It is differentiated from our knowledge of other human beings
by "our consciousness of not being, even in the depths of our
being, divided from its Object." In our experience of one another we are distinctly transcendent, but God, we feel, knows
the secret thoughts and intentions of our hearts. By this statement Webb does not mean to imply that we "introspect" (erleben) God's mind, but that in religious experience there is a sense
of being in more intimate relation with God than with other
people.[9] (2) The religious experience is differentiated from social experience by this further fact. In social experience there is
always the overt external action of human bodies, whereas in
religious experience no invariable overt external action is to be

8. C. C. J. Webb, lecture on "Our Knowledge of One Another," *The Proceedings of the British Academy,* XVI (1930), 290.
9. Cf. *op. cit.* (*The Hibbert Journal*), p. 26.

secured.[10] Perceived objects may evoke the experience of "something far more deeply interfused"; but not all perceived objects do invariably mediate this object, characterized by ultimacy and intimacy. " 'The mind of man,' 'all thinking things,' 'all objects of all thought' (Wordsworth), the different objects (in nature) which we have discussed, the apprehension of our fellows, the consciousness of self, our perception of the external world, all mediate the experience of something which is other than them all, yet can reveal itself in any of them all."[11] The religious object does not answer our prayers by overt external actions as our fellow human beings do; it responds mainly in the strength, nourishment, and communion which accompany our worship. The religious experience is not invariably connected with the overt activities of any specific physical object such as a human body; but such is not to be expected in the case of a reality which is "the innermost secret of ourselves and our environment."

Now it is this aspect of "intimacy" which causes men to react to the "spirit of the universe" as personal yet mysteriously so. Waldo Jewell-Lapan in a clear but naturalistic interpretation of religious experience[12] states that what renders nature (exclusive of man) so mysterious and incomprehensible to him is that nature is mysteriously like yet unlike himself. Although nature does not think, yet it displays order and intelligibility, and its order is appropriate to his thinking; although nature does not possess will nor purpose, yet it still achieves endings. It is incomprehensible to man because "without his faculties of willing or thinking, it yet brings forth ends, and possesses a structure which in its entirety is beyond his powers of apprehension." If, however, the innermost secret of nature (exclusive of man) and man together is experienced in the numinous experience so that the numinous object is not "wholly other" than man solely by virtue of its presence in nature (exclusive of man), but by virtue of its intimate connection with man, then there is no difficulty in understanding why man reacts to it as a "super-personality," and there is no conclusive reason for supposing that

10. *Ibid.*, p. 27.   11. Cf. *op. cit.* (*Proceedings*), p. 291.
12. "A Naturalistic View of 'Numinous' Experience," *The Review of Religion*, II, 30.

this reaction is illusory. For just as some men are more truly and fully representative of England than others, and the more representative Englishmen more truly representative of England at some times than others, so some men are more fully representative of the universe than others, and most men are more truly representative of it than other finite, nonhuman objects. This fact cuts beneath the base of both naturalism and pantheism. All finite objects, human and subhuman, are not equally representative of the innermost heart of the universe. Only the best men in their best moments can give the most adequate impression of the essential nature of the world. This principle holds true in far countries where foreign peoples derive their impressions of a nation from single representatives, and we believe that only the best representatives can give the fullest impression of a country, and only the best representative in his highest moments. So with respect to the universe, it is only the best men in their highest moments who give the most adequate indication of the world-spirit.

Two Acknowledgments: Numina Less Common than Sensa; Numina Involve Thought-Construction

It is necessary to relate this inadequate description of the object of religious experience to Tennant's criticism of *numina* as vague and as lacking specific quality. (1) *Numina*, especially of the high type which we have described, are not as common as sensa. Not as many people have "concrete" religious experience as sense-experience; this is true. (2) *Numina* involve a greater degree of thought-construction in order to be recognized than sensa; to recognize a reality characterized by "ultimacy" and "intimacy" requires a larger degree of experience-synthesis than that involved in perceiving a phenomena of the thing-type.

This fact, however, does not necessarily mean (*a*) that *numina* are totally thought-created; (*b*) nor that *numina* are derived from the manipulation of sensa, persona, and the empirical ego; (*c*) nor that *numina* are totally accountable in terms of antecedent beliefs or ideas derived from the social traditions of religious societies; (*d*) nor that *numina* are not unique and ultimate elements in what is "given."

Numina *Not Totally Thought-Created*

(*a*) There is an element of "confrontation" or "givenness," an awareness of objective stimulation, which gives the concrete moment of religious experience an inescapable character. The thought-recognition of *numina* cannot be created at will; it has to force its way into the consciousness of the individual and therefore carries with it a sense of direct presence and reality which is more than thought-given or thought-created. Such a "givenness" does not mean "infallibility"; error is always possible; but error enters into sense-givenness as well; and yet "givenness" is taken as a sign of objectivity. Error is not a feature which can be eliminated from subjective or objective "givenness."

Let us suppose, for example, that sensa are created by the subject, there still remains a difference between sensa which are more stubbornly "real" and those which are solely imaginal. No escape from the possibility of error is made by transferring all experiences from the objective to the subjective realms. Neither is there any escape from the possibility of error by transferring all religious experiences from the objective to the subjective realms. There is still a difference between *numina* which are "real" and *numina* which only seem to be. But the presence of the latter does not absolutely exclude all religious experiences which have the character of "givenness."

Numina *Not Derived Solely from Conjoined Objects*

(*b*) *Numina* may be apprehended in intimate conjunction with sense-objects, or other selves, or the self, but they are always more than these and possess qualities which are higher and more mysterious than these. Here it should be said that in moments of religious experience, the entire being of God does not stand revealed to the subject; neither does nature as an absolute whole, nor the universe as a complete whole stand revealed to a subject. But this is true of finite objects. Only aspects of sense-objects, other selves, and the self appear to a subject. We do not, therefore, conclude that we know nothing of these objects. The same is applicable to the manifestations of the religious object. Not all of the nature and qualities of God stand revealed in moments of high religious experience, but this does not mean that nothing is revealed, nor yet that there is no difference in quality between the manifestations of the divine object and the appearances of finite objects. Neither can the divine object be regarded as a totality of finite objects. "Thou, O Lord, art more than they" is the testimony of the religious consciousness.

Numina *Not Explained in Terms of Tradition*

(c) *Numina* cannot be solely accounted for in terms of ideas derived from religious tradition; otherwise to receive the idea from someone else would be to undergo the experience. This does not seem to be the case. Beliefs or ideas derived from social tradition do condition the interpretation of the experience. It would be impossible for a person to think of his religious experience as experience of the Trinity, or of Christ, or of Brahma without having acquired these terms and definitions from his religious teachers. But there is more to religious experience than the acquisition of these ideas and more to the experience than socially derived ideas tenaciously held with intense emotion. Certainly a teacher in a biological laboratory does not insure either that the student will find or recognize a specimen simply by telling him what he sees or should see under a microscope. Perhaps the student's failure to discern the object may be due to his deficiency of sight, but it may also be due to the fact that the object or a certain feature of the object is not there in the specimen. Only the presence in actuality of something to be recognized and of something comparable to the teacher's description can result in the judgment that a specific object has a certain forestated character. Something comparable to this is true in religion. Unless it is assumed that the ideas of religious teachers create the realities of religious experience in others, no matter how often errors creep into these interpretations, it is yet true that the realities which evoke the application of acquired definitions possess a certain stubborn independence of these definitions which they would not possess if the definitions were the sole cause of the religious experience. Furthermore, it is always pertinent to ask what caused the first experience of the first person who underwent a religious experience. From what social sources did he derive definitions which "created" his experience? The prophet or religious innovator is a comparable mystery. What current definitions give him his experience? Undoubtedly there are many subtleties here, but there is a common tendency to confuse antecedent belief (socially derived) with that a priori experience-synthesis which is an intrinsic or underived function of the mind of the individual.

Numina *Characterized by Ultimacy and Intimacy*

(*d*) *Numina* are unique moments in which a subject becomes aware of an object characterized by ultimacy and intimacy which concentrates its whole life upon him as its representative. This experience is above the level of rational thinking, not below it, but the object carries with it a "givenness" and stubborn "brutality" which causes the subject to assign its reality to something beyond himself and his thought. It is its "givenness" and its "ultimacy" and "intimacy" which make the numinous object unique, not vague, a fact to be accepted as objectively grounded as well as subjectively apprehended.

III. *NUMINA* ARE SO VAGUE AS TO ENTER VARIABLE, INCONSISTENT, AND SELF-REFUTING AFFILIATIONS

Numina are so vague and devoid of specific quality that they are connected with all kinds of objects throughout the history of religion. If all the objects which are perceived to be instinct with numinous power are actually thus endowed, then theism is refuted. If the divine power has selectively indwelt various objects, progress in theology has been made by successive denials of its actual presence in these objects.

The difficulties against the superhuman claim of religion [writes Baron Von Hügel][13] can conveniently, even though only roughly, be grouped according to the peculiarities in the objects thus presented to and apprehended by the human mind; the limitations, real or apparent, of these our apprehending minds; and the evils

13. Von Hügel, *Essays and Addresses*, 1st ser., p. 25.

which result, with seeming necessity, from all such belief in the Super-human.

. . . .

The first group, then, is busy with the objects, be they only apparent or be they real, presented to the religious human mind and soul. These seem to inflict a treble, an increasingly final, denial and refutation upon any and all superhuman claim.

For we can compare these experiences, in the past or even in the present of religion, simply with each other; and we shall then find them to present us with endless variations, and even grave contradictions.

The endless variations and contradictions in the object of religious experience to many thinkers cause them to dismiss the independent divine reality altogether. In Tennant's case, this variety is a major element in causing him to reject the evidential value of any specific religious experience. Horton quotes a student of Tennant's as saying:[14] "Tennant does not deny that there is religious experience, but he is sceptical about maintaining that this experience which is [phenomenal] effect is the result of a religious cognition of a [noumenal] cause without which the religious experience would have been impossible." This skepticism is so deep that it amounts to an absolute denial of any value to religious experience whatsoever in the court of philosophy. That there is great and serious difficulty here, no one would deny, but that the difficulty is as insurmountable or as negative in its implications, the following considerations are offered as sufficient rebuttal.

Variation, Illusion, and Inconsistency Pertain to Objects of Nature, Also, Without Utter Fatality

1. *Numina* are certainly not the only objects which are marked by variety, illusion, and inconsistency. Nature itself is, and has ever been, an object marked by the crudest ideas and illusory experiences imaginable. The solar system, rocks, plants, and animals have been fancifully regarded by men throughout

14. W. M. Horton, quotation from Dr. Bertocci, *Contemporary English Theology,* p. 89 n.

human history. Astrology, magic, and alchemy have infected early ideas about nature; the history of science itself is one long story of exploded hypotheses and concepts given to heat, light, gravitation, matter, and energy. A good case might be made out against the objective reality of the objects of nature by dwelling upon the confusion, the crudities, and the imperfections of human experience. Balmforth[15] cites a passage from

15. Henry Balmforth, *Is Christian Experience an Illusion*, pp. 65–66. "I have sometimes thought that the parallel between Science and Theology, regarded as systems of belief, might be conveniently illustrated by framing a refutation of the former on the model of certain attacks on the latter with which we are familiar. We might begin by showing how crude and contradictory are the notions of primitive man, and even of the cultivated man in his unreflective moments, respecting the object-matter of scientific beliefs. We might point out the rude anthropomorphism which underlies them, and show how impossible it is to get altogether rid of the anthropomorphism without refining away the object-matter till it becomes an unintelligible abstraction. We might then turn to the scientific apologists. We should show how the authorities of one age differed from those of another in their treatment of the subject, and how the authorities of the same age differed among themselves: then—after taking up their systems one after another, and showing their individual errors in detail— we should comment at length on the strange obstinacy they evinced in adhering to their conclusions whether they could prove them or not. It is at this point, perhaps, that according to usage we might pay a passing tribute to morality. With all the proper circumlocutions, we should suggest that so singular an agreement respecting some of the most difficult points requiring proof could not be accounted for on any hypothesis consistent with the intellectual honesty of the apologists. Without attributing motives to individuals, we should hint politely, but not obscurely, that prejudice and education in some, the fear of differing from the majority, or the fear of losing a lucrative place in others, had been allowed to warp the impartial course of investigation; and we should lament that scientific philosophers, in many respects so amiable and useful a body of men, should allow themselves so often to violate principles which they openly and even ostentatiously avowed. After this moral display, we should turn from the philosophers who are occupied with the rationale of the subject to the main body of men of science who are actually engaged in teaching and research. Fully acknowledging their many merits, we should yet be compelled to ask how it comes about that they are so ignorant of the controversies which rage round the very foundations of their subject, and how they can reconcile it with their intellectual self-respect, when they are asked some vital question (say, respecting the proof of the law of Universal Causation, or the existence of the external world) either to profess total ignorance of the subject, or to offer in reply some shreds of worn-out metaphysics. It is true, they might say, that a profound study of these subjects is not consistent either with teaching or with otherwise advancing the cause of Science; but, of course, to this excuse we should make the obvious rejoinder that, before trying to advance the cause of Science, it would be as well to discover whether such a thing as Science really existed. This done, we should have to analyse the actual body of scientific truth presented for our acceptance; to show how, while its conclusions are inconsistent, its premises are either lost in a metaphysical haze, or else are unfounded and gratuitous assumptions; after which it would only remain for us

Balfour's *Defence of Philosophic Doubt* to illustrate such a procedure. Actually, however, few if any except a solipsist, believe that variability and confusion of our experience of nature totally invalidate our human conviction that nature exists independently of our thinking. What this situation actually implies is that naïve realism must be rejected for a critical realism with respect to perception and to conception. The confusion is continually clarified by painstaking procedures, but confusion does not negate the entire existence of objective nature whatever in fact it may actually be. In like manner with respect to religious experience, confusion and variety do not automatically negate the entire existence of the reality to which the inconsistent experiences point. Certainly this conclusion cannot be drawn a priori or without wide consideration.

Variations Due in Part to Differences in Minds

2. Variation in the experience of nature and natural objects is usually taken to imply, at least from one angle, that the inconsistencies are largely due to the peculiarities, limitations, and inadequacies of the experiencing mind or the psychophysical organism of the individuals and groups involved. Inherent differences in aptitude and temperament, variations in stages of individual and social development in intelligence and character, cultural backgrounds of vast heterogeneity—these factors and many more account for variations in the subjective apparatus of those who seek to know the Real. Variation in observers cannot imply anything other than variation in the objects of experience. One single reliable object reflected in various mirrors, some of which are distorted, and some of which are perfect, will certainly give rise to as many different reflections as there are mirrors. But because the reflections vary from extreme distortion to remarkable resemblance, no sufficient reason is thereby given for denying that there exists any independent object of which these reflections are more or less copies; nor is there given any reason to deny that all reflections are equally good copies of that object.

to compose an eloquent peroration on the debt which mankind owed to Science, and to the great masters who have created it, and to mourn that the progress of criticism should have left us no choice but to count it among the beautiful but baseless dreams which have so often deluded the human race with the phantom of certain knowledge.

As a matter of fact, far from being a sign of the absolute
nonexistence of an object, variation may actually be a sign of
the object's stubborn reality. Oman has put the case thus:

Both in nature and in history, it is the illusions which have shown
mechanical uniformity. A mirage sun is merely a shining disc the
same for all and changing nothing of what anyone is observing;
the natural sun is a constantly varying object, giving to each observer a different impression of the world it shines on. To no real
experience do all men react in the same way; and only when dogmas
are mere forms of words can they be held with identical meaning.

. . . .

Even about the material world people can have the crudest ideas,
and they can feel towards it unnaturally and misuse it sadly. But
we do not argue that there can be, in that case, no stable reality,
and that it is a mere phantasmagoria of man's changing moods.
The variety of impression, on the contrary, is a very important
part of the manifestation of reality, for we rightly know any environment only when we have a mind to perceive it aright and a
will to use it well.[16]

Certainly a mirage lake does not have the same power of producing wide varieties of experience in various observers that a
real lake possesses. Variety is actually a sign of reality rather
than the reverse.

What is thus true with respect to our knowledge of nature
and of natural objects cannot automatically be denied to hold
true in the area of religious experience. The variety of impression is due to the variety, and variability in the variety, of many
observers over a long period of history. Far from negating the
existence of the religious object, variation here may signify the
vitality, persistence, and reliability of this object.

Variations Due in Part to Complexity in the Object Experienced

3. Not only does variety imply variation on the subjective
side of experience, but it also involves complexity on the objective side. For example, there are as many judgments and opin-

16. John Oman, *The Natural and the Supernatural*, p. 71.

ions of President Roosevelt as there are people who observed him, but not all the differences in judgment are due to the differences in observers themselves. Many of these differences arise from the complex nature and behavior of the President himself. One aspect of his nature he reveals to his wife and family, another to his Cabinet and intimate advisers, another to Congress, another to the invalids at Warm Springs, another to the naval officers who take him fishing. Opinions as to the character of Mr. Roosevelt will vary according to the particular side of it which he has displayed to various observers. Neither his existence nor his actual character are doubted because of this variation in self-revelation; neither are these supposed to be due to differences in observers; rather they are signs of his own many-sidedness and complexity of nature.

If this is true of a man, how much more should it be true of God. The divine being manifests Himself in nature, in society, in conscience, in the depth of man's soul. To no single individual does He reveal Himself entirely, nor to any in exactly the same way. That He is dependable, and reliable, we do not need to doubt solely because it is true that circumstances and differences in situation and medium of *rapport* cause Him to reveal Himself more directly and intimately to some—the prophets and Jesus, for example—than to others—people who occupy a less important position in the redemption of mankind. To some He may reveal Himself only as Creator, to others as Judge, to others as Saviour, to others as Intimate Companion; unlike Mr. Roosevelt, God may be capable of becoming intimate with all of His children (one can speak here only with great hesitation and with devastating consciousness of the anthropic character of the above symbols) ; but that some differences in self-revelation of a being as great and as complex as God must be, if He is God, is involved in the religious relation of God and humanity—that would seem to be true in the nature of the case. Certainly no complete knowledge of God could ever be attained or obtained by any finite person, for the object of this knowledge is great, complex, many-sided, and transcendent.

The Meaning of Development in Religious Experience

4. The foregoing discussion leads to a point which is involved in what has already been indicated but which needs to be ampli-

fied in a paragraph by itself; i.e., the fact that religious experience has been and is undergoing development from an early and crude stage into a later and more refined stage.

With respect to whatsoever grows and develops [writes Hicks],[17] it is the higher stages that help us to understand and to gauge aright that which is evinced in the lower. No examination, be it ever so minute, of the seed or embryo would enable us to predict what it will in the course of time become, unless we were already familiar with the distinctive lineaments of the full-grown plant or animal. Then, doubtless, when we trace back the mature organism to the germ from which it sprang, a study of the process of genesis throws a flood of light upon the nature of that which has ultimately emerged. But the point is that "in the first instance, at least, we must read development backward and not forward, we must find the key to the meaning of the first stage in the last." What, therefore, we have to look for is not a characteristic common to every type of religion, but rather "a germinative principle," as it has been called, underlying all types, "a motive power, working in the human mind, and essentially bound up with its structure." It is in their relation to this underlying principle, and not in any doctrines or external features which they possess in common, that religions have their basis of agreement. To a large extent the history of religious beliefs is, indeed, the exhibition of the constant conflict between the imperfections of the concrete imagery which the human mind calls to its aid in representing what it takes to be divine reality and the demands of the fundamental principle which that imagery obscurely embodies, a conflict in and through which the full significance of the principle itself gradually comes to recognition. The history of religions may, then, be said to be just religion progressively defining itself; and a clear discernment of its essence will be obtained, not by "peering into its cradle and seeking oracles in its infant cries," but by contemplating it in the more mature forms to which it has attained as the outcome of the entire process of its development. And no one, I take it, would seriously dispute the statement that the whole trend of the evolution in question has been towards a belief in God as one and not as many, manifesting Himself both in nature and

17. G. Dawes Hicks, *The Philosophical Bases of Theism*, pp. 35–36.

to the mind of man, yet revealing Himself most completely to souls of large spiritual compass and of strenuous moral power.

These words of Hicks are quoted to indicate what is cardinal truth with respect to any manifestation of development; namely, that we never are able to read a developing object "forward"; in the first instance we read the development "backward." We can only know what the germ of anything is or what it is capable of producing by first knowing what has been produced. If we did not know the latter first, we would never be able to predict the result solely by observations of the germ. Thus in the realm of religious experience the earlier stages must be continually held in the light of the later stages. This means that if there is any truth to the later experiences, some germinal truth however distorted by human crudity and infantilism, must be involved, at least upon some occasions, to some minds throughout the entire development.

Without assuming [writes Hicks][18] a continuous linear progress from the lowest to the highest, or attempting to trace, after the manner of Hegel, a necessary dialectical movement in the temporal development of religious systems, it can unhesitatingly be asserted that an impartial survey of the historical data leads unmistakably to the conclusion that advance on the whole there unquestionably has been to ever purer and loftier conceptions of God and of God's relation to the world. Moreover, although, of course, the consensus gentium is no guarantee of validity, although an Athanasius contra mundum may veritably be in possession of a discernment to which the Millionen cannot attain, yet an impressive fact certainly it is, and a fact not lightly to be discounted, that in every known period of history some kind of religious beliefs and religious observances have been in evidence, in tribes and nationalities the most unlike in other respects, too remote from one another to allow the possibility of mutual influence, and pursuing the most divergent lines of practical activity. This fact would seem to be, at any rate, sufficient to justify the assumption that religion is native to man, not a product of arbitrary or capricious surmisings, but a normal and universal expression of human nature.

18. *Ibid.*, pp. 37–38.

The least that can be admitted from the widespread occurrence of religious experience is that such occurrence means that God and man have been in some kind of *rapport* with one another. This is by no means to deny that the earlier stages have been defective, limited, and crude; it is simply to say that the presence of defectiveness and variety does not mean that even the lower forms of the religious experience are totally, universally, and absolutely illusory. These forms are germinally potent.

> Though Nature could not touch the heart of Peter Bell
> "By lovely forms, and silent weather,
> And tender sounds, yet you might see
> At once, that Peter Bell and she
> Had often been together."[19]

Something comparable to this is true of religious experience.

The Relation of the Foregoing Points to Tennant's Criticism

It remains to focus the light of the four points which have been drawn above upon Tennant's critical statement concerning the vagueness and variability of *numina*. While it is true that each and every object and connection of religious experience cannot be objectively real, there being no absolute numerical and existential unity of the two, it is not equally true that the experienced object is totally subjective and totally valueless as a sign of the presence of the objectively real presence of the divine. Thus it is oversimplification to say: "If all the objects which are perceived to be instinct with numinous power are actually thus endowed, then theism is refuted. . . . Refuted [we should say] so far as naive realism is concerned but not absolutely and finally refuted so far as a critical and universal realism is maintained." (By "universal" in this latter statement is meant a position which envisages the more developed with the less developed types of religious experience and which assumes that what is true in the developed experience is true in germ in the less developed experience.)

A comparable statement is appropriate to Tennant's further conclusion: "If the divine power has selectively indwelt various

19. *Ibid.,* p. 32.

objects, progress in theology has been made by successive denials of its actual presence in these objects." Progress in theology and in religion has indeed been made by refusals to hold that divine reality is entirely manifested exactly as naïve realism holds, but this cannot be taken to mean that none of these experiences is revelatory of reality.

IV. *NUMINA* ARE TOO PRIVATE, EXCLUSIVE, AND AUTOBIOGRAPHICAL TO BE CONSTRUCTED INTO COMMON OBJECTS

Numina are so private, exclusive, autobiographical that they cannot be constructed into common conceptualized thought-objects as sensa or *idia* can be. The meaning of this criticism is essentially this: whereas sense-objects are swiftly identified by practically all people and readily known to be experienced by all people, the religious object is not as quickly identified and as readily accepted by people generally as having an existence objective and common to all. This involves the common criticism that the religious object does not meet the requirements of a scientific object which is directly presented in prescientific, common sense-perception; which is repeatable, or repeatedly experienced, and experienceable by all observers—i.e., normal and properly equipped observers; and which possesses definite qualities which can be definitely described and communicated to rational beings. The lack of definite quality or the vagueness of *numina* we have already discussed. The question of commonness or communicableness requires examination at this point.

The Exclusiveness of All Types of Experience and the Meaning of Communication

1. A fundamental principle (absolutely accepted by Tennant) in connection with all experience is that minds as definite centers of experience are mutually exclusive and transcendent to each other. This fact means that one man does not live through another man's consciousness; neither does he "introspect" another man's empirical self as he may his own. Thus the objects which he senses are strictly his in a way in which they are not another's; and thus all experience becomes ineffable

in the sense that it cannot be communicated to anyone else unless that person has a capacity for experience. Seeing cannot be communicated to one who is not possessed of eyes or who is born blind; it is ineffable, private, unique. Hearing and the other senses are incommunicable to those who lack them; so also the higher faculties for free ideas cannot be communicated to a cow or to a moron. The process of communication consists chiefly in making it possible for another to exercise his capacities in such a way as to achieve an experience of an object which belongs or is owned by him; i.e., by his mind or consciousness. Thus a jeweler takes the large diamond from its hiding place in his safe and places it in the show window where those who have good eyes may see it. Thus the teacher places books upon the reserve shelf where the student may obtain his own information if he has the capacity to read and to understand written language.

The Communication of Religious Experience

The case is not essentially different from this in the realm of religious experience. Under no circumstances could Peter undergo or live-through (*erleben*) the religious consciousness of Jesus when Jesus intuited the "innermost Spirit of the universe" concentrating its love and demand upon Him any more than Peter could see or hear sense-objects with Jesus' own processes of seeing and hearing. The subjective processes by which the religious object is intuited are neither more nor less mutually exclusive from person to person than sense processes, and the method of communication in both cases is necessarily indirect. That is, to communicate experience of the religious object the saint or the prophet can only arrange the circumstances under which another may "see God" for himself, and even then the other will not "see God" unless he has the capacity and desire to do so. Sometimes the communicating function of the saint is to be himself the medium in which the numinous presence is offered to the other observer; sometimes it is to point out specific mediation-points in connection with which, and in the midst of which, the numinous presence may be "seen" by the observer; sometimes it means that the prophet cuts away the cataracts on the "spiritual eyes" of the observer so that where once he was blind now he sees. The religious leader's communicating function is to place another in the way of the object and to tell him how he can go about it to obtain the experience for himself. "Faith," says Dean Inge,[20] "begins with an experiment and ends with an experience."

The Evidential Value of Communicated Religious Experience

2. Hence if it is possible for the religious leader to put another in the way of divine power so that the other can obtain through his own experiment an experience of the divine, it follows that we cannot say as Tennant does that religious experience has no evidential value for indicating its validity to men generally, and that it is purely autobiographical, the private memoir of a few individuals; i.e., "few" with respect to the human race as a whole. For, while the religious object has its own peculiarities and differences from other objects, it is reported to have been experienced by many people of many different types in all ages of history. This in turn means that it has been widely though always indirectly communicated. This, in turn, gives some evidence for the actual existence of the object.

Such a fact does not prove absolutely that the divine object exists; neither does it prove that the divine object is everything that people have reported it to be; but this latter point as we have seen under our discussion of variation in religious experience does not mean that the existence of the divine object is absolutely denied and therefore eliminated; neither does the former statement mean that the absence of absolute proof is sign of the nonexistence of the object. For matters of fact as Hume long ago[21] pointed out are never susceptible to absolute

20. W. R. Inge, *Christian Mysticism*, p. 50.
21. Hicks, *The Philosophical Bases of Theism*, pp. 189–190, quotation from Hume's *Enquiry*. "All the objects of human reason or enquiry may naturally be divided into two kinds, to wit, relations of ideas and matters of fact. Of the first kind are the sciences of geometry, algebra, and arithmetic; and in short, every affirmation which is either intuitively or demonstratively certain. That the square of the hypotenuse is equal to the square of two sides is a proposition which expresses a relation between these figures. That three times five is equal to the half of thirty expresses a relation between these numbers. Propositions of this kind are discoverable by the mere operation of thought, without dependence on what is anywhere existent in the universe. Though there never were a circle or triangle in nature, the truths demonstrated by Euclid would for ever retain their certainty and evidence. Matters of fact, which are the

proof as are the self-evident axioms of pure reason. It makes no difference to mathematics whether a straight line or a perfect triangle exists in nature or not; as defined they possess certain self-evident theoretical meanings and have certain implications which are absolutely true. Truth here is not proved in the same way as it has to be when a straight street or a triangular green are proved to be existent because observed by someone to exist at some point in nature. Here the fact is coercively given from outside the mind, and here the report of the fact is to be verified by the reports of other observers, tests of the soundness of observers, and congruity with other reported facts. Verification in this instance is never complete, but it can be sufficient for all practical purposes.

What is true here is true with respect to the divine. God, being a "matter of fact" and not a theoretical definition like all matters of fact, can never be proved to exist in any such absolute sense as absolute proof is forthcoming in mathematics and the abstract science. It is rather a matter of checking, comparing, and systematizing the reports of various observers in an effort to obtain some substantial agreement as to what it is that they have experienced. Never is the evidence absolute or complete, but it is all that we have.

The Common Marks of Religious Experience

Now, obviously, if there were no reports at all, or no reports by reasonably sane, intelligent observers, there would be no ground for supposing anything to exist; neither would there be any reason for attempting to systematize the reports. But if there are reports, reports from intelligent people, reports from people in many different ages and in many different parts of the world, then there is some reason to suppose that they are

second objects of human reason, are not ascertained in the same manner; nor is our evidence of their truth, however great, of a like nature with the foregoing. The contrary of every matter of fact is still possible; because it can never imply a contradiction, and is conceived by the mind with the same facility and distinctness as if ever so conformable to reality. That the sun will not rise tomorrow is no less intelligible a proposition, and implies no more contradiction, than the affirmation, that it will rise. We should in vain, therefore, attempt to demonstrate its falsehood. Were it demonstratively false, it would imply a contradiction, and could never be distinctly conceived by the mind."

testifying to something which really exists, the experience of which is in some ultimate way "given" to them.

As a matter of fact, it is thoroughly possible to draw the lines of two widespread types of religious experience[22]—the "prophetic" and the "mystical" varieties of religious apprehension.

22. F. Heiler, *Prayer*, trans. by McComb. The following outline is given to suggest Heiler's description:

General Characteristics

Mystical	Prophetic
1. Fundamental Psychic Experience	
Pessimism, dissatisfaction with world, denudation of psychic life. Passivity, quietistic, contemplative.	Optimism, world as basically good, enhancement of life and will to live. Activity, ethical, vigorous, confident, trustful.
2. Idea of God	
Monistic, Oneness, undifferentiated unity. Static God.	One and many, God as living active will.
3. Valuation of History	
Static God outside of time. No revelation of God in history.	God as Creator, Speaker, Worker. History is revelation.
4. Attitude to Authority	
Authority in depth of individual soul. No objective fact of revelation.	God communicates His will through the prophets.
5. Sin and Salvation	
Sin, not violation of ethical standards, but thirst for life, desire, self-will, sensuousness.	Sin is breach of God-ordained order of values; a chasm between man and God.
Salvation is liberation from creaturely existence. Purification, illumination, union; asceticism, meditation, knowledge, nirvana.	Salvation is turning to God; trust in His redemptive deeds.
6. Relation to Ethics	
Moral action not good in itself, but an indispensable preparation for union with absolute.	Moral action is in itself a relationship with God and God's purposiveness; i.e., a form of religious experience.
7. Social Fellowship	
Individualistic or highly exclusive; tolerant but powerless to build social fellowship.	Social, consciousness of mission, intolerant at times. Powerful in building fellowship.
8. Relation to World Civilization	
Indifferent, withdrawal from world.	No absolute hostility; world to be transformed, redeemed.

(*continued on next page*)

The extreme manifestations of these two types are mutually exclusive and contradictory, but religious individuals and religious traditions do not run absolutely true to either type in its extreme. Outstanding figures such as St. Paul and the author of the Fourth Gospel combine the prophetic and the mystical (the transcendent and the immanent) experience in a rich creative synthesis. Religious experience may be characterized by a *rapprochement* of the mystic and prophetic word of God in and to the souls of religious men. "Men of acknowledged and pre-eminent saintliness agree very closely in what they tell us about God."[23] It is thoroughly possible to set forth the common marks of religious experience which distinguish it from all other types

22 (*continued*)

9. Hope of Immortality

Immortality, mergence in God now.   Personal survival, ultimate victory of good.

10. Final Distinction

Monism, loss of contrast, tension.   Dualism, vivid sense of contrast, tension.

Special Characteristics

1. Irregular experiences of visions, ecstasy: Upanishads, Yoga, Plotinus, Suso, Catherine, Teresa, Bernard, Francis.
Regular: Augustine, Aquinas, Eckhart, Tauler, Quietists.
2. Warm—emotion: Bhakti, Plotinus, Sufis, Augustine, Medieval mystics, Pietists.
Cool—unemotional: Upanishads, Buddhists, Eckhart, Quietists.
3. Simple—fanciful: Sufis, Bernard, Francis, Suso, Symeon.
Reflective, rational, theoretic: Upanishads, Sankara, Plotinus, Augustine, pseudo-Dionysius, Eckhart (mystic experience controlled by rational speculation). Yoga, Teresa, Angelus, Silesius, Quietists (mystic experience controlled by psychological analysis).
4. Erotic: Krishna mysticism, Bernard.
Purified: Augustine, Aquinas, Francis, Tauler.
5. Personal theism (loving fellowship with God): Bhakti, Christian mystics.
Impersonal, monistic (loss of soul in divinity): Upanishads, Sankara, Plotinus, Dionysius, Angelus, Silesius.
6. Devotional, prayerful: Bhakti, Christian mystics.
Pure absorption: Upanishads, Buddhism, Yoga, Plotinus, Tauler, Angelus, Silesius.
7. Cultural mysticism (external object of worship): Bhakti, mystery religions, Eucharistic mysticism of Middle Ages.
Non-Cultural: Upanishads, Plotinus, Augustine, Evangelistic spiritualists, Quietists.
23. Cf. *supra*, p. 132, quotation from Inge; cf. also *supra*, p. 95 ff., quotation from Broad.

of experience, and which make it highly probable that there is some objective reality, or aspect of reality, which corresponds to this experience. "The criticism that universal and objective knowledge cannot be based upon the data of 'inner' experience simply means that religious knowledge is not scientific knowledge. It is universal in the sense that it is possible to all; at least there is no evident reason why it should not be. It is objective in the sense that it has reference beyond self-consciousness."[24]

Our Common Experience of God Pseudoscientific

A judicious and astute statement of the position that a part of religious experience can be reduced to scientific formulation is to be found in Professor Macintosh's *Theology as an Empirical Science*.[25] Theology, in Professor Macintosh's view, is not a scientific study of religious beliefs or of the subjective psychological experiences of an individual or group. It is rather the theoretical formulation of the activities of a divine object which is known in a complex, subjective-objective, religious experience. The initial presupposition of all the empirical sciences is an assumption drawn upon the basis of prescientific common experience that the object of its observation exists. Common sense accepts the existence of the material world, living organisms, minds, and society. Chemistry, biology, psychology, and sociology accept the common-sense assumption that these respective objects or realms exist without dependence upon human knowing for their existence. Then they proceed to observe and to record the laws which are revealed in experimental procedures. In the same manner, theology accepts the deliverance of common sense that a source of religious deliverance exists independent of human awareness; then by experimental observation it proceeds to record the data and unravel their laws. Thus through the correct adjustment procedures, it is possible to verify the existence and redemptive character of the divine object as related to the needed deliverance of man from sin to such an extent that we can convert some of the common-sense presumption into reasonably valid knowledge.

The author thoroughly understands: (*a*) that there is a dif-

24. Waterhouse, *The Philosophy of Religious Experience*, p. 158.
25. D. C. Macintosh, *Theology as an Empirical Science*, pp. 25–46.

ference between the religious object and a sense-object, for the religious object is "spiritual" and valuable in a way in which natural objects are not; (b) that "apperception," rather than "pure-perception," together with appreciation of value, is involved on the side of the knowing process; (c) that strictly controlled laboratory procedures are not available, the trials and failures of religious techniques upon the stage of human history past and present having to supplant the laboratory equipment; (d) and that the verified data and laws are scientific only in the more generalized meaning of the term "scientific" as a reasonably sound body of information. He is not concerned to "prove" that prayers for rain (natural goods) are invariably answered by "overt external response" but that there is verifiable reinforcement of human ethical efforts whenever a correct adjustment is made toward a Power not ourselves which can be depended upon to assist our faltering efforts. He is not concerned also to "prove" scientifically all that philosophical theology means by the term "God"—i.e., Creator, General Providence, World Ruler; or that God is omnipotent, omniscient, and omnipresent throughout the entire universe; or that God is infinite and eternal. He is only concerned to defend the position that the "influence of the Holy Spirit"—to use an expression from classic Christianity—is open to reasonably universal and common verification. He would agree with Waterhouse to this extent, that religious knowledge is universal in the sense that in some manner it is a possibility for practically all people if they will make the adjustment, and that it is objective in the sense that it has a valid reference beyond self-consciousness.

Although Tennant has not—to the knowledge of the writer of this book—criticized Professor Macintosh's case, in accordance with his fundamental principles, Tennant would say: (1) that the religious object is too vague, too qualityless, too lacking in definite character to be an object of a science; (2) that the conceptual element in religious apperception is the distinguishing feature of the experience, that this is subjective in origin, not immediately "given," hence not verifiable in itself; (3) that there is no prescientific religious experience sufficiently common and universal to merit the assignment of any truth-value to the initial presupposition of theology as an empirical science; (4) that nothing like controlled laboratory conditions are available to advance the process of observing the religious object under rigorous, unvariable circumstances; (5) and that all of God cannot be scientifically verified and, therefore, the part that is claimed to be verifiable is insufficient.

This last point carries force enough to remove God from the area of "scientific" observation and verification. The fourth point likewise indicates that our control of the conditions of religious experience is far short of anything like that of the natural sciences. The social sciences also lack the experimental-controls of the natural sciences, but even in comparison with these, theology is less well favored, and an accurate body of verified information is much more difficult to obtain. But while theology cannot stand within the fold of the sciences, it can be pseudoscientific in the sense that some religious experience can be more or less generally observed and its claim to valid contact with the religious object honored with a specific place in the cumulative argument for the reasonableness of the religious claim. In other words, statements (1), (2), and (3) above may deny the name "science" to our common "knowledge" of religious experience, but it cannot eliminate such rough-hewn information from the courtroom of truth altogether. At least it is a witness, and a very important witness, in that institution.

V. RELIGIOUS EXPERIENCE IS PSYCHOLOGI- CALLY NOT EPISTEMOLOGICALLY IMMEDIATE

The experience of the "numinous" may be psychologically immediate, but epistemologically it is actually proven to be mediate. The confusion of psychological and epistemological immediacy pervades all mystical and intuitionalist theology and the majority of discussions of religious experience.

The Meaning of This Principle

The meaning of the first sentence is this: whereas every object of which any person is conscious is immediately before the subject psychologically, only one type of object is immediately experienced which is assuredly something more than a psycho-

logical idea or mental state. That object is the reality which is
known through sense-phenomena. The psychological process by
which this reality is known is not pure-sensation, but a process
in which an active subject exercises basic conceptualizing powers as well as receptive sensing powers. Sense-reality is, therefore, never known in its independent pristine purity, but only
under the selective and categorized shadings of sense and of
thought respectively. Though the cognizing process is complex,
and though the conceptualizing elements are "mediate" elements, nevertheless, the conceptual elements at the sense-per-
ceptive level do not destroy the statement that the reality which
is thus shaded is yet known with immediacy. At higher levels,
the independent reality is separated from the immediate experience of the subject by a thoroughly "mediate" *tertium quid*, a
concept or system of concepts which is supposed or believed to
represent the independent reality. The subject immediately experiences the concept; psychologically the conceptual object is
directly and immediately before the knower; but epistemologically, or metaphysically, the real object is across the ravine or
behind the screen.

The Application to Religious Experience

Religiously and theologically this means that God, being a
concept psychologically as well as a reality metaphysically, is
thus psychologically before the subject as a conceptual object
with "immediacy" and metaphysically beyond the intermediate
screen of thought with "mediacy." Inasmuch as God as metaphysical reality and God as conceptual idea are separated, there
is always a leap of supposition to be made when it is claimed
that the direct and immediately experienced concept is truly
representative of the metaphysical reality; and inasmuch as
any type of concept can evoke subjective feelings of certitude,
surety, and reality, there is always a danger of confusing the
immediacy and certitude of these feelings which are centered in
a conceptual object with an immediate and certain grasp of the
metaphysical object which careful analysis proves no one possesses. A religious person might have an experience of an idea
of God which evokes the emotions of worship, the activities of
service, and immediate assurance of reality, yet he still might

be completely mistaken about the actual metaphysical existence of God, and he always is mistaken about the immediacy of the metaphysical God to his mind.

The Application to Mystical Experience

Applied to mystical experience, this means that the mystic always directly and immediately experiences a concept of God and that he is always mistaken when he reports that he has "seen God face to face" with immediacy. Never does he experience any other type of God-concept than the one which he has acquired from tradition or authority before his experience; never does he return from his experience with report of God's being anything different from what he previously learned and thought God to be. The Christian mystic experiences Christ, God, or the Trinity, but never Mohammed, Buddha, Brahma, or Nirvana. He experiences what he thinks—i.e., his particular concept of religious reality; and nothing more can he be truthfully said to experience immediately, no matter how certain, or sure, or productive of fine results that experience may be.

Furthermore, the mystic cannot overcome the true mediacy of experience of God by claiming that he himself, in the depths of his soul, is "one with God"; that he is "partaker of the divine nature"; or that he is (existentially) Christ, or Brahma, or God. For, if he is God, he cannot be himself or know that he is himself; as God, he knows God, not himself. If he is himself, and knows himself to be himself, he cannot be God and know himself to be God. The mystic can never eliminate his own consciousness, for oneness always involves consciousness of oneness, and this means that he is conscious of the two who are one. It also means that if he is in any sense immediately conscious of his empirical self, he is not in the same experience without additional interpretation immediately conscious of God. That a subject is immediately conscious of his own states and objects without interpretation Tennant is willing to admit, but that he is immediately conscious of his own ideas and states of mind as being God's ideas and states of mind, this Tennant denies as contradictory to the facts of experience. Even in knowing the pure ego, a subject knows his own pure ego through a mediate process of interpretation or conceptual construction. To know God in the depths of the pure ego, however, is to know an object of still greater conceptual construction and to know an object in a thought process which is not God's thought process.

The Application to Intuitionalist Theology

Essentially the same truth holds true of an intuitionalist type of experience and theology such as that of Schleiermacher.[26] According to Schleiermacher, "the true nature of religion is an immediate consciousness of Deity as He is found in ourselves and in the world." The self and the world are interpenetrated by the universe or God and, therefore, in a person's immediate "feeling" of dependence upon God and His existence, he knows that God is himself or penetrating himself, and here he derives his greatest assurance of God's existence. But here, as Hicks points out, a number of difficulties break out, the central one of which is this—to "feel" my consciousness of an object is not to "feel" God's own consciousness of the same object with the same immediacy.

Whenever a person knows an object, he is conscious of an object and also of undergoing or living through (*erleben*) his own consciousness of that object. Even to live through consciousness of an object involves a difference in the complexity of the knowing process. To know one has lived through consciousness of an object is to discriminate this mental "undergoing" from other mental "undergoings" of his own and of all mental "undergoings" of his own from those of other persons. It also involves a passage of time, for the knowledge of the "undergoing" is second to the "undergoing" itself. Hence it is possible to distinguish the "undergoing" itself as a process of vague "feeling" and the knowing of the "undergoing" as intuition or cognition of a more complex type. When, therefore, according to Hicks,[27] Schleiermacher spoke of "self-consciousness in its immediacy," he was referring to the former process of "feeling" in the sense of awareness of "undergoing," but he was not entitled to imply that this type of immediate experience is experience of God or immediate "consciousness of unity with the Eternal." Certainly

26. In this paragraph the writer has followed the analysis of Hicks (cf. *The Philosophical Bases of Theism*, pp. 102 ff.) which is comparable in type to that of Tennant.
27. *Op. cit.*, p. 107.

the self's feeling of *Erlebnis* is not felt to be God's feeling of *Erlebnis*. If such were the case, then the self would feel it as God's and not as its own—a situation which is contradictory to the facts of experience. Furthermore, the self's complex thought of God as grasping the self is not God's thought of Himself as being united with the self. Self and God as experients are two distinctly transcendent realities; neither the immediate experiences nor the mediate experiences of the one are those of the other. Therefore, within or without, the self knows only a mediate conceptualized idea which represents God and the objects of God's experience and thought. Such analysis holds true of all religious experience of the mild as well as of the extreme mystical and of the intuitional type.

The Negative and Positive Elements in the Concept of Immediacy as Applicable to Religious Experience

If, then, Tennant's original statement is to be criticized, certain implications are not to be offered as component parts of the criticism. The criticism must not imply, (1) that the self lives through (*erleben*) God's own experiences; (2) that no element of conceptualization enters into the complex process of knowing God; (3) that God is known in isolation from all other objects (perceptual or conceptual). If there is to be any meaning to the term "immediacy," in religious experience, it must be an "immediacy" that is above the level of rational mediation and an "immediacy" which implies more than the presence of an idea before the mind of a subject. In other words, "immediacy" must mean at least the presence of a reality, or a part of reality, corresponding to the stimulus which grounds sense-presentations in something extrasubjective as well as, and along with, the concept which confronts the mind of the subject. Religious experience involves not simply the immediate apprehension of an idea by a subject but an immediate apprehension of a reality evoking, suggesting, and controlling the idea. It involves the noumenal in the phenomenal; God's metaphysical reality in the *numina;* and the "immediacy" with which the subject knows the phenomenal and the *numina* must include a reliable though perhaps partial and noninfallible grasp of the noumenal and the metaphysical religious reality.

The Grounds for the Assertion That Religious Experience Is Epistemologically Immediate

In other words, religious experience is not basically nonparallel to sense-experience. There are unique differences, but an "immediacy" which is essentially epistemological can qualify one as well as the other. At least such epistemological "immediacy" can be supported to the extent of allowing the claim of the religious man to epistemological immediacy for some of his experiences to stand on their own intrinsic merits, and of giving some genuine evidential value to this claim. If, as we have labored to show, religious experience, though different from sense-experience and social experience, is nonetheless not entirely the work of thought-construction or of concepts which are derived from tradition but carries its own unique contact with reality;[28] if, though displaying variety and inconsistency throughout history, the variety can be proved to be insufficient to support the contention that religious experience has no worthy claim to contact with extrasubjective reality whatsoever;[29] if, though religious experience is not as common as sense-experience,[30] it can nevertheless be found to be reasonably common (universal) and to exemplify certain common characteristics[31]—then it follows that Tennant is mistaken in his contention that religious experience is psychologically immediate but not epistemologically so, for the reverse would seem to be the case.

Illustrations of Intimate and Immediate Religious Experience

Without repeating the arguments to which the last four footnotes refer, certain additional points may be expounded. Whereas it may be fully admitted that the religious man does not experience God's own consciousness, it does not follow that there is no more intimate contact between the subject and God than that involved in a common medium of communication. An illustration will clarify this statement. In the intercourse of close friends or in the discourse of an orator, there is a personal influence distinct from the words spoken, which affects the

28. *Supra,* pp. 144–154.   29. *Supra,* pp. 154–163.
30. *Supra,* p. 151.   31. *Supra,* pp. 163–169.

minds of those to whom the words are addressed. This personal influence does not make the words of the speaker more true, nor yet more beautiful, nor more good, if true and beautiful and good they really are. What this personal factor actually does is so to quicken and stimulate the other person that his powers of seeing the truth, the beauty, the goodness of the words are enhanced. The case is not otherwise with a task to be done when an ordinary workman attacks a job with a capable and inspiring leader. The work is no less work in itself, but the presence of the leader strengthens and energizes the will-to-work in such a way that inertia and obstacles are overcome.

Something comparable to this situation is applicable to religious experience.

The Scriptural assertions of the indwelling of the Holy Spirit and of his mighty power in the soul [writes A. H. Strong][32] forbid us to regard the divine Spirit in regeneration as coming in contact, not with the soul, but only with the truth. Since truth is simply what is, there can be no change wrought in the truth. The phrases, "to energize the truth," "to intensify the truth," "to illuminate the truth," have no proper meaning, since even God cannot make the truth more true. If any change is wrought, it must be wrought, not in the truth, but in the soul. . . .

Even if truth could be energized, intensified, illuminated, there would still be needed a change in the moral disposition, before the soul could recognize its beauty or be affected by it. No mere increase of light can enable a blind man to see; the disease of the eye must first be cured before external objects are visible. So God's work in regeneration must be performed within the soul itself. Over and above all influence of the truth, there must be a direct influence of the Holy Spirit upon the heart. Although wrought in conjunction with the presentation of truth to the intellect, regeneration differs from moral suasion in being an immediate act of God.

It is false to say that soul can come in contact with soul only through the influence of truth. In the intercourse of dear friends, or in the discourse of the orator, there is a personal influence, distinct from the word spoken, which persuades the heart and conquers the will. . . . God has not made the human soul so that it is

32. A. H. Strong, *Systematic Theology*, pp. 453–454.

inaccessible to himself. The omnipresent Spirit penetrates and pervades all spirits that have been made by him. . . .

The view that God works only through the truth as a means, and that his only influence upon the soul is a moral influence— very naturally deny the mystical union of the soul with Christ.

By the phrase "mystical union of the soul with Christ," Strong does not mean a union which destroys the activity and personality of the believer.[33] The believer cannot say: "I am Christ." But neither does the phrase mean a union which is as exclusive as that of friend with friend. It is a mystical union, but "if we call it mystical at all," he writes, "it should be only because, in the intimacy of its communion and in the transforming power of its influence, it surpasses any other union of souls that we know, and so cannot be fully described or understood by earthly analogies."[34]

As physical science has brought us to the conclusion [writes J. L. Diman,][35] that back of all the phenomena of the material universe there lies an invisible universe of forces, and that these forces may ultimately be reduced to one all-pervading force in which the unity of the physical universe consists; and as philosophy has advanced the rational conjecture that this ultimate all-pervading force is simply will-force; so the great Teacher holds up to us the spiritual universe as pervaded by one omnipotent life—a life which was revealed in him as its highest manifestation, but which is shared by all who by faith become partakers of his nature. He was Son of God: they too had power to become sons of God. The incarnation is wholly within the natural course and tendency of things. It was prepared for, it came, in the fulness of time. Christ's life is not something sporadic and individual, having its source in the personal conviction of each disciple; it implies a real connection with Christ, the head. Behind all nature there is one force; behind all varieties of Christian life and character there is one spiritual power. All nature is not inert matter—it is pervaded by a living presence. So all the body of believers live by virtue of the all-working Spirit of Christ, the Holy Ghost.

33. *Ibid.*, p. 442.   34. *Ibid.*, p. 443.
35. J. L. Diman, *The Theistic Argument*, pp. 380–385, Strong's footnote (*op. cit.*, pp. 443–444) is used though the writer had noted it in Diman's book independently.

The above quotations have been presented to illustrate the point that there is a "mystical" element in religious experience which is not to be described in terms of the mutual absorption of the human and divine consciousness, but which is more intimate than the knowing of common Objects of truth, beauty, and goodness, and again more intimate than the magnetism of the personal, moral, and sympathetic relationship of human friends. This is another statement of the fact to which Webb refers when he characterizes religious experience as displaying the quality of "intimacy." Such "intimacy" of transforming power, according to Diman, does not have its source in the personal conviction of the Christian; it rather implies a real connection with religious reality.

Tennant's Criticism of Such Experiences

Without in any sense wishing to imply that Diman and Strong base their respective theologies primarily and inclusively upon the experience which is described above, it is correct to say that both of these men will allow a place in their systems for an experience of this type. Tennant might admit its possibility, but he would certainly give it no evidential value whatsoever, and quite probably he would deny it altogether. To know that the Holy Spirit is present to the subject, Tennant would say that a concept would have to be maintained in the mind of the experient; the conviction of the reality of the Holy Spirit's presence as far as philosophy is concerned is purely subjective certitude. There is no provable epistemological immediacy in this experience. What is to be said of this position?

Alternative Explanations of Religious Experience Must Be Faced

It should be understood that underlying this point of view is Tennant's conviction that the inward phenomena of religious experience are always susceptible to alternative, purely psychological explanations. Subconscious elaboration of religious ideas, the fatal operation of subjective interest, emotional and instinctive energies—explanations such as these are sufficient to account for the suddenness, the involuntariness, the "givenness," and the certitude which mark the appearance of religious phenomena in the mind. In view of these alternatives, Tennant believes that epistemological "immediacy" is most certainly negated and that the only recourse for theology is to deny the claim of these experiences to any validity whatsoever, until the existence of God is established by teleological reasoning controlled by facts first given in sense-perception.

Now, the appeal to "rational proof" from external nature does have important value. The naturalistic psychologist has no right to deny the validity of all religious conceptions simply by reducing them to subconscious operations, wish-fulfillment, autosuggestion, and heterosuggestion. Such reductions are valid only if the hypothesis of the reality of God is also ruled out on the grounds of rational, metaphysical argument. A naturalistic psychologist, who assumes that theism is disproved in general philosophy, or who just naïvely assumes that there is no real God without examination of the philosophical arguments and then reduces all religious phenomena to illusion, wins his case too cheaply. Certainly Tennant's position is a wholesome check upon psychologists of this type. No defense of religion or of theism can neglect this type of restraint upon those who prove their cases too easily. But the central question remains: does the religious apologist need to abandon the realm of inward experience altogether? Does he need to say that all religious experience is valueless as a true experience of God? Does he, while avoiding atheistic presuppositions, need to concur entirely with the results of the naturalistic psychological analysis of religious experience? To evacuate this province without an attempt to meet the claims of psychology to establish or to deny metaphysical truths on its own grounds is to avoid coming to terms with vigorous opponents. Certain critics consider this to be a serious defect in Tennant; it is believed that Tennant is wrong in assuming the psychological subjectivity of all religious experience prior to teleological argument.

The Grounds upon Which the Truth of the Religious Intellectualization of Experience Is Based

It is not the purpose of this chapter to examine the writings of various psychologists who disprove religious truth by various appeals to such entities as the "subconscious," "libido," and "suggestion." Some general statements must be made, however, with a view to justifying our conviction that some evidential value should be given to this type of experience.

(*a*) Alternative explanation and interpretations of "intimate" religious experiences are always possible; this is not to be denied. (*b*) Neither is it to be denied that the mental processes involved in religious experience follow certain law-abiding channels. Undoubtedly religious ideas and habits mature in subconscious activities of the mind and then "burst" into conscious realization at certain moments of outstanding significance. (*c*) The fact is, however, that both true and false ideas and habits mature in the subconscious; both true and false ideas result from autosuggestion and from heterosuggestion. It is wrong to assume that subconscious mechanisms characterize some ideas and not others, and that they infect some and not others. The central task is to discover what ideas and explanations are true and what are false, a task which can be done only if some ideas and explanations have characteristics which give evidence of truth where others do not. (*d*) The mere fact that a belief or explanation arises or exists is not sufficient to indicate its truth, neither is the mere fact of "givenness," for false beliefs are "given" as well as true. The "givenness" of a conviction must be connected with other criteria which are largely pragmatic.

Does this belief or explanation, for example, best intellectualize the experienced reality? Here is a moment of experience in which the subject feels gripped by a larger spiritual life than his own. High and noninstinctive moral ideals become intensely vivid; great energies are released of which the subject was not before conscious; the subject finds that he "can run and not grow weary," "walk and not faint," that he can achieve what he desires to achieve. Immediately he recognizes, formulates in words, intellectualizes this experience by saying that it is "not I who live, but Christ lives in me," or that he is "a partaker in the divine nature," or that he is "united with God." Such a formulation of terms may not be the only possible explanation, but it is one which has some relation to reality. It does not create the reality but represents it; and as a representation it does justice to features of the experience which other representations do not. It does justice, for example, to the depth, the "outside-ness," or the "beyondness," of the empowering life which does not seem to be man's own. These factors may be intellectualized as "libido" or "untapped reserves of energy already in the individual but unrecognized." It may be intellectualized as the "sublimation of energies repressed or suppressed or held back from other channels of expression." It may be rationalized as "the intensification of energies which come when one phase of the self is preparing to do battle with another phase of the self."[36] But it may also be assigned to the fact that "a universal life" has gripped the soul working in and beyond these natural energies. The rising tides of spiritual life and power may come from the ocean rather than far down the bay. Such an explanation does justice to the results of the experience.

Furthermore, drugs, illusions, magical creations of subconscious, and racial myth-making, in the long run, leave the self impoverished, regressive, infantile, and deficient in character. The experience of reality which the religious man rationalizes in theistic terms does not leave the soul thus but rather enriched, progressive, mature, and more fully and truly human. While we cannot say with crude pragmatism that any idea which works is true whether it represents reality or not, yet we can say with critical pragmatism that any idea which represents reality works, and works in the long run because it represents reality.

Again, if this rationalization of experience fits in with other intellectual formulations of other experiences, the experience of nature and of history, if this formula coheres with wider teleological considerations, then it gains additional probability. This criterion of validity does not replace the other two which have been noted above—justice to the appearances and practical confirmation—but it supports the others and makes it possible to integrate the interpretation of religious experience into a general world-view.

All of which leads to the final point; namely, if this represen-

36. According to Rivers, two psychological reasons are sufficient to explain the sense of power in religious experience. First, the increase in energy due to redirection of instinctive energies from their normal outlets into sublimated channels; second, increase in energies due to the occurrence of conflict in the self. Energies increase whenever a combat comes into view, and the opposing forces strengthen themselves for battle and victory. See T. H. Hughes, *The New Psychology and Religious Experience*, pp. 261 ff.

tation rationalizes religious experience of the type indicated, then it does so because at the moment of experience the reality is present to the representation, with "immediacy." Not simply an "immediacy" of subject and representation, but of subject and the noumenal through the phenomenal—this is the result which may be suggested as partial evidence for the validity of the theistic conviction.

VI. MOST DISCUSSIONS OF RELIGIOUS EXPERIENCE CONFUSE CERTITUDE WITH CERTAINTY

The experience of the numinous may be accompanied by a high degree of "certainty," but this may be simply a high degree of subjective psychological certitude and not of objective, reasonable certainty. The confusion of "certitude" and "certainty"—or of "certitude" and "probability," if complete objective certainty is impossible—also pervades most discussions of religious experience.

The Issue Stated with Reference to Ward

In an illuminating analysis of belief and certainty, James Ward states that belief is used in a narrower sense, excluding certainty, and in a wider sense, including certainty. From the epistemological standpoint, belief excludes certainty because belief is a private and personal matter whereas certainty is a characteristic of public scientific knowledge. For psychology, however, the difference between belief and knowledge is only one of degree, certainty or knowledge being the upper limit of personal belief. Epistemology, however, according to Ward, draws a distinction between subjective conviction and objective certainty or truth. Objective certainty or truth applies to propositions; subjective conviction applies to a state of mind. Psychology studies the causes and effects of subjective conviction, a state of mind; epistemology is concerned with objective certainty or the truth of propositions.[37]

37. James Ward, *Psychological Principles,* pp. 347–348. "Belief is sometimes used in a wider, sometimes in a narrower sense, the one including certainty, the other excluding it: the wider belonging to the psychological, the narrower to the epistemological standpoint. Epistemology has constantly to distinguish

*Tennant's Application of the Distinction Between Certitude as
a Subjective State of Conviction and Certainty as
an Objective Quality of Propositions*

The distinction between subjective certainty and objective
certainty is one which Tennant designates as certitude and certainty; certitude is a state of mental conviction, certainty a
quality of propositions. Obviously, when an objectively certain
proposition is believed with subjective psychic conviction, truth
and assurance coincide at a maximum degree, but truth and assurance must always be distinguished.

The burden of Tennant's analysis of scientific knowledge is
to show that no scientific proposition is absolutely certain or
true, for scientific conceptions, facts, and generalizations are
all derived from an interpretation of a nonlogical "given" element in sense perception. Of this reality which is presented in
sense-experience for conceptual interpretation by the mind, the
scientist can have only probable truth. Propositions about reality are never self-evident, but only relatively evident, or probably certain. They depend objectively upon the control of sense-
given data, and subjectively upon a volitional faith or trust in

between belief and knowledge as differing in kind, since belief is always, and
(scientific) knowledge is never, a private and personal matter. Psychologically,
however,—for the individual that is to say—his belief and his knowledge (or
certainty) differ only in degree. Certainty is then regarded as the upper limit
of such personal belief: it may be represented by unity, lower degrees being
represented by fractions, as in the 'odds' of betting transactions, for example.
But epistemology also contrasts knowledge with probability in a similar fashion, save that the difference is then referred not to the psychological causes of
belief but to its logical grounds. With these the epistemologist is exclusively
concerned; the psychologist, however, not at all. His business is primarily
with the believing, together with its causes and effects, as subjective, not with
the grounds of the belief itself, as objective: what interests him is a living process, not a logical structure. Despite this wide difference the one term 'certainty'
is often applied to both; though they are distinguished as respectively subjective certainty and objective certainty: so we say indifferently 'I am certain
of' and 'It is certain that.' Such phraseology is often convenient; yet where
scientific exactness is important it is to be avoided, and there are better terms
available. At all events psychology is not interested in objective certainty or
truth as such, but only in subjective certainty or conviction. Truth belongs entirely to the universe of propositions: certainty implies a complete state of
mind. In this state propositions enter not as true or false but simply as believed
or not believed. Whether propositions are believed or not is to be ascertained
not by considering them but by observing the feeling they produce and the active attitude to which such feeling leads."

the applicability or correspondence of the mind's creative interpretation to external reality. Subjective believing or certitude
(an act of will) enters into every interpretation of reality as
well as objective constraint, so that "probability" comes to
mean a matter of degrees, both of objective constraint and subjective believing. Simple propositions about sensorily perceived
facts carry the highest degree of objective constraint and the
least actual degree of subjective venturesomeness—though subjective emotional conviction may also be at a maximum. Progressively complex propositions about the reality behind the
sensorily perceived facts carry progressively less objective constraint and progressively greater degree of subjective venturesomeness or faith—psychological conviction varying from high
to low degree of emotional conviction. The test of the probability
of these propositions is one of pragmatic working; i.e., do these
propositions enable us to adjust ourselves to reality? do they
contradict other propositions and other practically certain
facts? in what respects do some propositions interpret the facts
more appropriately than the possible alternatives? Objectively
this sort of criterion is the only type of constraint that science
can obtain as it passes on to more complex interpretations of
propositions about propositions which are relevant to sensorily
perceived facts. Subjectively, faith in the relevance of these
interpretations to the metaphysically Real is progressively
greater and greater in degree. Faith in this sense is certitude,
but certitude which represents an act of will rather than degree
of emotion.

Now it is Tennant's conviction that pragmatically verified
propositions of the sciences lead on to all-inclusive propositions
about the world as a whole. Reason struggles to create these
propositions which faith holds to be relevant to the actual independent world. Such world-propositions are plural in number, and theism is but one of possible alternatives. If the theistic
proposition pragmatically interprets the less complete generalizations arising out of perceived facts more appropriately than
the alternatives, a certain type of objective certainness or probability characterizes this proposition which merits a faith-venture in its plausible or possible truth. When such a proposition
is satisfactorily argued and defended, it may then be held with

the greatest intensity of emotion and acted upon with the greatest subjective conviction and assurance. In other words, all lesser facts and experiences may be interpreted by this master proposition, which together with reactions of feeling and will may give us religious experience which we can justly call valid.

The Representative Propositions Arising from Religious Experience May Be Characterized by Some Degree of Objective Certainty

In Chapter II it has been argued that the process by means of which, according to Tennant, the mind creates or constructs its idea or concept of "other-self" is false unless in the first instance there is a basic "extra-spective" connection or intuition of "other self" upon which the analogical inferences and comparisons may rest.[38] In like manner the concept of "divine self" is constructed out of finite factors and analogies which have no basis upon which to rest[39] unless there is a fundamental, truly immediate "extra-spective" connection or intuition of the "divine self." The general principle upon which this insistence of a basic extraspective intuition is founded is that an object can be declared to be comparable and analogous to some other object only if it is first experienced to be actual and present. To say that God is like man in certain respects and unlike man in others is to have some prior acquaintance with God. Some basic realization of the presence of the reality of God to the interpreting mind of the subject is a fundamental part of the process by which man's idea of God is constructed. The process of recognizing the presence of God is one in which the mind eliminates analogies or previously recognized objects as not holding true, and retains others as applicable. If the resulting representation contains characteristics which, upon the grounds of practical applicability, rationalizes the experienced contact more adequately than other representations, we may assume that there is a greater validity to the one than to the others. This furnishes the objective constraint of the representation, or representative proposition, which is needed to ground subjective conviction as more than sanguine emotion.

38. Cf. *supra*, pp. 113 ff.   39. Cf. *supra*, pp. 130 ff.; also p. 98 ff.

The Criteria of Objective Certainty

Now the difference between Tennant's position and the one which is being defended in this essay is that Tennant denies all claims of validity to all the representations of the specific experiences of individuals and groups of individuals of the divine reality. These have no claim to validity until a conceptual representation has been constructed to interpret masses of fact, which in themselves are first devoid of the divine presence and later are found to convey suggestions of the greater reality which determined the world-as-a-whole. Now whatever may be said to establish some objective probability for the truth of this general theistic proposition, it does not guarantee the specific experience of one or more individuals who find themselves gripped by a larger, redemptive life than their own. The representations (or representative propositions) of such specifically religious experiences are objectively indicated to be true or false upon the basis of their appropriateness to those features of the experiences which they intellectualize more adequately than other representations, just as the appeal to the appropriateness of the cosmic theistic representation to intellectualize our experience of the world-as-a-whole is a factor in the complex criteria by means of which this proposition is judged. Such is not by any odds the whole criterion. The recognition of the "givenness" of the appearing reality, and the claim that valuable results confirm the connection of the idea with reality rather than with illusory reality are also factors in judging representations of specific experiences as true rather than false.

If these criteria hold, then objective grounds for truth are found for specific representations which are not to be confused with subjective certitude. Thus with respect to Tennant's distinction between certitude and certainty, it is possible to substantiate a claim to "objective certainty" as a characteristic of specific representative propositions which intellectualize specific experiences. "Certitude" does not need to be confused with "certainty" if the meanings are unconfusedly applied. Upon the other hand, it should be pointed out that psychologically "certainty" may also involve the maximum of "certitude"; the two aspects shade into one another at points, and hence, in a wider sense, it may be said that we only have certitude at best.

The Communication of an Inclusive Certitude

This leads to the final point which may be presented in this connection. Making it possible for a person to obtain an experience of contact with Something which can be intellectualized by him as representing the real Presence of the divine, redemptive Reality is a far superior way of imparting the highest type of certitude, the synthesis of "objective certainty," and "subjective certitude." Tennant believes, of course, that the best "apologia" at the present moment is one which emphasizes the former and not the latter;[40] i.e., rational and general argument, rather than experimental adjustment and personal experience. That there is an important place for such a philosophical argument, we have no reason to deny. But to the knowledge of the present writer, Tennant has converted none of his Cambridge colleagues to acceptance of his argument as true, and the situation is not otherwise, it may be believed, beyond this circle, in the midst of which his theory has been constructed and defended. The truth is that rational argument never ends in personal acquaintance; it is rather personal acquaintance which facilitates the acceptance of the rational defense.

VII. RELIGIOUS EXPERIENCE INVOLVES NO UNIQUE FACULTY OF COGNITION AS SOME WRITERS MAINTAIN

Religious experience involves no unique faculty of cognition as certain mystical and intuitionalist writers assert. It is impossible to distinguish this so-called higher faculty of mystical apprehension from certain subliminal functionings of mind or from anesthetic and hypnotic revelation.

The Aim and Types of Special Faculty-Arguments

In order to bring criticism to bear upon this position, certain preliminary issues must be clarified. It is best to begin with a statement of the purposes to be obtained by those who insist upon special faculties of God-apprehension. The general aim of all these theorists is to establish the truth-claim of objects which

40. Cf. *supra,* pp. 26–28.

are known by means of peculiarly distinct and trustworthy processes of the mind. According to Knudson,[41] the so-called "religious argument" for the existence of God, that is, the argument from religious experience, takes three forms. First, that religion is an "instinct" by means of which a person adjusts himself to his environment. In being an "instinct," religion is "proven" to be a natural endowment of human nature, and its object is "proven" to be valid because an instinct presupposes the existence of the object toward which it is directed. This argument is not a direct argument from the conscious experience of a subject but from structural tendencies in human nature, more deeply embedded than consciousness itself. The goal obtained, if such an instinct can be "proven" to exist, is that God's existence is thus validated.

The second form of the religious argument, according to Knudson, is an argument from the a priori element in the religious reason. In this argument, the biological analogy of the first form of the argument is relinquished, and religion is regarded as a structural or formal element in reason itself rather than an instinct. Historically this argument is linked with Troeltsch who tried to set forth the rational, a priori categories of the religious understanding. Schleiermacher and Otto have contributed elements in the evolution of this doctrine which is recently argued by Knudson[42] and, in separate form, by Griffiths.[43] The objective for which this argument is drawn is again the validity of the God-idea. If religion is truly a priori, if it is a form by means of which the reason creates the objects of experience, and if the structural capacities of human reason are trustworthy, then the object is as valid as the capacities are trustworthy. Religion is self-validated; faith (creative reason) creates religious experience, and religious experience validates faith. As long as man is rational, as long as his rational nature does not decay, just so long will religion endure and be valid. "God hath set eternity in man's heart," preached Knudson,[44] and so long a man's heart or mind is inherently prone to create religion, there is no need to fear its invalidity.

41. Cf. Knudson, *The Doctrine of God,* pp. 219 ff.
42. *The Validity of Religious Experience.*
43. *Op. cit., God in Idea and Experience.*
44. The Wesleyan Chapel, 1935.

The third form of the religious argument, according to Knudson, is the empirical form of the argument. God is given as an object of experience, as sense-objects are given to sense experience. Discontinuing our reference to Knudson, it may be said that this form of the argument does not invariably imply any special faculty for the apprehension of God beyond the normal powers of the normal human mind. In some forms, however, a special organ of religious knowledge is implied. Some mystics, describable as "exclusive" rather than "comprehensive" mystics, lay claim to a special religious faculty often termed "the divine spark" or the "inner light" which operates above, and in separation from, the normal processes of sense and of reason. Other theologians define the religious sense as "feeling" or special intuition of some unique type. Such experiencing power enables a person to perceive the divine so directly that there is no uncertainty as to its existence. To see God face to face is to know with absolute certainty that He is. God to the exclusive mystic is known in a presentative, partially representative experience. In both cases truth is established.

A. THE APPEAL TO RELIGIOUS INSTINCT

Having thus introduced the forms and purposes of the various "special faculty" arguments, the question must be faced with respect to each: do special faculties exist? and if so, how far do they validate theism? First, religious instinct. The consensus of opinion among psychologists is that religion is not an instinct, and Tennant shares this view. If "instinct" is given a strictly defined and precise meaning as it is in some psychological writings, manifestly this judgment is substantiated. "Instincts" when more or less strictly defined are supposed to exemplify the following characteristics: (1) psychophysical tendency; (2) hereditary transmission; (3) relative unmodifiability; (4) absence of acquired learning; (5) definiteness of function; i.e., practically automatic; (6) independence of higher activities of reason; (7) universality. Sex, self-preserving activities such as food-taking and self-defense, and gregariousness may be selected as examples of instincts, but not religion.[45] Un-

45. Cf. J. E. Turner, *Essentials in the Development of Religion,* pp. 96 ff.; K. Edward, *Religious Experience, Its Nature and Truth,* pp. 36 ff.; E. S. Conklin, *The Psychology of Religious Adjustment,* pp. 15 ff.

less the term "instinct" or "instinctive" is to be defined in some vague way as indicating a general tendency in human nature to experience in a general way something which is in general designated as religion, religion cannot be said to be an instinct. And if this vague definition of instinct is employed to describe religion it is too vague to be valuable in any serious discussion of the subject. Certainly an appeal to this type of instinct can never fully establish or validate the actual existence of the divine being. What may be meant by the term instinct as applied to religion is something not far removed from the "religious a priori" which Knudson and Griffiths discuss. The term "religious a priori" is a more intellectualistic term for the same characteristic which may be designated as instinct; namely, an original endowment or capacity of human nature. To an analysis of this we now turn.

B. THE APPEAL TO THE RELIGIOUS A PRIORI

(1) A. C. Knudson's Argument

The second form of the religious argument is the a priori argument. Knudson's position may be summarized as follows.[46] Human reason is essentially active and creative as Kant maintained. The mind constructs experience, thus making it possible, and it does so (Kant to the contrary), along four distinct lines—scientific or theoretical, moral, esthetic, and religious. At least, humanity enjoys sense-experience, moral experience, esthetic experience, and religious experience, and this is possible only because the mind has four inherent capacities of producing such experiences upon the occasion of its stimulation. Each capacity is unique and underived from the other, and each is basically trustworthy or autonomously valid; therefore God exists.

Knudson's underlying epistemological assumption is absolute dualism. The mind never passively receives impressions from without, or witnesses independent reality with immediacy, or photographs the actual world. A stimulus comes to the mind from without and the mind then creates ideas and values; i.e.,

46. Knudson states his case in *The Validity of Religious Experience*, chap. iv; in *Studies in Philosophy and Theology*, pp. 93–127, edited by E. C. Wilm; in *Present Tendencies in Religious Thought*, pp. 244 ff.

experience. The dualism is so sharp that the mind is responsible for content as well as form. "There is more or less of both form and content in all actual experience. And both the formal structure and the material content are mental products."[47] Primary, secondary, and tertiary (values) qualities are all mind-created. Their validity is based upon their inherent residence in human nature universally, and a universal faith in the trustworthiness of the human mind's basic ways of reacting to objective stimulation.

The Meaning of the Phrase: Religious A Priori

More specifically the religious a priori may be characterized negatively and positively. (a) Negatively the term, "religious a priori," does not mean that the mind has innate ideas of religious realities which exist prior to any experience. The term rather refers to hidden, unconscious capacities of mind which manifest themselves only in and through experience. From the conscious experiences of sense, beauty, goodness, and religion, we infer hidden capacities for such experience.[48] (b) The term does not mean that religion is a faculty separate from other faculties; it rather refers to one of the four fundamental modes of the mind's activity. The mind is a unity, not a bundle of separate entities, and within its unity, it exhibits four types of reaction, one of which is the religious.[49] (c) The term, religious a priori, does not designate any psychological theory of religious experience. It does not refer to the emotionalistic, mystic, moralistic, intellectualistic, or eclectic types of religious psychology. The religious a priori underlies all these psychological aspects of the religious consciousness. It is a hidden, creative capacity operating in and through the whole mind to make possible the experience which comes to consciousness in feeling, idea, and will. It is the ground of all the appearances which psychology discovers in the empirical experience of the religious mind, but it is identifiable with none of these.[50] (d) The term does not enable one to decide whether or not religious experience is ultimately perceptual or inferential. It undergirds a theory of direct

47. *The Validity of Religious Experience,* p. 148.
48. Cf. *ibid.,* p. 147.   49. Cf. *ibid.,* pp. 152–153.
50. Cf. *ibid.,* pp. 166–167.

religious perception and indirect religious reasoning.[51] Upon a dualistic theory of knowledge, perception of any type, sensory or religious, always involves an inference from the immediately perceived object to the metaphysical object, so that all experience is inferential to a degree, and this is sustained by the a priori religious capacity.

Positively, (e) the religious a priori is a unique capacity of the human spirit for the creation of religious value. Intrinsic religious values are twofold:[52] the passive values of peace, optimism, and confidence, which are grounded in the sense of trustful dependence upon God, the Creator and Sustainer; and the active values of moral inspiration, love, and righteousness, which arise from the assurance that in all the evils of life "we are more than conquerors through Him who loves us," and from the conviction that "we can do all things through Christ who strengtheneth us." The religious a priori is used in an elastic sense to cover a capacity which is as complex as the essential elements which are found in conscious religious experience. If mystical, esthetic, and ethical elements are essential features of the conscious religious experience, they are also descriptive features of the hidden a priori or religious capacity.[53] Fundamentally, however, Knudson's major insistence is upon the rational character of the a priori, for it is only by insisting upon the rational nature of religion that the danger of subjectivism may be averted. If emphasis is placed upon the emotional, mystical, or volitional aspects of the religious capacity, the capacity is regarded as purely subjective and consequently it will not validate the experience.[54]

(f) The power of the rational, a priori, religious capacity to validate autonomously its own creation is the final positive feature of its description. Just as the scientific, moral, and esthetic capacities of human nature validate their respective experiences, so does the religious a priori. Logic creates none of these, and logic cannot disprove any of them. Knudson quotes Bowne with full approval—"Whatever the mind demands for the satisfaction of its subjective interests and tendencies may be assumed

51. Cf. *ibid.*, pp. 167–168.   52. Cf. *ibid.*, pp. 110–116.
53. Cf. *ibid.*, p. 165.
54. Cf. *ibid.*, p. 162. Knudson thus shies away from Schleiermacher at this point and for this reason.

as real in default of positive disproof."[55] The intelligibility of
the world and our ability to understand it are assumed by science, and it is not otherwise with religion. Each type of experience justifies itself—to be sure each type of experience must
undergo criticism and guidance, but the essential validity of
any type of experience lies in the trustworthiness of the capacity
which creates it. Religion like the other three types of experience is practically universal throughout history, a fact which
indicates that it is structural to the human mind as such. That
such a basic capacity or interest should be valid is an example
of the true principle which is indicated, but inadequately stated,
in pragmatism. If profound needs and interests are satisfied by
beliefs, then those beliefs may be regarded as true. This is the
true principle in true application. Whereas pragmatism argues
that certain consciously experienced, practical values of religion are either its truth or signs of its truth, a position which
is intellectually inadequate, the exponent of the religious a
priori argues that the basic capacities of the human mind exemplified in religious experience and values are valid because
they are satisfied; or should we say—must be satisfied.

Three Criticisms of Knudson's Position

The central issue which evokes criticism of Knudson's position is this: Does the religious a priori actually substantiate its
claim to be a superior way of validating the existence of God?
Does it really convey superior assurance that religion is non-
illusory? That the answer to this question is negative appears
to be correct for the following reasons. (a) The difficulties which
confront the truth-claim of the religious object are equally
present to an extreme generative theory of the object as they
are to be an extreme selective or realistic theory. The difficulties
are applicable in a different manner, but they are still there to
be reckoned with, and no superiority is gained by this type of
validation.

For example, instead of saying that some objects of religious
experience are illusions and others are real (a situation which
causes the rejection of extreme selective realism), we now have
the alternative—some capacities of human nature generate

55. *Ibid.*, p. 176.

ideal-religious-objects which are illusions and some capacities generate the objects which truly represent the independently Real. Some criteria must be produced for deciding which capacities are trustworthy and which are not. The fact is that error is a stubborn factor which confronts the generationist as much as the selectivist. Furthermore, untrustworthy capacities must exist throughout all humanity for no human mind is totally free from the possibility, if not the actuality, of error. Knudson is quite clear on the reverse side of this. The universality of the trustworthy capacity for religion is practically extensive with humanity throughout history and the test of the trustworthiness of this widespread capacity must be an introverted pragmatism; i.e., the basic structural interests, needs, and powers of the human mind are satisfied, therefore the object of that satisfaction is true. The appeal to pragmatism is said to be justified, however, in this case where it is not as well justified in a more empiricistic theory. But this statement is deniable on the basis of the fact that error infects capacities as well as the products of capacities. If practical value does not completely guarantee one, it does not completely guarantee the other.

(b) Again, the extreme emphasis of Knudson's theory upon the creative activity of the mind, a creativity which gives both form and content to experience, is virtually a denial of all revelation of any reality except idea, hence the superiority of this a priori validation is rendered suspect from another angle. An absolute dualism between idea and reality does not do justice to the fact of knowledge, as is shown in Tennant's own theory of our knowledge of physical objects in sense-perception. Tennant is never willing to admit that the object of sense-perception is a mental state or a purely subjective idea. The object of sense-perception is a metaphysical-reality-in-the-relation-of-appearing-to-an-apprehending-subject. Not absolute dualism but duality is his position; not two separate particulars—idea and thing—but a connected relationship—thing in relation to subject as appearance—is what Tennant believes to be the nature of sense knowledge. Such a theory makes possible a foundation for asserting a correspondence between idea and thing, and hence Tennant, unlike Knudson, does not accept Berkeleyan idealism. Knudson's dualism leads him to a denial of the metaphysical reality of physical things; these are ultimately the creative will of God. More than ideas in God's mind, physical things are aspects of God's creative activity whereby he stimulates the mind of man into creative idealization. The physical object is, therefore, idea, and as physical appearance it apparently gives a false impression to unsuspecting realists. Only the idealist knows that physical things are direct acts of God.

Now, here is an example of the result of accepting an extreme doctrine of the creativity of mind and an absolute dualism between idea and thing. Why is there still not grave danger that the creativity of the religious mind might falsify the higher results of that particular type of stimulus which is responsible for evoking the higher religious values? How do we know that the stimulus is not different from what our best creative religious thinking makes it out to be? If there is no real revelation of the divine love; if the mind creates the idea of the divine love, can we be sure that the idea is valid of anything which exists beyond itself? Is the only revelation that we have an idea created by mind itself?

It is not the purpose of this writer to deny the constructive power of mind in our knowledge of reality. There is no meaning to a revelation which impresses itself upon the mind in such a way that mind has no active part in receiving and recognizing. To argue this would be to negate personality altogether and to make man a subhuman instrument. If God's relation to man is a personal relationship, then God will never arbitrarily thrust ideas or energies into a person's mind. Respect for personality means that God awaits the responsiveness and insight of the persons to whom He addresses His creative Word. Just as one man cannot directly thrust his ideas into the mind of another, but states his ideas in words in the hope that another will hear and discern their meaning for himself, so God cannot force His ideas directly into a man's mind, but must communicate His meaning in a divine language in comparable hope that man may discern the meaning which "the words" convey. Language is always a frontier between two private centers of consciousness, and these respective centers are active and creative on their respective sides of that point of contact and of resistance. There is no point to denying the creative discernment of mind, but the discernment is not pure creation of the meaning; it is still a discernment of a meaning that is given to be discerned. There may be considerable variation between the meaning as given and the meaning as discerned, but insofar as truth is attained the latter must contain the former. The latter must be controlled by the former to a greater extent than Knudson's theory will allow. Truth is discerned not by trusting one's capacities for discernment, but by regarding the empirical signs that the given meaning is correctly discerned. This is largely a matter of observing future consequences and practical adjustments. From observations of experience we learn that our capacities are trustworthy or not; but we do not pass from an assumption of the trustworthiness of our capacities to a conclusion that these confer an autonomous validity upon our discernment.

(c) Another reason for doubting the superiority of the a priori method of autonomous validity of religious experience rests upon the fact that the charge of "vagueness" is as quickly ascribed to the a priori capacity for religion as to the object of experience. One of Tennant's reasons for rejecting the object of religious experience as being as truly "given" as the object of sense-experience is that the religious object is vague and qualityless, so vague, in fact, that it can be connected with all sorts of objects throughout history. Reasons have been given to modify the force of this objection, but it should be said that it can be brought with equal force against the a priori capacity for religion. Knudson gives this a priori capacity elasticity enough to cover whatever one decides to be essential in religious experience. It must be a cognitive capacity primarily, but ethical, mystical, and other elements may be ascribed to it according to one's conclusion as to the nature of conscious religious experience. Certainly "vagueness" is chargeable here, and more easily so, if one reflects that the variations of religious experience throughout history must in turn mean variations in this a priori capacity also. No doubt an answer can be framed to meet this charge, but it is Knudson's claim that the a-priori-capacity-theory has a greater power to validate religious experience than the empirical theory, and this claim appears to be unfounded.

In spite of the fact that the claim to superior assurance must

be denied to Knudson's theory, certain merits may be ascribed
to it. Religious experience does imply a capacity for it, and a
trustworthy capacity when its trustworthiness is decided upon
empirical grounds. Furthermore, religious experience does not
imply a separate faculty of the mind, but rather a capacity of
the normal human mind working as a unity in the discernment
of religious reality. No necessity is placed upon the theologian
or psychologist to revert to an outmoded faculty-psychology to
account for religious experience. Distinguishable potentialities
there must be, but not utterly isolated and disparate faculties.
These insights are acceptable features of Knudson's discussion.
Tennant would undoubtedly accept the denial of a separate religious faculty; he would affirm the capacity of the discursive
reason to apprehend and to validate a reasonable inference from
the world to God; but he would not base the validity of the inference upon the capacity for it. Such validity would be based
upon the character of the inferences themselves.

(2) Rees Griffiths' Argument

The next example of the validation of religion by an appeal
to the a priori nature of man is Rees Griffiths' *God in Idea and
Experience* or (subtitle) "The A Priori Elements of the Religious Consciousness." Although Griffiths has worked his position out in the light of many different theorists, his guiding
genius is W. E. Hocking—*The Meaning of God in Human Experience;* perhaps one other might be added, E. Caird—*The
Evolution of Religion;* in other words, his affinity is with the
absolute idealists rather than with the personalists and the rationalists of the a posteriori type, and this characterization may
serve to introduce a brief statement of his position.

The Nature of the Religious A Priori

Griffiths, after aiming a chapter of criticism at the Freudian
theories of religion, first labors to show that no argument a
posteriori from the world which is known to science or to morality can ever establish the existence of God. Such arguments
are unable to establish theism, because they assume that the idea
and experience of God originates in the order and manner in
which the a posteriori proofs proceed. That is to say, man begins

with the facts of science or of morality, none of which bespeak anything of their connection with God, and then by inference from these purely secular, naturalistic, "atheous" facts, he produces the idea of God as a magician takes a rabbit from an apparently empty hat; the experience of God then follows the emergence of the idea. To Griffiths, this is an impossible interpretation of the process; for unless God is in the experience of nature and of morality from the beginning, as an a priori element of self-conscious experience, no amount of juggling can produce the idea or experience of God thereafter. Furthermore, unless God is originally connected with all types of experience —scientific, moral, esthetic, and also the "numinous"—no possible way of connecting these respective types of experience with one and the same God can follow. Thus he denies that we can infer or experience God as the author of the ethical or numinous consciousness separately and then afterwards state that the same God is the author of nature and all other phases of experience. God must be an original, underived, a priori element in self-consciousness itself in order to be inferred from various departments of experience, or in order to be connected with each and all departments of experience respectively and unitedly. The principle which makes possible, or in Kantian language, which constitutes religious experience, the principle by means of which the mind categorically clothes experience with religious meaning, is formulated by Griffiths in the following fashion:[56] "Self-consciousness is only possible in so far as I am able to find in the object not only a reality other than myself, but a reality expressive of Another Mind which knows me through my awareness of the object . . . to be aware of myself as a subject who knows the world outside me implies that I should confess that through the world I know there speaks a voice which apprehends me even as I am able to apprehend the world." The idea of God, which Kant regarded as merely a regulative Idea of Reason, was according to Griffiths adequately made into a constitutive principle by E. Caird.[57] To Caird, self-consciousness had a religious not a secular character; self-consciousness only arose in an awareness which overarched the subject-object

56. *God in Idea and Experience*, p. 187.
57. Cf. p. 186; also p. 208.

relationship; i.e., consciousness of God. Reason constrains man to know himself only as he is aware of a Knower in nature who knows both nature and self in one transcendent unity.

Griffiths' Dependence upon Hocking

Support of this description of the a priori religious principle Griffiths derives from Hocking.[58] He quotes Hocking's statement:

(a) It seems to me that the original source of the knowledge of God is the experience which might be described as an experience of not being alone in knowing the world, and especially the world of Nature. . . . (b) At the source of all religion, so far as our analysis can discover, we find an experience of God as another Knower of our world, already in close relation to self, and also in some natural bond with our social and physical experience.[59]

Griffiths points out that according to Hocking we cannot know our fellow men by immediate experience. The source of our belief in the reality of our fellow men lies in an original idea of Other Mind, by means of which the communicable symbols of the Other are interpreted. This original idea of Other Mind cannot be mere idea; it must be an actual experience of Other Mind, for the only ground upon which the idea can be judged as "mere idea" is by being aware of another actual Mind which is not my own. The idea of Other Mind can arise from nothing but an actual experience of Other Mind. It arises, however, not from an impression which is made by Other Mind upon the self, but rather from an inward idea which is at the same time the actual experience. Through intercourse with natural objects a self becomes aware not only of natural objects but of natural objects which are shared by the Other Mind and the self. "We cannot genuinely conceive ourselves as mentally alone in this cosmos."[60] Our awareness of Other Mind is fundamental social experience, which is not inference but immediate experience, that is, it is concrete a priori awareness. It accompanies all our

58. Cf. pp. 189–206. Griffiths leans heavily upon Hocking.
59. Griffiths, p. 190; cf. Hocking, *The Meaning of God in Human Experience,* (a) p. 236; (b) p. 240.
60. Griffiths, p. 195; cf. Hocking, p. 278.

awareness of the world, and it is the fact that an Other Mind knows the world which we know that guarantees the objectivity of the world to us. In other words, it is God who guarantees the world as objective to us.

So far, Griffiths has been quoting and vigorously assenting to Hocking's argument, but now he states that Hocking falls short of what he believes to be the full a priori principle of religion. To Hocking, consciousness of an object in nature implies consciousness of Other Mind which knows the same object. To Griffiths, this is a more accurate statement of the case than to say that consciousness of the object is simply consciousness of the object and no more, but even this is not enough. The religious a priori demands not only that the Other Mind knows the object which the self knows but that the Other Mind knows the self also. In knowing the Other Mind I am also known; the Other Mind must be truly God who knows me as well as the object. "I must be aware," writes Griffiths, "that in my knowing I am known, that in fact through all my knowing, the world, because of the Other Mind which indwells it, is creating me and knowing Itself through me."[61] Here we have the full immediate consciousness of religious community, a unity which Caird found to be present in every self-conscious act. This religious self-consciousness, Griffiths goes on to state, is not an achievement of "my own mind alone." "It is achieved through the Other Mind's knowledge of me. In so knowing me It makes the Unity underlying the subject-object synthesis a spiritual and intelligent reality instead of a bare unity of Knower and Known. It becomes a Divine Unity because the antithesis is resolved, not by me only, as the subject who knows the object, but by the object itself which I am constrained to deem a Subject who knows me and creates me in my knowledge of the world."[62]

Four Criticisms of Griffiths' Position

The general question now arises: Is this position, which has been so baldly stated, true? Obviously if there is such an a priori rational principle by means of which the mind in every act of self-conscious knowing knows God, all the heart-breaking

61. *God in Idea and Experience,* p. 200.
62. *Ibid.,* p. 202.

doubts and alternatives which beset the a posteriori position are overcome, and we are more than conquerors through the principle that knows and creates us. But the question is: Does this principle withstand criticism upon reflection?

The following reasons are sufficient to reject it. (a) This theory fails to face the epistemological difficulties which infest its assumptions about nature as the common content of the human and divine minds. This theory states that in knowing a natural object, a tree, for example, the self knows not simply a tree, but another mind which knows the tree. It is assumed that the tree is content of Another Experience, and thus, objective to the self. From the standpoint of the self, the tree is what naïve realism takes it to be—totally independent of me; from the standpoint of the Other Self, the tree is what subjective idealism takes it to be—dependent content of the Other Self; from the standpoint of the self, the tree is experienced as a content of Other Mind; from the standpoint of God, the tree is created in the self to be a content by means of which God knows Himself through the self. Certainly there are puzzles here which Griffiths does not face at all. If the tree is independent of the self which knows it, and knowing makes no difference as naïve realism maintains, then it follows that "real trees" and "illusory trees" are equally objects independently existing in the world beyond the Knower. Equally independent also are all the primary, secondary, and tertiary qualities, real and illusory, which are ascribed to these trees. Thus we acquire a bundle of difficulties with which to confront us when we examine the next step. All these real and illusory and various trees with variable qualities are known to be contents of Other Mind. Griffiths, following Hocking, tells us that the self does not directly experience the experience of the other's mind, but only objects which are common to both. Categorically, however, he does have consciousness of these objects as objects of another's experience, and this idea of another's experience is not "mere idea" but experience. Therefore, it would seem to follow that if he does experience another's experience, he directly experiences the content of his mind. And if he directly experiences the content of the other's mind as the other experiences it, then what he experiences, the other experiences, and his illusions are the other's illusions. This, in turn, reflects badly upon both the self and God. The self creates erroneous and defective contents in God experience, and worse still, God creates erroneous and defective contents in the self, knows the self by means of these contents, and, what is more, knows Himself through this self. These implications are not pleasant to contemplate, but so far as Griffiths' book is concerned no attempt is made to meet them.

(*b*) A second major difficulty arises in connection with Griffiths' theory of the relation of God's experience and man's experience. If God knows man and creates man in man's knowledge of the world, then what becomes of man? Man and the world are both contents in God's mind. If man is more than content in God's mind, then he is not to be regarded as "mere content," but something of which that content is a representation. In like manner, if the world is more than content in God's mind, the world also is something of which that content is a representation. But the theory makes no explicit distinction between reality and ideal representation. Both the world and man become absorbed in a transcendental unity of divine self-consciousness. In knowing the world and self, man knows the contents of God's mind; in knowing the world and self as content of His own mind, God knows Himself; man has no independent status at all. Perhaps Griffiths has an answer for these implications, but a reading of his book has not provided it for this writer.

(*c*) A third difficulty which besets Griffiths' theory is the continuous assertion and implication that mind in creating ideas thereby constitutes objective experience or independent reality. To say that the mind by inherent principles of activity generates an awareness of an objective world which is content of another Knower's mind who knows the self in return is to say that the mind generates ideas of God and the world as His thought. It is not self-evident that such ideas are also metaphysical realities; neither is it true that all ideas generated by mind are actually experiences of independent reality. Suppose, for example, that a person has a clear idea of another person; there still remains the arrival of that person to confirm the idea. Idea and reality are not universally and eternally conjoined, so that the existence of one implies the actual presence of the other. Idea-of-a-thing and idea-of-a-thing-as-existing are both ideas, and it is dogmatism to ascribe existence to the latter in any ontological sense. Experience though constituted by thought still involves something more, which thought alone does not create. The "more" is not given by the a priori.

(d) A fourth difficulty which confronts one who reflects upon Griffiths' theory is this—why is not everyone religious? If such an a priori principle determines that man in every act of self-conscious knowing experiences God as indwelling his world and as knowing him, why is not everyone conscious of God and assured of His reality? Undoubtedly religious experience is a widespread and persistent phenomenon, but there is sufficient lack of recognizable religious experience to give pause to acceptance of its assignment to an a priori, a universal, and imperative principle in the mind. The task of the religious leader and missionary ought to be considerably less difficult than it appears to be, if the imperative call to prayer is as "a priori" as Griffiths claims. Furthermore, why have not more theologians and philosophers forsaken the a posteriori and empirical ways of validating theism if this a priori principle is convincing as it is to Griffiths?

The Theories of Griffiths and Knudson Compared

These four difficulties are reasons for rejecting Griffiths' theory as it is presented. It is comparable to Knudson's theory in stressing the creativity of mind along structural religious lines, but it differs from Knudson's theory in being monistic, whereas Knudson is dualistic in his epistemological interpretation of the object. Knudson evokes a pragmatic test to validate his a priori capacity whereas Griffiths does not, and in this sense, Griffiths is much more intellectualistic in his approach. Both, however, are basing religion upon a rational capacity in the human mind, and neither of them dislocates the unity of the mind by defending separate religious faculties. Needless to say Griffiths' theory would not be acceptable to Tennant, and Tennant's position is sustained by the above argument.

C. THE APPEAL TO SPECIAL INTUITIVE FACULTIES

The third form of the religious argument may involve an appeal to special intuitive faculties. One of the aspects of religious mysticism has been the claim to possession of a special faculty for the immediate apprehension of God. By use of a technique, the phases of which are widely known to nonmystics, the mystic is permitted to rise out of the ordinary levels of sensuous, intellectual, discursive, and moral consciousness into a state of supernormal spirituality wherein and whereby, through the grace of God, he may hold spiritual converse with Deity. Here upon this high-place of life, above the life of the body and the life of the mind as it functions in reason and in conscience, the mystic "sees God face to face." God is a presentation not a representation, concrete reality not an abstraction, directly experienced not inferentially known. Such experiences are always transient and impermanent; often they occur in minds of pathological tendency; usually there are variable aspects of imagery, thought, emotion, and volition which accompany both the upward movement to the state of reception and the downward movement from the high moment of communion.

A Rejection of "Exclusive" Mysticism

In his *Philosophy of Religion*, Caldecott[63] distinguishes between "exclusive" and "comprehensive" mysticism. Exclusive mysticism is the extreme, exacting type, in which the lower orders of human experience are sundered from the upper level of spiritual converse. Comprehensive mysticism is the milder, less arduous type, in which the higher level of spiritual intuition is not derived from the lower, but the lower levels are articulated with the higher. Knowledge of God is the consummation of all lesser knowledge; it is not the terminus of a discursive argument; neither is it a priori in the transcendentalistic sense (an example of which was found in Griffiths' theory). It is rather a direct experience of the empirical type which, when possessed, sheds its light upon all other aspects of experience, so that the world, men, the self, body and soul become instinct with new meaning and declare a new glory. In other words, ordinary life becomes sacramental, the outward symbol of a divine life and grace known in beatific vision.

For "exclusive" mysticism, no defense will be undertaken. As we have indicated before, the "oneness" of the mystic and God is open to the serious contradiction that if he becomes God, he

63. *Op. cit.,* pp. 86–87.

cannot be himself and know himself; if he is himself, he cannot be and know as God. Furthermore, man does not introspect the states of another mind as he does his own; hence the mystic cannot say that he knows God in the immediacy of self-consciousness. Again the denial of all existence and value to the lower orders of experience is contradictory to all normal apperception, as far as man is concerned, and to the creativity and redemptivity of God, as far as God is concerned. The doctrine of creation implies that the world exists and is good, while the doctrine of redemption implies that the world though imperfect is yet being perfected. Any mysticism which denies the existence and value of the world as a revelation of the creation and redemptive activity of God can never be integrated into a comprehensive world-view. Neither the object of such mysticism nor the special faculty by means of which it is apprehended merits our defense.

A Defense of "Comprehensive" Mysticism

For "comprehensive" mysticism, a practical defense may here be stated. The valuable element in "comprehensive mysticism" is that truly adequate religious experience is something more than the conclusion of a discursive argument. Religious experience on its cognitive side is still "reason," but it is reason exercising a synthetic and intuitive mode of awareness rather than a discursive and volitional awareness. The results of discursive thinking are never absent from intuition, but the intuition is more than this; it is an act of accepting reality as present to the mind.

Discursive and Intuitive Consciousness

To develop the meaning of these statements further, the difference between discursive and intuitive consciousness must be drawn. First, in discursive consciousness, there is a passage of the mind from one item to another; the procedure is transitional from aspect to aspect in a labored, additive manner. In intuitive consciousness there is no consciousness of transitional, additive passage, but a direct consciousness of the whole object before the parts are distinguished. Thus we may say that intuitive consciousness is totalistic and nontransitional, whereas discursive consciousness is additive and transitional. Second, in discursive consciousness the mind is active, striving to attain some more inclusive comprehension as it passes from part to part. In intuitive consciousness the mind rests upon its object not in the sense that the mind has ceased to think but in the sense that it rests in its object without immediate striving for another. Third, in discursive consciousness there are always elements of doubting and questioning whereas intuition stands above the level of doubting and questioning. Intuitive awareness carries with it a finality, wholeness, contemplative-security, from which the questioning phase of consciousness is absent.[64] Fourth, in discursive consciousness emotional and valuational elements are at a minimum, whereas in intuitional consciousness there tends to be an accompaniment of sympathy and of valuation.

Another aspect of intuitive consciousness which needs to be presented is its realistic reference. Perhaps this can be best illustrated by Thouless' description of the stages of prayer. The first type of prayer, according to Thouless, is the prayer of the understanding or ordinary mental prayer,[65] in which the thought of the person is directed toward the idea of the religious object. What occurs in services of public worship and in voluntary private devotions is more or less prolonged discursive meditation about a religious idea. Sometimes this will be accompanied by strong emotions, but it need not necessarily be so. If, however, the meditation is sustained for sufficient length, the prayer of the understanding may become the "prayer of simplicity"[66] or of "acquired contemplation," in which directed thinking ceases, and the mind is permeated with the single idea of God. This type of prayer comes involuntarily, but it can be dissolved by simple redirection of attention. The final stage of the process is completed when the prayer of simplicity passes over into mystical prayer,[67] wherein the object of prayer is not an idea, nor an idea of a present reality, but a directly perceived reality. This is called by Thouless, deoversion.[68] Other mental activities are temporarily suspended, and the experienced con-

64. Cf. Price, *Perception*, pp. 150–154.
65. Cf. Thouless, *An Introduction to the Psychology of Religion*, pp. 179, 236.
66. *Ibid.*, p. 166.   67. *Ibid.*, pp. 226–227.
68. *Ibid.*, p. 237.

tact with God cannot be voluntarily attained, nor voluntarily terminated by simple redirection of attention. At its best God-centered introversion is followed by God-inspired extroversion, wherein valuable work is done, and the world is illumined with the idea of divine presence and purpose.

"Comprehensive" Mysticism and Intuitive Consciousness

Obviously, here we have a description of "comprehensive" mysticism at its best, but the point is that there is a point in this process where contemplation passes over into intuitive acquaintance. This may be false, but to the one undergoing the experience it does not appear to be, nor are the results demoralizing to character. A further point is that this realistic intuition is not confined to extreme mystics but is found in ordinary religious exercise by ordinary people. Dean Inge writes: "But if we realize, as is certainly the truth, that what is called mysticism is only a further development of a universal religious practice, that of prayer, we shall put aside these attempts to discredit religion at its base."[69] Again this experience comes as an intuitive discernment of the cause and source of the highest objective standard of truth, beauty, and goodness, together with a discernment of support and succor. Hence religious experience is beyond the limits of discursive reasoning, not in the sense that no discursive reasoning has ever taken place, but in the sense that in the moment of experience the discursive characteristics of consciousness are in abeyance, and the intuitive attributes of totality, rest, unquestioning, sympathy, and realistic discernment are there. Thus religious experience is complex, comprehensive, and relative to appreciation of the highest standards of value. The complexity, however, reflects the complexity of the object of experience and not simply the creative capacity of the mind. The intuition like all intuitions is susceptible to error, but validation does not take place by discursive argument below the level of this experience. It rather comes by intellectualizing this experience as it appears and testing it for reality by the results which follow in life.

Thus we are led to the conclusion that the capacity for reli-

69. Joseph Needham, ed., *Science, Religion, and Reality*, p. 385.

gious experience is more than discursive capacity. It is rather the whole mind, in a unity, intuiting the divine strength and stay of those who seek that strength in the pursuit of values, which are also willed and known by God. Upon an empirical basis, Hocking is acutely suggestive when he states that religion is the sense that we are not alone in knowing, and, we may add, in willing and in working for values in the world. But this is an experience which does not blur the distinctions between the world and values as at once, and the same existential semiindependent entities and content in either the divine or human minds. Such "immediacy" as this experience possesses resides in the togetherness of these elements. It is a "special faculty" only in the sense that it is more than discursive; that it is comprehensive personal acquaintance with an object which is intellectualized as God. From this fact of experience we may infer that the mind has a capacity to apprehend religious reality in experience. From the validation that the rational representation of this experience can achieve from the characteristics and results of this experience, we may conclude that the capacity is trustworthy. Trust is in the validity of the experience, not primarily in the capacity which conditions it.

Application of the Argument to Tennant

Applying these considerations to Tennant's statement that there is no special religious faculty, we may say that insofar as this applies to exclusive mysticism the statement is acceptable, but insofar as it applies to all religious experience, it must be rejected for an intuitive awareness, which rises above the discursive reason to grasp the reality of God. This grasp is not infallible, nor complete, but it is subject to its own type of empirical verification and as such has a place in a comprehensive theology.

Summary of Chapter

At this point a summary of the arguments which have been developed in this chapter is in order. Negative criticism of the points in Tennant's rejection of religious experience as having no unique value for validation of theism has been developed

from a positive standpoint which has been constructed in piece-
meal fashion to meet the respective points which have been
raised by Tennant.

Against point number I, that sensa are our sole, original, underived immediate contacts with independent reality, it has been
argued (a) that Tennant does not deny the term "epistemological immediacy" to thought-constructed sense data, hence
thought-construction is not in itself a negation of immediacy;
(b) that the implication of the genetic method, namely, that
greater thought-construction involves greater untrustworthiness as well as supposition, must be denied; (c) that thought-
constructed awareness of other selves is a true example of epistemological immediacy and therefore here, and possibly also in
religious experience, is denial of the assignment of epistemological immediacy solely to sense-objects.

Against point number II that *numina* lack specific quality,
after an exposition of religious experience had been rendered,
and after acknowledgments of the facts (1) that *numina* are
not as common as sensa and (2) that religious experience involves some thought-construction, it was argued negatively that
the thought-element in *numina* does not mean: (a) that *numina*
are wholly thought-created without any element of metaphysical "givenness"; (b) that *numina* are derived solely from the
phenomena in conjunction with which they are "given"; (c)
that *numina* are not originally accounted for in terms of ideas
derived from social tradition, both their "givenness" in experience and their originality being incomprehensible upon the social acquirement theory;—but positively that *numina* have the
unique qualities of "intimacy" and "ultimacy"—an active presence not remote, nor inferred, nor indifferent but which "disturbs" the subject in ways which have peculiar force and character—the response of the innermost reality of the world and
the self to us.

Against point number III that *numina* are so vague as to
enter into variable, inconsistent, and self-refuting connections
so that progress in theology came by progressive denials, it was
argued (1) that wide variations and inconsistencies occur in
the thought-construction of natural objects and nature; that
these do not negate all reality in this realm; and that therefore

wholesale denial of reality on a basis of inconsistency is not valid; (2) that variations imply differences in subjects, but these instead of signifying illusion rather imply the actuality and vitality of a real object; (3) that variations imply also differences in the manifested aspects of a complex reality; and (4) that progress and development in religious knowledge must not be taken as a "reading forward" of objects that are successively denied, but rather a "reading backward" from the highest experience to the lowest, with the realization that if the highest experience is valid, the lower stages of this experience while for the most part illusory are nonetheless germinally sound.

Against point number IV that *numina* are not readily constructible into common Objects, it was argued that owing to the mutual exclusiveness of experiencing minds, no experience can be directly communicated; that all communication involves assisting another to obtain his own experience for himself; that if this can be done, any type of experience has evidential value. Religious experience does have common features; it can be indirectly communicated, though not with such accurate control as to be characterized as "scientific"; and it can be verified to a high degree of practical adequacy.

Against point number V that religious experience is psychologically but not epistemologically immediate, it was assumed that immediacy in religious experience does not mean (*a*) introspection by man of God's consciousness, or (*b*) absence of thought-construction, or (*c*) isolation of divine reality from finite objects, but it was argued that there is a type of intimate religious experience which is more adequately intellectualized as experience of God than as experience of the subconscious, or suggestion, or some other conceptualization of naturalistic psychology. It was further argued that "immediacy" of the epistemological type characterized the experience inclusive of its intellectualization, and that the truth of this is decided on the practical adequacy of the intellectualization to represent the given features of the experience.

Against point number VI that empirical theology confused certitude with certainty, it was argued that this distinction is acceptable, but that the intellectualization of religious experience can be characterized by practical certainty of the objective type, and by a certitude which includes a measure of objective certainty which is not derived entirely from the objective certainty of a world-explanation which excludes religious experience.

Against point number VII that there is no special religious faculty, it was argued that there is no religious instinct in the strict sense of the term instinct; that there is no a priori capacity which guarantees the truth of its object in the superior way which Knudson indicates; that there is no a priori principle of the type Griffiths supports; that there is no support for the supernormal intuition of the exclusive mystic. But it was argued that religious experience of the milder type is a unique function of the whole normal rational mind as it makes an empirical contact with religious reality. The validity of the conscious experience reflects a valid trust in the capacity for religious experience which underlies it. The idea of religious experience as the result of discursive reasoning either explicit or implicit is rejected.

THE VALIDATION OF THEISM

General Orientation: the Argument Thus Far

IT is the purpose of this chapter to set forth the interrelated grounds upon the basis of which our knowledge of God may be reasonably verified. The burden of Chapter II was to reveal the fact that Tennant's conception of the process by which religious belief may be validated is fallacious because his implied conception of the origin and nature of religious experience is false. To Tennant, the truth of religious belief can be established only by general philosophical argument from the sensorily perceived facts of common knowledge, and religion is the emotional and volitional response of the self to the theistic hypothesis or idea. According to this essay, religious experience is not merely a reaction of the self to a discursively reasoned hypothesis or world-explanation. It may involve such hypothesis, but the experience is more direct, personal, and realistic than this. Tennant's argument was shown to be inadequate in its explicit statement, and thus its implicit character was taken as inadequate. The analogy of the inferential and analogical processes by which man first develops his idea of God to comparable processes by which he comes to know other selves was shown to be inadequate to the complexities of the situation. Upon the basis of analogical inference, it was argued that we can never come to a consciousness of other self in this fashion, and that, in like manner, we can never first come to awareness of God in this fashion. Noninferential, nonanalogical contact with God is first essential to an initial awareness of God. If this is present then a foundation is given for constructing thought-representations of what is there. Without this, the inferences are unsupported.

Furthermore, Tennant's explicit argument manifests certain other weaknesses. The whole teleological argument according to Tennant implies that God is Creator. He admits that man has no empirical analogies for this conception, and his admission is fatal for a theory which denies any direct religious experience and professes to build upon and to be controlled by facts of a world which is originally known in sense perception. Again, extrapolations of the data by means of which his full theistic inference must be sustained are not easily justified in the eyes of those whom, devoid of religious experience, this theory aims to convince as more objectively reasonable than the alternatives. The difficulties which were shown to beset Tennant's general argument are sufficient to convince us that the case needs to be reconsidered. In the reconstruction of theistic defense which follows, no attempt will be made to vindicate the multitudes of specific issues which arise on every side. It will be assumed that the general lines of procedure are valid. Another volume would be necessary to argue in behalf of specific issues. The main purpose of this chapter is to reveal the interconnection and interdependence of the principle arguments for theism.

I. RELIGIOUS EXPERIENCE THE PRIMARY GROUND OF THEISM

The first and central point of departure must be a direct religious experience, the nature and validity of which have been defended in Chapter III. As N. Kemp Smith[1] and C. C. J. Webb[2] have pointed out, the first requirement for making the divine existence credible is to start with the initial experiences which make that belief possible, because no amount of argument will ever "prove" the existence of God to those who lack the experience. Given an initial experience of God, the arguments then acquire new significance, in that they help confirm and integrate this experience into a more comprehensive world prospective. Without religious experience the general rational arguments do not lead to a validation of the God of religion. This is a major weakness, and nothing will replace the primary experience of religion.

The experience occurs to different people under various circumstances. Canon Raven describes the experience as it emerges in the confrontations of nature and of Christ, i.e., the confrontations of overwhelming Beauty and Goodness. He writes:

1. Cf. *supra*, p. 91.   2. Cf. *supra*, p. 93 ff.

We all have known moments when the overwhelming beauty of a sunset flooded the whole of our being, when we were vaguely aware of something "beyond," of a presence in it, yet not of it, when we were stirred with a joy not far from tears. Stars and sea, great architecture and great music have the power to produce this mood in most of us—in each according to his temperament. The poets are full of it, and not only those who can be set down as eccentric or neurasthenic. Few men have been more sane, more virile, in a way more ordinary than Browning or Walt Whitman; and yet not Wordsworth himself has a clearer apprehension of the mystery beyond the universe. And common folks know it—gardeners and seamen, and young labourers, before the struggle of life dulls their sensibilities and binds them fast on the wheel of things, and nearly all women, especially mothers of little children, and all lovers. In intensity their perception will vary from a faint sense of wonder as at something not wholly of the earth, to the clear conviction that for a timeless moment they have been rapt into union with infinite reality. Probably there are not many who have not at some time known such rapture breaking in upon a moment of quiet after a period of effort, and effecting a characteristic temper, marked at once by a sense of detachment, so that one contemplates oneself and the world objectively and in vivid perspective, and also of sensitive sympathy and kinship with all that is. For a time one lives among the familiar scenes of one's home as if one were a guest from elsewhere, a stranger to whom everything was new and unexpectedly delightful. Then nothing is common or unclean; unattractive people, dreary surroundings, monotonous tasks are transfigured: we discover a fresh appetite for simple pleasures, joy in what we have hitherto taken for granted, friendliness for those who are too often mere conveniences—the postman, the lift girl, the railway porter. Like young lovers, we face life with a smile, and life smiles back at us. And yet, though we are in it and thrilled by it, we are also very obviously elsewhere. A secret presence accompanies us; in a secret world we are at home; and though outwardly we behave much as usual, indeed at our best, we have constantly the feeling that we are spectators as well as actors; and often the drama seems almost unreal—so incongruous as to touch our sense of humour, so unimportant that we are surprised at those who find its events of engrossing interest. Yet withal there is neither boredom nor absentmindedness; we are overflowing with vitality, alert, observant, intelligent beyond our normal level, fulfilling with ease duties that would else tax all our powers, handling situations with tact and intuition, quick to understand, to pardon and encourage.[3]

This "moment of union with infinite reality," this "cosmic emotion," this emergence of the eternal in communion with men at their highest moments of integration may be illusion, but Raven points out that the unexpected and immediate quality of its emergence, the inability to explain what has suggested it, the failure of attempts to treat it as pathological, the fact that multitudes have it give it a sanction as strong as any other experience or conviction. It is an experience which is more easily "felt" than described, it brings detachment from self, sensitivity and kinship with all "that exists," a vitality of personal life which makes men in considering the impact of this aspect of the universe upon them slip inevitably into the language of personality. God is Light and Life and Love.

Raven also believes that when a person strips off his pretensions and allows the personality of Jesus to make its impact upon him, Jesus, like nature, strikes every note in the scale of his experience. Here again, in high moments, the experience of union with infinite reality emerges within him.

As with the universe, so with Him, the categories of beauty, truth, and goodness seem commonplace and inappropriate. We feel that He has given a new meaning to them, a meaning which we are not big enough fully to grasp. There is in Him a poise and balance, a sense of wholeness, a raising of all our powers to their highest level, an adjustment with the orbit of a single and consistent self. We see Him as it were in sections: at one time His volcanic energy, at another His superhuman restraint, His shattering severity and His overwhelming gentleness, His dauntless fortitude and His intuitive compassion, His loneliness and His sociability, His sub-

3. C. E. Raven, *The Creator Spirit,* pp. 205–206. Another excellent example of cosmic religious experience is to be found in Sir Francis Younghusband's chapter, "The Mystery of Nature," in *The Great Design,* pp. 237–239, ed. by Frances Mason.

limity and His delight in common things. His character seems a series of contrasts: it ought surely to be a jangle of discords. And yet the qualities we analyse and differentiate are in Him united and harmonious; each element takes its fitting place, each is essential to the full-orbed majesty of the whole . . .

Like Nature, He strikes every note in the scale of our experience, and draws from them the music of the spheres. That is why the doctors of the Church have called Him Man rather than a Man and have dwelt upon the universality and representativeness of His Manhood.[4]

Specific moments thus arise in which man finds himself confronted with overwhelming beauty or goodness or truth, with something more also, which transcends his imagination, fills his heart with awe, baffles his understanding, and demands an utter offering of himself to its service. This is religious experience at its highest and best; and it is not easy for anyone to interpret or to intellectualize such experiences in terms which adequately convey to others just what has transpired. Certainly the imagery or conceptual processes by means of which it is interpreted cannot convey it directly to another. Experience is truly exclusive of minds, as we have continually insisted, and communication is always by concepts or representations, though sometimes the presence of one richly experienced friend inspires another to see the object of surpassing value more readily. The interpretation alone is linguistically conveyed, and it is the interpretation which is dependent upon the culture and background of the experient. Often this is anthropomorphic in the worst sense; often it involves illusion and misunderstanding; but when the experience is truly there, it is difficult to avoid the highest personal interpretation. In the case of high religious experience, as Raven says, "here is Life, Life with unlimited energy, Life from which pulses boundless vigor, Life which thrills and enfolds, and saturates us." Raven goes on to state that for some this "mystical experience" guarantees the concept of personality of God,[5] whereas the rest of the universe makes it permissible only.

4. *Ibid.*, pp. 232–233.   5. *Ibid.*, p. 220.

II. PHILOSOPHICAL CRITICISM NEEDED TO DIS-
TINGUISH VALID FROM FALLACIOUS RELI-
GIOUS EXPERIENCE; RELIGIOUS EX-
PERIENCE INSUFFICIENT BY IT-
SELF TO VALIDATE
THEISM

The problem of which interpretation this experience guarantees leads at once into the subject of the relation of reason to
religious experience, or, in other terms, the relation of philosophy to the argument from religious experience. Reason or
philosophy is called upon to perform an important service for
men of religious experience. Religious experience, like all other
types of experience, is subject to error and to illusion. No experience is absolutely infallible. Hence wherever error is possible, there reflection must set up some standard for judging
truth or falsity in experience. Furthermore, not only must
truth be discriminated from error, but the relation of the principle of this type of experience to the principle exemplified in
other types of experience must be established, and this is the
office of reason and philosophy.

As Hicks has said,[6] "fundamentally there is only one way of
knowing. . . . Wise men and simple, scientific and unscientific,
contemplative and practical, all employ ultimately the same
means of ascertaining the truth or falsity of what seems to be
offered in experience, and of determining what are the actual
facts." This "means" is thought or reason. Reason whether used
by common sense, science, or philosophy is analytic and synthetic—analytic in breaking up or discriminating elements in
presented experience; synthetic in uniting these discriminated
elements in ways in which they do not at first seem to be united;
i.e., by reference to wider principles which they exemplify. A
collection of facts is not science; only facts which exemplify
laws, concepts, hypotheses can constitute a science, and the same
is true of religion. To the philosopher as a religious man the
facts of the world exhibit principles which are not explainable
in terms of mechanism but in terms of a Supreme Mind. The

6. *The Philosophical Bases of Theism*, p. 159; cf. pp. 159–163.

critical examination of explanations relevant and irrelevant to various aspects of the world of fact and value is a task which religious experience in itself does not supply.

The failure of uncriticized religious experience to yield infallible truth is the first reason why a simple appeal to religious experience cannot validate theism. Some effort must be made to identify true religious phenomena from the false; common characteristics of this experience must be isolated; and the intellectualization of this experience must be assigned some reasonably greater probability for accuracy than other possible explanations. This task was undertaken in the last chapter and need not be repeated here. It will suffice to say that many people have had these experiences; that these experiences come with a unique "given" quality; that they leave behind them results of great value in the development of personality. As Raven points out, the Eternal is not our Nurse or Mother but Light, and Life, and Love; the cross is in it as well as joy; it is not a swooning experience; it is not Nirvana but Beatific vision; not Valhalla but Gethsemane. To call it fear is to forget that it is awe-inspiring; to call it "narcissus" or "libido" is to overlook its "otherness"; to restrict it to some abstract symbol such as "First Cause," "Unity of Universe," "Activity," or "Eternity" is to impersonalize the experience into abstraction. The highest religious experience has a claim to accuracy which reflection may sustain.

III. PHILOSOPHICAL ARGUMENT NEEDED TO SUPPORT THE IDENTIFICATION OF THE OBJECT OF RELIGIOUS EXPERIENCE WITH THE GROUND OF THE UNIVERSE

But there is still another limitation of religious experience which needs to be met. As Webb says, mature religious experience is unsatisfied until the God of religious experience is also the "Absolute," the ultimate ground of all that is. This statement does not mean that God must be the God of absolute idealism, but simply that the God of religious experience must be the one Supreme God of all creation. The highest religious experience cannot acquiesce in the "polytheism" which James suggests

in his *Varieties of Religious Experience*.[7] Religious experience
in itself does not establish the Creator of the material universe
or the Designer of nature; such concepts represent a greater
degree of thought-construction born in conjunction with other
experiences and included in the interpretative rationalization
of religious experience. The weighing of the evidence for this
wider concept is the task of philosophy; in other words, it is the
task of philosophy to validate the conviction that the God of
religious experience is the God of the universe.

A. NEGATIVE CRITICISM OF THE NATURALISTIC INTERPRETATION OF SCIENCE

It is in connection with this larger task that Tennant's theology is of great importance. On the negative side, Tennant has
developed the "higher-criticism" of science with a view to denying the presumptions of naturalistic philosophy masquerading
as science. Scientific facts are often taken to be absolutely objective and final realities; from the psychological aspect, the
knowing mind is thought to "make no difference" to the experience of physical facts; from the standpoint of the apprehended
physical object, no interpretive presuppositions are realized;
and the tendency to regard certain aspects of reality as the
whole of that reality is great in the minds of pseudoscientists.
In other words, science involves a dual process of abstraction,
an abstraction or omission of the knowing mind, and an abstraction of certain aspects of reality for the purpose of observation,
interpretation, prediction, and experimental control. The
physiologist, for example, selects certain aspects of human beings for the purpose of observation, reflective analysis, and synthesis. He may observe, classify, and legalize the blood circula-
tion of any man, friend or foe. The facts of friendship and
"enemyship" do not enter into his consideration because they
do not enter into his purpose. If he tends to neglect the multitude of other aspects of the complex creature, man, for the purposes of his science, he must not fail to realize that these other
aspects exist and are real also. To interpret man as a physiological mechanism and nothing more is a false absolutizing of a

7. *Op. cit.,* p. 526; also pp. 131–133.

methodological procedure. "Science" then becomes crude materialism and naturalistic philosophy. A methodological omission is transformed into a denial. If, on the other hand, the physiologist assumes that the facts of his science are totally independent of himself as knower, if he is unaware of the part played by his own mind in the psychological processes which enter into experience, here again he may be tempted to rule mind out of his interpretation of reality. If, furthermore, he remains unaware of the vast assumptions of nature's uniformity, dependableness, and intelligibility, he may forget the elements of pure faith which enter into the foundations of his science and assume that his science is absolute and certain knowledge. Thence he may decide that science is absolutely certain knowledge, whereas philosophy and religion are insecure meanderings of obscure and deluded minds.

Six Points at Which the Naturalistic Interpretation of Science Breaks Down

The naturalistic or humanistic interpretation of science has the following roots. (1) Methodological procedures are regarded as complete and final accounts of reality; methodological omissions are transformed into denials of the religious interpretation of the world. (2) Science neglects the individual and deals with the general, repeatable, conceptual aspects of the flow of reality. (3) Science omits all reference to ends and purposes accomplished or in the process of being accomplished by a divine controlling personality. (4) The knower and the knowing are thought "to make no difference" to the objects of scientific study; the self is thus denied, and an uncritical realism becomes absolutized. (5) Presuppositions which are not inductively derived nor inductively verified are taken for granted and assumed as absolutely certified, objective experiences. (6) Nature is thought to need no explanation beyond itself; that is, it is assumed that the explanation lies in nature itself.

In order to establish the truth of the naturalistic interpretation or philosophy of science, it is necessary to prove that a certain selected aspect of reality is the final and ultimate reality; that this reality accounts for individuality and history; that no reference to purpose is necessary to final explanation; that absolute realism is the only valid epistemology; and that the uniformity and the intelligibility of nature are empirical facts satisfying no human need and needing no explanation beyond itself. Once the implications of these statements are set forth, it appears that the case cannot be established.

(1) Methodological Omissions

Let us suppose that physical entities as studied by physics and chemistry are taken to be the final realities of the universe. A thoroughgoing mechanistic philosophy results, but this philosophy must prove that all the facts of consciousness with its content of sensa, interests, purposes, and values are explainable in terms of physiology and, ultimately, in terms of matter in motion and quantitative measurement. The mechanistic philosophy must show that mind is not a true cause and that consciousness has no function in the evolutionary process. It must show how truth and error, moral goodness and sin, beauty and ugliness are explicable on the theory of materialistic determinism. Actually this is impossible.

(2) Neglect of the Individual

Materialistic naturalism must account also for the entire course of history by reference to economic trends and to power politics. Creative personalities must be absorbed into statistical averages and predictable tendencies. Individuality, genius, and values of truth, goodness, and beauty must be definable in terms of measurable energy-units and organization and their occurrence or realization predictable in mechanistic terms. Obviously this too cannot be successfully accomplished.

(3) Teleological Indications

Mechanism must account for the suggestion of design or purpose in nature as a whole. Events and processes seem to accomplish ends or objectives; they seem to subserve future goals. Mechanism must account for the functions of parts of nature in working toward ends. In other words, matter in motion must become extremely clever matter to accomplish unconsciously results which the majority of men consider important. It is impossible for materialistic mechanism to account for the world without importing into the theory potentialities which are far removed from the vigorous meaning of the concept of mechanism. Hence the pristine concept breaks down as a final explanation of the universe.

(4) An Extreme Realistic Epistemology

Again, the naturalistic philosophy must prove an extreme, realistic epistemology if it is tacitly based upon such a theory. It must also validate its denial of the creative functioning of the subject in knowing. The difficulties here may be briefly expanded, the first of which are epistemological and concern the nature of sensa.

There are, it appears, two opposing general theories as to the nature of sensa; selective or generative. The selective theory is held by such realists as deny that psychophysical conditions of awareness affect the sense-object in any way. Awareness does nothing to the object; awareness is not responsible for the existence of the object. What the subject does in perception is to contemplate the qualities of independent objects. The generative theory, on the other hand, is held by those who maintain that psychophysical conditions of awareness do make a difference to the sense-object apprehended. These conditions are at least part of the total causal determination of sense-objects. An extreme generative theory would omit the words "at least part of" in the above sentence. The subject in this case does not contemplate an object but creates it. The subject is not responsible for the awareness of the object but for the existence of the object.

(a) A Critique of the "Selective" Theory of Sensa

Neither extreme form of the two theories can be settled by direct appeal to the data apprehended. It is only after a consideration of indirect evidence and of the respective advantages of each theory that one can be preferred to the other. The extreme selective theory has certain advantages. (1) It accords with the naïve "look" of things. The qualities we perceive do seem to be out there independent of us. (2) It avoids all the complexity and the difficulty of explaining what the process of generation must be. A creational theory is always at a loss to state just where and how generation occurs. (3) It avoids also the pendulum-status of sensa, which causes the less extreme generative theory much difficulty. That is to say, a generative theory of the less extreme type commits itself either to the proposition "sensa are particular existences which correspond to other particular existences" or to the proposition "sensa are independent objects-in-the-relation-of-appearing-to-a-subject." In the former case, there results a dualism between sensa and thing with the charge of agnosticism dangling over it; in the latter case, the theory is perpetually on a fence falling now to the subjective side and now to the realistic side in an endeavor to escape extreme realism, on the one hand, and solipsism and agnosticism on the other.

These advantages are all to the good, and if a selective theory could be made to work, it would be an easy matter. But the selective theory has severe disadvantages. (1) The major disadvantage is the overwhelming complexity and diversity of qualities which it assigns to the independent world. Among normal people the differences in colors, shapes, sizes, temperatures, etc., are enormous. Can the same independent object have all these qualities at the same time? The differences do not seem to be reducible to a part-whole relation. What each person perceives is part of the whole object, it is sometimes argued. Add all the sensa of different people or of the same person at different times and places together and you derive the thing as it is in itself. But, when to normal people are added abnormal people or normal people in abnormal conditions, the independent world must then contain all the objects which we ascribe to dreams, hallucinations, and disease, for all these qualities have the same objective look, and we have denied that psychophysical conditions make a difference to independent reality. Faced with these facts, a selective theory places a tremendous strain upon one's credulity. Science which deals with public and common Objects becomes impossible because real objects are too variable to be admitted to the realm of permanent fact. Therefore, the extreme selective theory must be rejected.

(2) But another difficulty faces the selective theory too. We know from scientific investigation that a complex process of psychophysiological activity does occur whenever perception takes place. We know that there are differences in time between

the moment a stimulus is given and the moment sensa occur as, for example, when we see the smoke of a gun before we hear the report, or when we see the light of a star which has left it thousands of light-years ago. It is difficult to believe that a sense-object which occurs at the end of a complex process is the independent object which occasions the stimulus or which is contemplated by the subject.

For these reasons, it seems necessary to agree with Tennant that a selective theory cannot be accepted. It seems further necessary to agree with him that there is no way to compromise and hold a composite selective-generative theory. Science, for example, tends to hold a generative theory of secondary qualities and a selective theory of primary qualities, but this does not avoid the disadvantages of the selective theory which apply to primary qualities as well as to secondary qualities. Both stand and fall together; if the selective or extreme realistic theory falls in one case, it falls in the other.

The "Generative" Theory of Sensa Difficult but Inescapable

One who feels forced to reject the selective theory becomes then involved in the difficulties of the generative theory: (1) contrary to the look of things; (2) mysterious process of generation; (3) opposing dangers of subjectivism and agnosticism. With respect to (1) there is real difficulty. Experience tends to indicate that the "look of things" is often incorrect, but it indicates also that the appearances of things are characterized by inescapable external control. Theoretical justice must be done to the fact of error, but it also must be done to the fact of truth. The appearances must be saved even though they are impure. Generation then must be held in connection with its dual sources. It, therefore, does not mean absolute creation on the part of the mental source alone. The external "look of things" is in some sense essentially valid or relevant. This is inescapable. With respect to (2) it is necessary to admit that the process of generation cannot be completely described. The ultimate nature of both the subject and the metaphysical object is not completely known in the moment of experience. The generation-process is an "ultimate" which we simply have to accept. Finally with respect to (3), it is probably true that if complete, photographic knowledge is demanded, this position has an agnostic tinge. But there is some more or less direct basis for realistic belief. We find it impossible in practical life to doubt that our sensa give us contact with something independent of ourselves and that independent reality stands revealed in sensa. Our sensa are not created at will; they are forced upon us in such a way that we have to accept them. They are not utterly chaotic appearances but orderly, law-abiding, and controlled from the extramental pole of the knowledge-process. For these reasons we cannot believe in pure subjectivism; our belief in a real physical world is grounded in a stubborn external control, and we can say that we know the noumenal through the phenomenal.

It may be that we are forced by an extreme dualistic form of this theory to face the possibility that, as Berkeley held, this system of interacting things is ultimately a system of ideas in the mind of God, or the further possibility, which Ward held, that this system of interacting things is ultimately a world of spiritual monads. This issue is not absolutely settled without other considerations. The problem of evil, for example, forces Tennant to rule out Berkeley's hypothesis, whereas a tendency to accept the scientific theory of electrons or comparable units of physical energy causes Tennant to exclude the claim of Ward's hypothesis to absolute validity. With respect to the ultimate units of the world, Tennant is semiagnostic with leanings toward a metaphysical realism rather than a spiritualistic pluralism. Yet his duality-theory of perception leads him to believe in one-to-one correspondence between phenomena and noumena; it drives him to state that we know the noumenal through the phenomenal and to reject from the beginning of his analyses the bias to idealism which was fostered by Cartesian dualism. This means that the agnosticism of extreme dualism is virtually overcome in valid sense-experience before the additional considerations of evil are brought into the decision.

To return now to materialistic mechanism. Mechanism usually starts with an acceptance of the selective theory of primary qualities if not also with a selective theory of all qualities. Often the difficulties of this position are not examined and the microscopic world is regarded as a completely known physical mechanism. To prove this in the face of epistemological considerations and recent developments in physical science is the task to which naturalism must direct itself. The difficulties are obviously insurmountable.

(b) A Critique of Extreme Realism's Rejection of the Creative Subject

The second point with respect to which the issues need expansion is the creative activity of the subject in knowing. Mechanism must first prove the proposition that consciousness of an object and the existence of an object are one and the same thing. This is a logical impossibility for by no rule of logic is "to be a thunderstorm" the same as "to be conscious of a thunderstorm." Awareness introduces a new factor into the situation which is an ultimate, given element irreducible to any other. Awareness, however, is always awareness of something by a being which undergoes or lives through the awareness. This being or subject of awareness is not identifiable entirely with the occurrence of sensa, or of a flow of sensa. For example, the awareness of a patch of yellow color is meaningless in itself until it is thought to signify an existing object, let us say, a box of crackers. To make this identification there must be added to the sense-datum a greater element of thought-interpretation. Ideas of former experiences must be brought to bear upon the sense-datum before it can be recognized and classified as an object which exemplifies a certain character beyond what is given. Such a synthesis is made by an agency which is capable of bringing ideas of past experiences into conjunction with present experiences. The agency must be one which endures throughout successive experiences; otherwise the bearing of ideas of past experiences upon present experience could never be made. A succession of absolutely separate agencies could never bring the ideas and sense-experiences of one into connection with those of another. Some enduring single agency is necessary to account for the recognition of a yellow sensum as a cracker box. To define recognized objects in terms of separate sensa or a flow of sensa without thought-interpretation and without an active agency of connection is to omit elements which go to make up any experience of an object of fact at all.

Now mechanism at the extreme denies not only the reality of the agent but consciousness as well. Consciousness is the shadow of physiological reactions to the environment; it possesses neither power nor influence in the concourse of events. Such a position needs to be proved in the face of disconcerting facts; obviously this cannot be done. Neither can a less extreme naturalism successfully prove that there is no difference between sensa and thing; thought and thing; sensa and thought; and sensa, thought, and agent. To identify either sensa or thought with thing is to put illusion and contradiction into things. To identify the agent with thought or sensa is to deny the unifying activity which makes experience possible and to destroy knowledge altogether. For, if the knower is the known object, he cannot be the knower any more than if the mystic becomes God in the moment of ecstasy can he then be himself or know that he is himself.

(5) *Unprovable Assumptions*

The fifth difficulty which naturalism must face is the unprovable assumption which undergirds all scientific endeavor; namely, the assumption that nature is uniform, its sequences regular and repetitious, and, in spite of appearances, its regularities discoverable. Certainly this assumption that nature is orderly and intelligible throughout is not given in any one bit of experience. No one has examined nature as a whole to know whether or not uniformity prevails throughout the universe. Furthermore, there are signs of genuine indeterminacy in physical theories of nature which may or may not be assignable to uniform sequence. This assumption that nature is orderly goes far beyond experience. To the naturalist it cannot be derived from a priori factors in mind. To such a person, it is a pure act of will based perhaps upon the desire to discover or to explain facts according to the causal sequences, and upon the practical need to know such sequences in order to predict future events from observed conditions. This situation gives the lie to any assertion that science is free from assumption and from human interest. As a matter of fact, science is based upon both faith and human needs. Naturalism is unable to prove its claim to absolute certainty and absolute disinterestedness.

(6) *Nature Needs Nothing Beyond Itself to Explain It*

The final point which naturalism needs to prove is that nature needs nothing beyond itself to explain it. So far as science is concerned, it is sufficient to confine explanations of events to the circumstances, antecedent conditions, and causes of events. To impose this position, however, upon philosophy is another matter. For philosophy, the problem is to discover why nature is this and not that, an order instead of a chaos, a system which develops values and not a disorganized, unprogressive jungle. The answer which naturalism makes to this question is simply that nature happens to be what it is, an orderly system; that is all that can be said. In other words, naturalism tells us that there is no explanation. Not that the explanation is there but unknown, but rather that there is no explanation there at all. All of which means that in the last analysis, naturalism denies the assumption of all science; i.e., that there is a reason, an explanation for everything no matter how confused the appearances. To say that nature is inexplicable by anything beyond itself is to declare that the central assumption of science is an illusion; it is to rest in inexplicability, chance, or the position that "it happens to be that way." When these implications of the naturalistic view are drawn out, it appears that naturalism contradicts its basic faith by declaring it a deception.

B. POSITIVE STATEMENT OF THE FACTS WHICH DEMAND COSMIC EXPLANATION OR THEISM

The conviction that nature needs something beyond itself to explain why it is this and not that leads on to the positive case for the theistic world-view. That the world of experience exhibits principles or tendencies which mere mechanism leaves inexplicable and which may be accounted for by the presence of a supreme directive mind—such is the contention of theistic philosophy. With certain modifications, Tennant's cumulative teleological argument for theism may be sustained.

(1) *Nature Adapted to Thought*

The first fact to be noted is that nature is adapted to human thought and reason. It is conceivable that nature might be a chaos in which similar events never occurred and processes were never repeated with regularity. In such a state there would be no universals or concepts, no application of the categories of thought, and no relationship of the world to the principles of logic. In fact, if thought is derived from nature, there could be no thought and no rational mind. Nature, however, is not a chaos but a cosmos, an order closely correlated with thought. Nature is a medium through which thought and meaning are conveyed to the human mind. It is as if nature itself sought to convey thoughts which are first entertained in a mind within nature. A thoughtless mechanism would scarcely seem to be capable of conveying such meanings and values as nature is found to convey. Hence the theist infers that the intelligible world is the work or communicative medium of an intelligent mind or God. This inference is not the origin of the idea of God; neither is it an absolute proof, for other alternatives are not logically excluded. Mindless mechanism, chance integrations, unconscious generation are conceptual possibilities which may be placed beside theism as explanations of the orderliness by means of which nature is adapted to human thought. The major question is whether or not these alternatives to theism can successfully explain the order of nature without tacitly importing into these conceptions potentialities which they do not rightfully possess. Mechanism, chance, and instinct become extremely clever in producing an order which conveys meaning and principle to human minds; so clever in fact that they exhibit the powers of intelligence and are thus transformed beyond recognition.

(2) *Adaptation of the Cosmic Environment to Living Organisms*

The next fact calling for explanation is the adaptation of the cosmic environment to living organisms. Following Henderson's study of the successive physical changes in the cosmic environment which preceded and made possible the existence and growth and evolution of living organisms, the theist infers that these changes subserved an objective or end which was consciously foreseen and voluntarily imposed upon the physical processes. Out of countless possible elements and distributions, just certain elements (carbon, hydrogen, and oxygen) in sufficient quantities and temperatures were selected to compose an environment in which living organisms can dwell. The selection may have been the outcome of chance or of unconscious purpose, but to the theist the collocations are too complex, unusual, and intricate to be the outcome of chance, and the selectivity involved is too complicated for simple instinct to accomplish. Though the theist cannot exclude the conceptual possibilities of other explanations than his own, he can indicate their improbability by reference to appropriate analogies. Neither chance operations nor instinctive activities devoid of intelligent direction and control are sufficient to account for extremely complicated adjustments over long-time periods. Intelligent selection by a mind which is conscious of alternatives, and a will which exercises the results of judicious choice, this appears to the theist to be the more probable explanation.

Broad's Objection Weighed

At this point it is appropriate to weigh Broad's objection[8] that in a universe of vast extent in space and time, it is not antecedently improbable that collocations chanced to occur which made this small world which we know a place which is suited to living organisms for a relatively short period of time. First the fact that "collocations" do not exist, so far as we know, in the larger areas of reality beyond the small universe which we know, or the fact that there is no environment for living organisms in the unknown universe, cannot be taken to mean "thoughtless negligence" upon God's part. Such would be the case, as Hicks points out,[9] only if it were possible to point to a world in which there were living things without an environment to support them. Otherwise the point is meaningless. Second, it is a question whether or not the conditions of collocation are as local and temporary as Broad implies. The present suitable environment is the result of long changes in geological ages, which in turn root back in remote astronomical periods and conditions. This tiny portion of the universe has ramifications which involve the vast universe. It is not absolutely isolated or cut off

8. *Supra*, p. 135; cf. Broad's "Review of Philosophical Theology," *Mind*, XXXIX, 476 ff.
9. Hicks, *op. cit.*, p. 205.

from the wider areas of reality. Third, if the vast universe were
not only without collocations but without law; i.e., if the vast
universe were a chaos in which cause-and-effect sequences did
not hold, it is difficult to see how such a state could fail to effect
the tiny ordered fragment. A wild surrounding world would
certainly break up the collocations of a tiny pocket within it in
a very short time just as a hurricane cripples a city. The truth
appears to be that the large world permits the smaller world to
exist without molestation. One cannot be separated from the
other; they are interrelated. Fourth, as Tennant states, we have
no knowledge of the formation of many universes by successive
throws of the cosmic dice all of which were unsuccessful but one.
If dice were thrown, if chance did operate, it looks as if the dice
were loaded, as if the outcome were intentional. In other words,
the "collocations" appear to involve too intricate combinations
and adjustments to be the results of the lawless operations of
chaos. That they may be is a conceptual possibility, but it is not
a plausibility or a probability to a theist.

(3) The Progressive Development of Organisms

Not only is it highly plausible that the gradual adaptation
of the environment to the possibility and existence of organisms
is the outcome of rational design, but the general trend of the
evolution of organisms from lower to higher types suggests a
comparable justification in teleology. It should be noted that
the fact to which attention is called is the general fact of direction or progressiveness in organic evolution, not a particular
adaptation of some specific organism or species to the environment or to itself. Undoubtedly specific adaptations call for
teleological interpretation too, at least the general assumptions
underlying the immediate explanations of specific adaptations
by mechanistic biology require explanation, but for the purpose
of establishing the God of the cosmos the wider fact is of greater
significance.

When Paley developed his teleological argument, Darwinism
had not come into existence. Regarding organisms as completely
constructed machines with all adaptations of organs to organism, part to whole, and whole to environment "ready-made,"
Paley correctly argued that the demand for purposive explana-

tion is overwhelming. But when Darwin substantiated the fact
that organisms and organs have been developed not only gradually over long periods of time, but by minute, mechanical, and
chance changes as well, he demolished the basis of Paley's argument. The sting of Darwinism resides not in its substantiation
of "gradualness" but in its suggestion that mechanical and
chance-changes are sufficient to explain the adaptations of organisms. "Gradualism" as a basis for minute mechanical explanation and, by implication, complete mechanical explanation, represents the real threat of Darwinism. If Darwin's
mechanical principle of explanation represents the complete and
final truth of organic evolution, then teleology is unnecessary;
if it is not the final truth, then Paley's theistic conclusion and
his idea of means and ends as distinct from the idea of cause
and effect are still applicable to the gradual evolution of organisms.

An extensive examination of Darwinism has cast grave suspicion upon the finality of its mechanical explanation. The difficulties reside not so much in the theory itself but in the assumptions which underlie it. Darwin assumed not only the continual
occurrence of variations but their progressiveness and transmission. It is obvious that, after variations occur, some may
prove advantageous in the "struggle for existence" and be
strengthened. But what caused the variations to occur? The environment may determine what variations will stand, but it does
not determine what will arrive. Either the occurrence of variation is due to pure chance, or else it is due to purpose, conscious
or unconscious. To assign variation to pure chance is to say
that there is no cause behind the effect, a denial of the central
assumption of science, or else, if it is assumed that every effect
does have a cause, the appeal to pure chance is actually an appeal to ignorance.

Now variations not only occur, but they occur in more or less
definite directions. Are we to assume that the long series of
changes involved in the development of organs which function
usefully in the economy of an organism are the results of pure
chance occurrence, or are they changes according to a pre-
arranged order or plan? If they are the operations of pure
chance, why have they not gone astray? From all practical ex-

perience, pure chance might be responsible for several lucky throws of dice, but not for continual success. Continual success means that the dice are loaded or that the dice have been subject to design. So also "continuousness" in the construction of organs which serve a needed function is a sign of the presence of purpose.

With respect to the transmission of variations, there are also many difficulties. Whenever a person breeds horses, he has to exercise continual care that a talented animal mate with another talented animal rather than a mediocre mate. Such breeding is never left to chance but, in the realm of nature as a whole, we are to suppose that the breeding of animals with comparable valuable variations takes place by chance. This seems most improbable to many. If the transmission of variations is a matter of chance combination of qualities in embryonic forms, then the problem is complicated, but it is no easier to understand the operation of chance in the microscopic realm than in the molar realm. If variations appear in many animals all in one generation in the form of "mutations," the occurrence may be coincidence, but the extent of the occurrence bespeaks design.

When we proceed to answer the larger question whether or not the central trends of organic development from simple-celled animals to intelligent animals are the result of pure chance operations, we become hesitant about answering affirmatively; especially so when we realize that the development of organisms has taken place with corresponding favorable conditions in the environment; i.e., within an environment which is relatively stable, yet, not static but constantly varying and evoking new adaptations. It is difficult to believe that complicated, interrelated variations and changes could take place over long periods of time without the guidance of a large-scale plan. Such a plan in no way destroys the mechanical processes involved; it rather fulfills and completes the mechanical explanation. In other words, a mechanical explanation or an explanation in terms of second causes and effects may be sought and found, but nothing is lost, and much further illumination is gained if a teleological explanation or an explanation in terms of means and ends is also sought and found. The cause of an effect is then not only the antecedent material factors in existence, but the idea or plan for which these antecedent factors are put into mechanical operation and selectively guided toward an end-result. Given the necessity of a plan on behalf of which material processes operate, it is open to one, of course, to infer that such a plan is unconsciously held by nature. Such a possibility is logically thinkable, but it fails to be practically probable or understandable. Blind instinct accomplishes relatively simple goals without too great obstacles to overcome; only fully rational minds accomplish complex objectives against severe obstacles. The problem of world-making and general progressive evolution is too complex and too hazardous to be accomplished by anything analogous to the instinct of lower animals searching unconsciously for food to satisfy hunger. From practical experience, conscious mind or God is the only plausible solution.

The Problem of the Soul's Origin

An exceedingly important problem emerges at this point in connection with the teleological argument; namely, the problem of the origin of the human soul. Is the human soul derived from the souls of human parents in the process of generation, or does it come from God by creative act at a point in the growth of a new human organism? The issue recalls the classic theories of Tertullian and Pelagius, traducianism and creationism. Obviously, the question cannot be settled by an appeal to experience; certainly it cannot be settled here. But Ward[10] and Tennant are led to adopt the creationist position for two major reasons: (1) the impossibility of conceiving how mental life can be derived from physical structures; and (2) the difficulties of supposing that the mental life of a child is derived from the minds of its parents. In the case of the body, there is definite physiological continuity between the body of the child and the bodies of its parents, but there is no comparable continuity in the case of its mind. Minds and, particularly, character do not split off the parental minds as bodily parts. True, there are inherited tendencies, but character is not inherited. The child has definite individuality. His mind is influenced by the inherited composition of his organism, but it is still something in itself,

10. Cf. Hicks, *The Philosophical Basis of Theism*, p. 212, for Ward's motives. Tennant's are doubtless the same.

and genius may be best accounted for by supposing that the endowments of genius come by creative act of God. The emergence of a new soul is best conceived as an emanation from the mind of God. This supposition involves no contradiction to the facts of psychology; it is consistent with the pure-ego doctrine; and it is a conceivable hypothesis.

The General Relation of Value-Arguments to the Teleological View of Nature and to Religious Experience

The teleological evidence which we have been considering to this point has been drawn largely from the integrations of the physical world, physiological organisms, and the relation of orderly processes to rational minds. Attention is now to be given to esthetic and moral values and to value-arguments for theism. The general position of these arguments must be cited in their relation to the natural evidence given above, and also to the primary evidence of religious experience from which, as has been argued, theistic defense must start. Value-arguments are not sufficient in themselves to establish theism. They need the support of the teleological view of nature, on the one hand, and the validated religious experience *sui generis* on the other. For, without the support of the teleological view of nature, a theism based upon value-arguments alone opens itself to a charge comparable to the one which Broad brings against Taylor;[11] namely, that many people believe that in our present state of knowledge there is cumulative evidence that the naturalistic view of nature and human nature is true; that the conditions which make the fulfillment of absolute, unconditional obligations are not actual; and that, therefore, the person who is lured by impossible perfections instilled in him by well-meaning nurses should be psychoanalyzed and adjusted to reality. Broad rightly adds that doubtless people have been bluffed into accepting the naturalistic view as inevitable, but Taylor has not attempted to disprove it. This is the weakness of all arguments for theism from moral values alone; namely, they do not disprove the naturalistic view of nature on the negative side nor advance evidence for the spiritual or teleological interpretation of nature on the positive

11. Cf. C. D. Broad's review of A. E. Taylor's "Faith of a Moralist" in *Mind,* XL, 367–368.

side. Unless this is done; i.e., unless there is mind expressing its purposes through the processes of physical nature, there is no basis for the further hope that even the rudimentary conditions for the ultimate realization of value are actual.

On the other hand, value-arguments alone are inadequate apart from direct religious experience. Let us suppose that it is possible to establish the metaphysical objectivity of moral and esthetic values, it is still another step to the position that values are the ends of spirit. As far as objectivity is concerned, values might simply constitute a realm of subsistence or essence without any ground in God. The step to God must be taken by religious experience, not by way of rational inference or by a priori ideation, but by direct *rapport* with religious reality. If there is a direct communion of spirit with spirit in the medium of values, then the moral argument by way of inference from values can confirm the experience of religious communion. Hence we conclude that the argument from values to theism cannot stand alone; it must be correlated with basic religious experience and the teleological view of nature. With this general orientation in mind, the evidence and implications of values may be indicated.

(4) The Realm of Subsistent, Unactualized Forms and Values

Before noting the theological implications of the fact that nature is a realm of "actualized," "realized," or "expressed" values, it is necessary to face the difficult question of the status and theological bearings of forms or subsistences in general. Tennant insists that the abstract formulae of pure mathematics, propositions in logic, and abstract values of goodness do not *exist*; i.e., they are not independently real in the ontal world. His position can be clarified only by attempting to define in our own way such terms as "existence," "subsistence," and "reality." "Existence" is a much narrower term than "reality";[12] it refers to individual things or events which occupy a definite position in time (i.e., minds) or in time and space (i.e., physical things in nature). Such things or events are active causes apprehended through the senses or through immediate introspection or "ex-

12. The writer is following Hicks at this point. Cf. *The Philosophical Basis of Theism*, pp. 220 ff.

traspection." There are entities which, though real, do not come under the criteria: individuality, temporality, sometimes spaciality, activity, and perceptibility (as distinct from conceivability). Some of these entities are universals, relations, forms, propositions, or truths of logic and mathematics, esthetic and moral values. Blue things exist but the abstract universal, blue, does not *"exist"* though it is real in the sense (1) that it is not exhausted by any single specific blue thing; (2) it is not constructed or changed by the will of thinkers; (3) it is not a temporal or spacial individual in the process of nature; (4) it is conceived, not perceived, through the senses. Logical forms such as the principle of contradiction have certain comparable characteristics in that they do not derive their truth or validity from the mental act of thought or belief. Tennant gives explicit admission of this when he states that psychogenetic method and analysis presupposes the use of "only a few empty forms."[13] Yet he rejects the extramental reality of abstract forms of other types.

But certainly mathematical propositions do not derive their truth from either being believed by mental act or from being exemplified in "existence." The proposition: $2 + 2 = 4$ is true whether believed or not. No mental construction or supposition can make $2 + 2 = 5$. Neither is the meaning of the proposition exhausted by any particular manifestation of it in the realm of existent physical process. There is a stubborn necessity about mathematical rules which insist that our thinking conform to them. Hence we say that they have "reality," meaning by "reality" that they are not made valid by an act of thinking nor are they exhausted by any specific manifestation in existence. In this sense, forms or truths may be regarded as "subsisting" or as constituting a realm of "essences." Clearly essences may be manifested in connection with existent individuals in the temporal process, but the temporal process does not exhaust their reality, neither does their nonexistential reality become exhausted by being ideas in human minds. The difficulty with Tennant's position is that forms when not manifested in existence have reality only in human minds whereas the position here developed is that their necessary, insistent validity is not due to

13. *Supra*, p. 38.

the human mind but rather a stubborn reality before which the human mind must bow. Therefore, they have a reality independent of human thinking as well as in some sense independent of any particular manifestation in existence.

It should now be noted that the unactualized values of goodness and beauty occupy the same status as logical and mathematical truths. Beauty and goodness are manifested in existent individuals, but there is a standard of beauty and goodness which is not exhausted by these specific manifestations. The unexhausted standard, however, does not derive such reality as it further possesses from being an idea in some human mind. Human tastes, desires, and mental constructions do not make beauty and goodness really and validly beautiful and good. In fact, the perfected form of the beautiful and the good is not yet conceived by any human mind. The manifested values are elements in a structural system of beauty and goodness which is much more complete and perfect than the sum of the manifestations. What actually seems to be true is that the manifestations derive their intrinsic character from the inclusive standard. Such standards are real though they do not "exist" in minds or in nature.

It is clear that to Tennant we have no right to affirm that such unactualized standards "exist" if they do not "exist" in human minds or in nature. In accordance with our definition of "existence," we must agree that absolute values do not "exist"; but we do not agree with Tennant's insistence that such values do not belong to the realm of reality. The structure of unactualized, unconceived values possesses a stubborn, necessary reality so that any further developments in our conception of values must conform to the real, absolute pattern. Just as our thinking must conform to the patterns of logical truth, so must our future appreciations conform to the perfect pattern of the highest, absolute values. Otherwise any future, higher value-construction is equally true which means that there is no true good or beauty at all or that man is the measure of all things.

If, however, we refuse to accept these implications and hold to the extramental reality of absolute values, the question then arises, do these values simply subsist alone or are they grounded in a supreme mind and will. Certainly materialistic mechanism

cannot account for them; they are neither physical nor mechanical. Hence, either they are the result of a chance integration of essences or subsistences, or they are the intended values
of the divine spirit whose nature is absolute goodness and absolute beauty as well as absolute truth. Such values are known
and willed by God, from whose nature or spiritual capacities
they derive their reality. We as human beings do not comprehend them, but in the moment when our creative vision beholds
through a glass darkly the constraining pattern underlying our
forthcoming conceptions of higher values, we apprehend not
only the underlying pattern but feel also the inspiring presence
of the divine nature. This is the religious experience at its highest, an experience which involves a relationship with the spiritual nature from which the values derive their reality. Granted
the authenticity of this deeper religious experience, the argument from absolute values to a source confirms this experience.
The religious experience is not first a causal inference or hypothesis from values; but the inference does sustain the theistic
interpretation.

(5) *The Saturation of Nature with Beauty*

Proceeding now to values which are actualized or realized in
nature, it is necessary to note the fact of manifested beauty and
to indicate the implications of this fact for theism. Both inorganic and organic nature exhibit beauty; i.e., they exhibit not
simply secondary qualities but a certain texture, delicacy of
blending, or harmoniousness which we term, beauty. Such delicacy may be contributed by the human mind to the stimulation
of ontal nature, or it may be a characteristic of ontal nature itself. In the former case, beauty is phenomenal and subjective;
in the latter case, it is ontal and objective. In Tennant's judgment, the issue need not be settled with finality, for in either
case beauty may be regarded as the expression of the divine
purpose. Tennant insists, however, that if beauty is phenomenal,
there must be something in the structure of the ontal to evoke
it in minds which stand in relationship to actual nature. This
represents an application of duality-theory to esthetic appreciation and implies that beauty is not a purely subjective state

in the mind without any objective control. Either beauty or its counterpart characterizes ontal nature beyond the subjective shading of mind. Some such objective reality of beauty must be maintained; otherwise, there is no true beauty manifested in existent things and situations. If the diverse appreciations of various people are equally true of any single manifestation of beauty, then there is no real beauty; mistaken beauty or partial ugliness is beauty; and there can be no basis for common agreement as to the true value whatsoever. Such implications are not easy to square with our normal conviction that Shakespeare's plays, the statue of Venus, a mountain peak, are beautiful whether anyone thinks so or not, that such objects ought to be appreciated as beautiful, and that there is an intrinsic value in the object insistently calling to be appreciated truly.

Certainly in the case of beauty in the inorganic world it is difficult to understand how the mental appreciation of beauty could have evolved unless something in the environment persistently evoked it. In the case of organic beauty, sexual selection is not sufficient to account for the manifold beauty of organisms. Beauty is more than brightness or intensity of color; it is delicacy, exquisiteness, harmony, and blend of color and hue. To assume that insects and animals are attracted to mates who possess not simply brilliance of color but delicacy of shading is to assume that these creatures have an esthetic taste which is rare among human beings. Beauty is not a utilitarian quality; it has an intrinsic character; and it saturates the entire realm of nature.

What then is the cause of this widespread presence of beauty in nature? Mechanism, in the human realm, is not invariably beautiful. More often than not man-made machinery is hideous. Can we then suppose that mechanism has an invariable, intrinsic quality of beauty about it? It is possible that this be true but not practically probable. Is beauty, then, an outcome of chance? Here again such interpretation is possible but practically improbable. If the manifestations of beauty were sporadic or seldom discoverable, it might be easy to accept the chance-hypothesis, but its actualization is too continual and too widespread to convert possibility into practical probability. The more reasonable inference is that a supreme artist has expressed his genius, plan, and inspiration in the individual things and situations where beauty is found.

Perhaps, as in the realm of human art, a large part of the delight which we experience in appreciating a masterpiece resides in our appreciation of the inspiration and genius of the artist, so in the realm of nature, much of our emotional excitement is due to our deeper recognition of the genius and purpose of the creator. Such recognition assumes the religious apprehension of the divine presence manifesting its ideals in the beauties of nature. Beauty, of course, might be conceived as constituting a realm of subsistence without any grounding in the divine life and nature, but this position must be relinquished if the religious experience which accompanies the esthetic experience is valid. The experience of actualized esthetic value is fulfilled and completed by direct religious awareness of the divine spirit. The inference from actualized beauty to a divine source confirms this experience by more adequately accounting for the value than mechanism or chance.

(6) The Actualization of Moral Values

Two major issues are confronted when the theological implications of moral values are defended: first, the question of objectivity with the attendant issues of origin, validity, and authority; and second, the problem of the relation of nature to the realization of moral values; i.e., is the world hostile, friendly, or neutral as far as man's struggle for moral ideals is concerned? With respect to the first, the answer may be reconstructed from a criticism of Tennant's position. To the unsocialized individual, according to Tennant, "the good" refers to "the desirable" and not to an objective quality of an act. "The desirable" is "the pleasurable," first to the bodily and then to the inner self. When the individual becomes socialized, he becomes aware of that which is good or desirable to others, achieves a social standard, and applies this standard to his own conduct from the vantage point of a socialized spectator. The psychological drive behind his effort to obey the social standard is sympathy. Sympathy and creative idealization result in oversocial refinements of the common standards to which he pledges inward obedience. Standards are thus subjective creations of socially experienced minds.

The truth of this theory is open to suspicion on the following grounds: (1) moral standards have an obligatory character which is equivalent neither to desirability nor to sympathy. When in human life, one experiences the obligation, for example, to speak the truth though the heavens fall upon him, he is not experiencing an impulse of pleasure; he is not speaking the truth in order to secure future pleasure; and he is not acting out of sympathy for others. He is rather facing an unconditional "must" or demand, which cuts across his desires, his feelings, and his sympathies, and which is required for its intrinsic rightness. Irrespective of results, the moral man obeys the insistent demand of his conscience to speak the truth upon a specific occasion because it is right to speak the truth. By no psychological alchemy can an "ought" be produced out of pleasurable feeling, desire, and sympathy. (2) If there is any true right or good action in a specific situation, it can never be created out of socialized desires. Not all desires of an individual are truly right and good, neither are all the desires of the collective community of individuals. Neither, also, is it true that common desires are invariably right or good. In the intellectual sphere truth is neither equivalent to the opinions of various people nor invariably equivalent to the common opinions of a majority of people. Neither is the truly good equivalent to the preferences of a majority of people. Whenever we say that Jesus, for example, is a truly good individual, we mean by that statement more than the fact that many people think so. We mean that Jesus is good whether many people or even whether anyone thinks so or not. We imply that there is an intrinsic quality in Jesus which all men ought to judge good whether they do or not. Undoubtedly the widespread judgment on the part of many people helps an individual to attain his own judgment of good conduct, but the truly good is something more than the sum of opinions and preferences. It has an intrinsic, objective, necessary character which compels mental acts of recognition. This compulsion is not analogous to physical coercion which annihilates the individual will and drives the individual irresistibly ahead of it by overwhelming power and might. It is a compulsion which awaits recognition by the individual, permits misconception and error, and allows the consequences of recognition or error to follow. In this respect it is comparable to the truth, $2 + 2 = 4$. One may think that $2 + 2 = 5$, but consequences follow this belief, and the truth is there stubbornly insisting upon recognition. Human freedom is not abrogated if the human mind does not make the truth true or goodness good. The creative freedom of the mind resides in its power to generate opinions about the truth and preferences of the good.

For two reasons, then, Tennant's theory of moral value must be rejected. It does not provide for the true character of obligation, nor does it provide for real, objective standards. Granted then that there are objective standards of good and right realized and actualized in the conduct of existent individuals, the question arises, from whence come these standards which individual minds do not create out of themselves alone, but which they recognize through their judgments and realize in conduct? As in the case of esthetic values, several possible explanations are available. They may be the outcome of chance coincidence, but this seems unlikely in view of the widespread experience of moral values. They may have reality apart from any ultimate ground, but the religious experience of men who catch intimations of the divine presence in conjunction with the experience of obligatory moral values offers a basis for making the rational inference that objective standards are grounded in the nature of God. Certainly mechanistic materialism cannot account for moral standards, for these standards are not material in character. Furthermore, if materialism is the true explanation of the world, then no standards can be moral for there is no free will in man; his choices are the automatic functions of his brain; and whatever he thinks right is right because necessary. Theism is thus the most plausible explanation of objective moral standards.

The second major problem in conjunction with the theological implications of moral values must now be indicated. Is nature friendly or instrumental to the realization of moral ideals? Certainly the first consideration of importance is the fact that man is "organic to nature," or, in other phraseology, man is the "child of nature." If it be true that man's soul comes directly from God, noumenal man cannot be conceived as coming from nature. Phenomenal man; i.e., his bodily organism, is clearly the product of cosmic evolution; man's organism represents the goal and crowning achievement of the whole course of inorganic and organic development; hence, in this sense we may say that man is the "child of nature." So complicated, however, are the adjustments of this evolutionary process that it is practically impossible to think of them as the result of chance or instinctive operations. Yet, whether we draw the theistic conclusion or not, nature is at least friendly enough to man to produce his organism. Nature is not absolutely hostile nor is it absolutely neutral.

The second point of importance is that nature supplies the background and stage upon which human beings play the roles of moral creatures. Nature cannot be thought to supply man with ethical ideals and maxims, but rather with a general existential background. Nature is largely law-abiding, uniform, and dependable. As such, nature often causes suffering and pain to embodied minds, but if nature were pure chaos, no intelligent understanding of the external world would be possible at all, no ideas or universal principles would hold true of nature at all, and no intelligent life would be possible. Insofar as moral life presupposes the relatively stable existence of life and a basic intelligent comprehension of the natural world, nature which supplies these conditions cannot be considered either hostile or neutral in relation to moral life. In fact, much of the unpredictable, chance hardships, which seem to occur in nature, in reality prove to be the conditions of moral achievement. If nature were an absolutely static system, no growth in triumphant character would be possible. Obviously, nature is not adjusted to secure perpetual pleasure for everyone, but there are possibilities in all types of circumstances for human beings to react morally and to do their duty for its own sake. Hence by supplying the conditions of intelligent thought and the opportunities for moral response, nature may be said to be friendly to ethical man.

Perhaps a further word needs to be said with respect to the bodily appetites and animal impulses of man. It may be charged that these are responsible for perpetual sin and crime on the part of man, and hence prove that nature is hostile to moral living. But, as Tennant has said, morality presupposes raw materials which can be constrained by will into ideal patterns. Nature puts a premium upon health, vigor, temperance, and self-control. Animal impulses, though exacting at times, offer the conditions of moral achievement. This being the case, it cannot be said that nature is entirely hostile to morality nor entirely neutral. It is friendly in the sense that it supplies the conditions which make moral living to some degree possible.

The larger question as to whether nature will continue indefinitely to support such realization of moral values in view of the prospective extinction of our environment in solar death is not to be answered easily. This question ultimately rests upon the existence of God whose perfect goodness finally rests upon the fact that He will preserve the conditions of indefinite moral progress in the world or else sustain the lives of worthy men in an immortality wherein the moral achievement of individuals is continued and sustained. That such is the case we have no widespread empirical evidence. Hence unless we are tacitly to inject a future possible experience into the evidence of the present, in which nature is roughly able to sustain the realization of some moral ideals, we must admit that the perfect goodness of God cannot be proved by natural theology. With the evidence we have available, it is not improbable that there is an intelligent designer of nature whose purpose it is to make nature instrumental to moral realization, but that progressively higher ideals will be realized must be a matter of valor grounded in the hope that a God, who is great enough and good enough to make the world as it is, is great enough and good enough to sustain the personalities and the moral achievements of men through whatever crises and catastrophes nature may bring them. The only validation which is open to us then resides in the practical value which is discovered in living on the basis of a hope. If life lived on this basis proves to be richer and more complete in ethical character than a life lived upon some other basis, then some evidence is given for the ultimate truth of this hope and faith. Certainly in practical life theories which do not make a valuable difference in action are not ultimately found to be true. Applying this test to antitheistic theories we may suppose that in the long run they destroy morale by introducing pessimism and despair. Hence if such is the case, serious doubt must be entertained as to their truth. Conversely the ability of theism to sustain morale and moral optimism is some evidence of its truth.

Summary

Thus by diverse channels, theism comes to be a more reasonable world-explanation than mechanism, chance, or unconscious purpose. The office of reason has been first to break up the objective maze of experienced reality into certain general areas of factual and valuational structure, second to ask whether or not these lines of evidence are practically explicable by reference to mechanism, chance, or unconscious purpose, and third to indicate wherein theism is the more reasonably adequate principle of explanation. Such a principle of explanation, it has been persistently argued, is not the actual reality of religious experience; it rather confirms the supposition that the God of religious experience is also the God of the cosmos. This, in summary, is the nature of the validation offered by a teleological explanation of nature and values. The arguments from nature and value are inadequate without the primary fact of religious experience which is confirmed by rational argument within its own sphere. Religious experience, on the other hand, cannot establish the theistic world-explanation by itself. Neither can the moral argument succeed apart from the teleological interpretation of the physical world. These three types of reasonable validation are interdependent though religious experience is primary and practical-value-for-living the final confirmation of the complete and perfect goodness of God.

C. THE PROBLEM OF EVIL, ITS CHALLENGE TO THEISM AND A REASONABLE ANSWER

At this point the problem of evil thrusts itself into the situation as the chief source of doubt as to the finality of the theistic explanation thus confirmed and validated. The problem arises in theology from an attempt to be loyal to three distinct assertions: (1) the sovereignty of one God, the creator, sustainer, and controller of the world's destiny; (2) the reality of natural and moral evil in the world; (3) the goodness of God; in such a way as to deny no one of these and yet find some significant meaning which will include all of them. The difficulties of the solutions offered in the history of theology bear a direct relationship to the strength of the emphasis which is first placed upon any one of these propositions. If, for example, the sover-

eignty of God is stressed, and if evil is still considered to be a
reality, then strict consistency leads the exponent to assert that
God who is asserted to be good causes evil as a part of his pre-
determined plan, thus leaving us with the theoretical puzzle of
calling the author of evil good. If, on the other hand, the goodness of God is stressed and His sovereignty is also maintained,
consistency of emphasis will lead to the transfiguration of evil
into (a) an illusion, or (b) a deprivation or absence of good, or
(c) a necessary discord in the larger harmony of the whole, thus
presenting us with a denial that evil is really evil. If evil is an
illusion then our normal value-judgments are false, and the
evilness of the illusion or of the wrong standpoint is still left
unexplained. If evil is simply absence of good, we have to face
the apparent fact that evil is often a very positive force and
that our judgments falsify its real character. If it is a necessary
discord in the larger harmony of the whole, then it is either still
real discord, or it is an illusory discord, and our value-judgments are false. If, on the other hand, emphasis is placed upon
the reality of evil, and the goodness of God is also asserted, consistency leads to the recognition of a challenge by one or more
forces to God's complete sovereignty. An absolute dualism will
maintain that God is confronted by an evil principle which is
self-existent and independent of God. This principle of evil may
be a spiritual being; i.e., a devil, or a material being; i.e., re-
fractory matter. Absolute pluralism would, of course, involve
a denial of God entirely, thus dissolving the problem of evil but
only dissolving it to replace it with the problem of good which
theism solves more adequately than alternative theories. But the
results of absolute dualism are: (1) a dethroned God; (2) a
second God or factor whose existence is ultimate and unexplica-
ble in terms of God; and (3) an assertion that evil is as ultimate
as good, a fact which makes such unity as we have in the world
a dire mystery and arrests our hope for an ultimate victory of
good over evil.

Believing that God is the only truly independent power in the
world and that all other forces are ultimately dependent upon
him, holding to the reality of evil, and, still, to the goodness of
God, some theists try to trace the extramundane conditions of
the necessity of evil without relinquishing God's sovereignty or

His goodness. An attempt is made to find an inferior devil, as it were, which arises as a by-product of the creative purpose of a good God who chooses to make an evolutionary world. This is the way of relative dualism, the way which Tennant takes, and the way which, in this, or modifiable form, must be taken if all three factors are to be held and there is to be any explanation of evil at all.

Natural evil is in large measure the unavoidable by-product of a natural order which is necessarily an order and not a chaos; otherwise no life or development would be possible in an indeterminate world. Moral evil is the unavoidable result of an order of free persons whose freedom of choice implies freedom to choose evil as well as good if moral character, the only final good, is to be achieved. If God's central purpose; namely, the progressive development of moral personalities, is good, and if evils are inescapable in making a world in which the attainment of this good end is possible, God is still good in character even though real evil enters this world as an unwelcomed condition.

Yet it should be noted that not all the evil in the world order is explainable upon the basis of this by-product theory of evil. There is apparently a surplus of evil which presents us with dark and awesome mystery. Facing this ultimate, inexplicable darkness and placing an emphasis upon its inexplicability, some theists insist that the problem of evil is insolvable and that the ways of God are utterly transcendent. They will charge a position comparable to Tennant's with easygoing optimism, rationalism, and anthropomorphism.

But certainly Tennant is not unmindful of the mystery of evil. If, in early stages of his argument, he seems to be oversanguine, as, for example, when he states that evil does not come out of good but good may and often does come out of evil, or when he insists upon the benefits of a rigidly determined order of nature, it must also be remembered that the end of his argument is characterized by a discussion of what he calls "the trial of faith," or the evil which passes understanding. Furthermore, at no point in his argument does he undertake a demonstration of the providential purpose of specific evils. He insists that the just distribution of evil with respect to moral merit is not evident, and contends that God cannot be conceived to be morally perfect unless He grant immortality to human spirits. For immortality, there is no evidence other than our hope in the existence of a perfectly good God. For the existence of a perfectly good God, there is no coercive, self-evident assurance, but only a faith which has "probability" enough behind it to be hope not utterly blind though sorely tried. Certainly this is not easygoing optimism. It is optimism, true enough, but not in the sense that evil will ever be entirely eliminated from this world. Evil there will be as long as nature is uniform and human wills are free. Yet there is no such pessimism in Tennant as would allow the expectation of absolute evil or utter destruction of good in the earthly future. Tennant is too much of an evolutionist to feel that moral progress will not be made in the future. His optimism is undismayed by the possibilities of solar destruction; in fact, it is in this connection that he appeals to the unknown universe for restoration of energies when he has denied previously that the possibilities of the unknown are able to deny teleology throughout the whole universe. His optimism does not necessarily rest in earthly progress, however, for it is really in immortality that man's future hope resides, and it is to immortality that he is really committed in his personal faith.

Thus it is plain that, while Tennant realizes the surplus mystery of evil, he does not emphasize that mystery to such an extent that he can give no explanation for its presence in a world created and directed by a good God. It would seem to be true that if one is optimistic enough to venture forth on the presupposition that the problem is in any measure reasonably solvable, it is along the line Tennant has taken. His theodicy does not relax the necessity for moral struggle; it rather lends that struggle an encouraging background. It does not declare evil to be an illusion or an appearance of good. It accepts evil as real but not as an absolute principle on a par with God. In other words, it maintains a relative as against an absolute dualism. Unless it is possible to support a position of "relative dualism" or "semidualism" as being mainly reasonable, there is no alternative but "absolute insolvability" and transcendent mystery, if evil is Real and a good God exists.

Rejecting the position of utter insolvability and accepting the position that relative dualism or semidualism is basically reasonable, it is important to note two criticisms which are brought against Tennant's theodicy. The first is this. While it is logically correct to argue, as Tennant does, that you cannot have the advantages of a determinate order of nature without the accompanying disadvantages, the real question is: must all determinate systems involve as much evil as the one which we know does involve?[14] If God is great enough to be Creator of the universe, and if He is as good as Tennant believes Him to be, is it not conceivable that such a Being could have, and perhaps ought to have, brought into being a determinate system which would have less natural evil than there apparently is in this one?

Such a question as this has little significance to Tennant. He maintains that we have no knowledge of possible determinate systems, and that we have no right to think of God as entertaining ideas of various possible universes before He brought this one into being. We have this universe before us and no other; we derive notions of possible universes from this actual universe and not actual universes from possible ones. God is ground of the actual world; the two are coeternal; and the conception of God-without-a-world entertaining thoughts of possible worlds is not legitimate, according to empirical principles of theological procedure.

This answer is partially convincing, but it requires certain modifications. In order to be consistent with its principles, it requires a straightforward acceptance of the eternity and self-existence of primitive matter. For, if matter is not eternal, then empirical analogies to the creation of the world are valueless, and if empirical procedure—empirical in Tennant's sense of keeping perpetual touch with sensory experience—is deserted for speculative analogies and mysteries, then there is no ground to insist upon the truth of the coeternity-of-the-world-and-God-together and the falsity of the orthodox doctrine of God-without-the-world-before-creation-of-the-world-in-time.

Certainly there is nothing illogical about a beginning of the ontal world in time. If emergent evolution is true, there certainly has been a time when God existed without aspects of the

14. This criticism is Broad's. Cf. review of *Philosophical Theology,* II, in *Mind,* XXXIX, 483.

world which we know through science. Of reality prior to the
"primary collocations" with which the evolution of the known
world began, we certainly have no empirically elaborated knowledge. Hence there seems to be no point to holding that empirical method necessitates the ruling out of the idea of God-without-a-world. If empirical analogies fail to be applicable to a
divine creator, and if he is truly independent of the world, there
is no necessity for holding to the theory of eternal creation,
against orthodox theism. If this be true, there is likewise no
reason why the actual world restricts the possible worlds to one,
and also, no reason why God could not have entertained conceptual possibilities prior to creation. In other words, against orthodox theism, Broad's criticism is appropriately severe.

There is a conception which needs to be carefully scrutinized
in Tennant's theory, and that is, the-indispensability-of-this-
world-to-God. This world may be indispensable to man's knowledge of God, and the conception of evil as following necessarily
from a determinate order of nature and from human freedom
may also be an important element in theodicy, but the use of the
indispensability-of-this-world-to-God to overrule God's consideration of other possible determinate systems and the idea of
His-existence-without-a-world is fallacious. It restricts God's
sovereignty by introducing an absolute dualism in reality if not
in name, and does so without a basis in empirical procedure. If
such a dualism is held, it must be established upon true empirical analogies; namely, the idea of "creation" as the organization of primitive, eternal matter by the will of God working in
accordance with plan and purpose. Then it can more legitimately support an answer to the criticism that God ought to
have made a less evil determinate order than the one which exists.

Acceptance of such a dualism must face the implications of
extensive limitation to God's sovereignty, but no dire results
follow. To admit that primitive matter is self-existent and eternal is no more unreasonable than to accept the indispensability
and coeternality of the world-and-God, or the creation of physical, quantitative reality out of God who is pure spirit. Matter
and spirit being such unlike realities, it is slightly more reasonable, probably because more empirical, to maintain the coeter-
nity and relational independence of both. Such a position does

not cut off all hope of a final victory of good over evil, for matter in itself is not evil, though it may cause suffering. If God, as spirit, be perfectly good, He can still work out a progressively suitable physical situation and provide immortality for persons. In other words, no ethically disastrous implications need follow from the semidualism here suggested.

The second criticism of Tennant's theodicy is this: While theism must make some place for the moral freedom of man, Tennant emphasizes the freedom of man to such an extent that the operations of divine grace upon an impotent human will are practically ruled out of the picture. Tennant is Pelagian in his belief in the potency of the human will and in his moralistic emphasis. This criticism[15] comes from religious people rather than secularists who raise the first objection; i.e., must all determinate orders be as evil as the one we know? It comes from people who believe that insight into the divine ideal and an experience of the saving, redeeming influence of God comes to man not by virtue of a willed effort on man's part to achieve his own ideals with the idea of God as a general background or orientation, but by virtue of the prior act of God upon the blind and impotent spirit of man. In other words, the criticism implies that the religious experience of grace has no significant, necessary place in Tennant's philosophical theology.

This, of course, opens another line of discussion which is irrelevant to the general acceptance of his theodicy in the face of secular challenges. One comment may be made, however, which represents an opinion only, and that is this. In the history of Christianity, Christian leaders have always maintained two incompatible positions: human freedom and human bondage broken by acts of grace. No reconciliation of these opposites is completely possible; the tension is partially relaxed by an emphasis upon one position or the other. Paul, Augustine, and Luther placed the emphasis upon the impotency of man and the action of divine grace. They undoubtedly discovered the psychological advantages of turning the mind from its own imperfect performance toward the gracious redemption of God's spirit in the heart of man. Yet, on the other hand, while they emphasized

15. Cf. review of *Philosophical Theology* by R. Mackintosh, *The Congregational Quarterly*, VIII, 374 ff.; also *The Expository Times*, XL, 348 ff.

divine grace they did not practically deny the necessity of voluntary exertion of the will. The Catholic position in the main has been semi-Pelegian. In any case, the freedom of the will has not practically been denied even when theoretically overruled as in Calvinism. Genuine human freedom is basic to Christian theism, and this implies the possibility of evil, as Tennant rightfully states.

A Final Review of Epistemological Issues with Reference to Santayana

Accepting Tennant's theodicy as essentially sufficient to overcome such doubt as would completely reject theism, one final problem may be reviewed; namely, the epistemological issue of monistic or dualistic realism and the definitions of "immediate experience," "intuition," knowledge, and faith. The issue is this. Is there any sense in which we can "immediately experience" or "intuit" a metaphysical object, or do we "immediately experience" or "intuit" a phenomenal object (other terms for which may be "datum," "sensum," "essence," "idea") which is existentially and numerically distinct from the metaphysical object and know the metaphysical object only by inference (mediate and analogical)? The argument of this book has been that it is impossible, starting with an "immediate experience" of sensa, to achieve an apprehension of a metaphysical object by mediate, analogical inference. This is true of metaphysical "things" or substance-causes; it is true of metaphysical other selves; it is true of a metaphysical God. The term "metaphysical" is used in the sense of "ontal" as referring to an existent reality which exists independently of its being known. In the case of other selves and God it has been argued that, unless something more than mere sensa are "given" to the subject, no possible way to apprehension of other selves and God is open by mediate, analogical inference even though the subject may have experience of one living self, namely, his own. It has been argued that "immediate experience" or "intuition" of other selves and God is fundamentally necessary and prior to any "mediate analogical inferences" from sense-experience and introspection. It has been persistently insisted that we have "immediate experience" of other selves and God which is not simply experience of phenomena but of noumena through the phenomena; that if in sense-perception experience of the noumenal through the phenomenal can be described as "immediate," then it is necessary to apply the term "immediate" to the experience of the noumenal through the extraspectively personal and religious phenomenal. Sufficient dualism has been allowed to make room for error and conceptualization. Sufficient duality has been insisted upon to make knowledge possible. Knowledge may be faith or belief, but it is "immediate," "direct," "intuitive" faith which involves independent reality as well as the phenomenal datum. The terms "immediate," "direct," and "intuitive" are used to designate a type of cognitive act which is not inference, explicit or implicit, and not simply awareness of sensa, persona, or *numina*. The definition can be illuminated by reference to the writings of certain critical realists who deal mainly with knowledge of the physical world.

To Santayana,[16] no account of knowledge is adequate unless it draws a distinction between existence and essence; i.e., between noumenon and phenomenon, independent reality and the given datum of awareness. The subject intuits the essence; he believes in the existence of an independent reality of which the essence is a qualitative characterization. The essence is not the independent existent; it is not a mental state; neither can it be said to exist in the mind. It is neither physical nor mental;[17] i.e., neither intrinsically thing, nor a thought, nor the spirit's act of intuition.

"Intuition cannot reveal any fact, it is pure fancy"; "in order to reach existence intent must transcend intuition and take data for what they mean, not for what they are."[18] Existent facts are experienced first by belief or animal faith in their existence and then by the affirmation and description of their bare existence in terms of essences which are intuited. Belief in an existent thing is never "direct perception" or "intuition";[19] intuition of essences is not "knowledge" nor "experience" of facts.[20] Essences are immediate and unsubstantial;[21] the distinction between truth and error does not apply to them. Illusions are essences as well as other character-complexes which are correctly believed to describe existent facts.[22] "Intuition runs no risk of

16. *Scepticism and Animal Faith.*   17. *Ibid.*, p. 92; cf. pp. 128, 130.
18. *Ibid.*, p. 65.   19. *Ibid.*, p. 167.
20. *Ibid.*, p. 138.   21. *Ibid.*, p. 90.
22. *Ibid.*, p. 46.

error for it has no ulterior object."[23] Animal faith in existent
fact always precedes the intuition of essences in terms of which
the existent is described.[24] Nevertheless, essences are indispensable terms in the perception of matters of fact and renders
transitive knowledge possible.[25] Essences are "vehicular,"[26] the
terms by which the animal thinks of the existent. Essences do
not *resemble* the existent; they are *relevant* to the existent;[27]
i.e., the essences are not the same in nature as the qualities of
existent fact. They are, however, good symbols or descriptive
words which more or less accurately describe the believed-in-
existent. Knowledge is always perception of a reality which
transcends the essences, yet to which the essences are relevant
descriptive symbols.

Before attempting to criticize Santayana's conception of essences, it is necessary to ask if the term "intuition" must necessarily be restricted to awareness of essences only. Other critical
realists apply the terms "intuitive" and "immediate" to the primary, prior belief in existent fact, however later described by
the symbols of given data. A. K. Rogers states that there are
two main forms of "intuitive or primitive belief."[28] By an intuitive or primitive belief he means a "belief that rests on its own
bottom and does not depend upon security borrowed from other
beliefs."[29] He distinguishes "intuition in the stricter sense, where
confidence seems to depend on the immediate seeing that a thing
is self-evidently so"[30] and belief in another sense; namely, the
conviction that sensations, geometrical intuitions, logical demands, and remembered events actually give information about,
and apply to, a real world of things and forces. This latter belief in a real world of existent facts is described in the following
manner: "Any assurance that I may have about an independently existing world may be intuitive in the sense that it is simple, immediate, and strongly self-confident; but it can never be
self-evident, for the reason that, as such a world never is directly identified with its description as an idea in my mind, I
can conceive myself mistaken in my reference."[31]

23. *Ibid.,* p. 70.   24. *Ibid.,* pp. 107, 179.
25. *Ibid.,* p. 80.   26. *Ibid.,* p. 81.
27. *Ibid.,* pp. 84, 88.   28. A. K. Rogers, *What Is Truth?,* p. 7.
29. *Ibid.,* p. 7.   30. *Ibid.*
31. *Ibid.,* p. 40.

Apparently belief in independent reality can be described as intuitive, instinctive, primitive, simple, immediate, and self-confident, but insofar as error is always possible the belief that any experienced-content describes independent reality cannot be characterized by invariable self-evidence. Santayana, therefore, uses "intuition" and "immediacy" in the narrow sense to describe the act by which a subject is conscious of the given-data before it. Rogers permits the term in a wider sense to designate what Santayana describes as "animal faith."

From this it is apparent that the terms "immediate experience" and "intuition" which have been employed in this treatise to describe physical, extraspective, and religious perception are used in the wider, inclusive meanings of Rogers to cover not only awareness of data but also consciousness of independent realities. The possibility of error has been persistently admitted in physical, personal, and religious awareness, but insofar as perception is true, we "immediately experience" the noumenal or independent reality through the phenomenal. "Immediate experience" may be an act of animal, moral, or religious faith, but it is not an inference, implicit or explicit, from data which are absolutely dislocated from the stimulating presence of independent reality, and it is not composed solely of awareness of independent data or essences. If it be clearly understood that knowledge involves a noninferential direct awareness of independent reality through the configurations of data; then it is not incorrect to call knowledge "intuition," or "faith," or "belief," or "immediate experience," as long as such terms mean or involve this type of awareness.

Turning now to Santayana's conception of essence more specifically, certain difficulties may be set forth. It does not seem correct to define essences in such a way that there is no difference between essences which are illusions and essences which are truly relevant character-complexes applicable to independent objects. If independent objects never come into the range of direct experience, and if independent objects have no part in determining what the essences are, then what basis is there for validly believing that some essences characterize existents whereas others do not. Santayana makes exceedingly confusing statements about the relation of an existent fact to the essences in terms of which it is described. Essences "are not given until attention is stretched out upon the thing, which is posited blindly in action; . . . they come as revelations or oracles, delivered by that thing to the mind, and symbolizing it there."[32] Yet essences are never existent objects themselves, nor any part of them; "essences are not drawn out or abstracted from things."[33] "Essences, in order to appear, do not need to beg leave of what happens to exist, or to draw its portrait."[34] "In themselves essences have no genesis; . . . In seizing upon any particular essence first, discourse is guided by an irrational fatality."[35] Intuition arbitrarily assaults the realm of essence,[36] yet upon the occasion of attending to a thing in the environment, it selects essences which have neither genesis nor psychological or physical existence, and the subject believes that some of these characterize the existent object in some cases truly and in other cases falsely.

It is legitimate to ask: What basis does one have to believe that certain essences are true and others false if existent objects do not reveal themselves in the essences? By intuiting nonexistent essences no one can intuit or infer existent things; if attention is first directed toward existent things, there must be signs other than essences to mark their arrival before the act of attention. But the essences are the only signs which come before the consciousness of the subject; therefore, the existent must give itself in the garb-of-existent-essences. Therefore, also, existent-essences must differ from imaginary-essences; percepts must differ from images; otherwise there is no real world at all. Knowledge of the real world is always impure and colored by the dark glasses of the embodied mind, but no matter how colored the vision of the real world may be, the real world is still seen through the glasses darkly. An absolute dualism between essence and existence is utterly impassable even by faith; a relative duality-in-unity, though difficult to maintain, nevertheless makes faith possible. Such faith, we have maintained throughout this book, is possible in the existence of substance-causes, other selves, and God.

32. *Op. cit.*, p. 94.   33. *Ibid.*, p. 93.
34. *Ibid.*, p. 97.   35. *Ibid.*, p. 132.
36. *Ibid.*, p. 132.

BIBLIOGRAPHY

CHRONOLOGICAL LIST OF TENNANT'S PUBLISHED WRITINGS

The following published writings of Frederick Robert Tennant constitute the source material employed in this book. (Listed according to date of appearance.)

Book: *The Origin and Propagation of Sin;* Being the Hulsean Lectures Delivered Before The University of Cambridge in 1901–2. Cambridge, University Press, 1902.

Book: *The Sources of the Doctrines of the Fall and Original Sin.* Cambridge, University Press, 1903.

Lecture: "The Child and Sin" in *The Child and Religion,* ed. by Thomas Stephen. London, Williams and Norgate, 1905.

Essay: "The Being of God, in the Light of Physical Science," chap. ii, *Cambridge Theological Essays,* ed. by H. B. Swete. Cambridge, University Press, 1905.

Book: *The Concept of Sin.* Cambridge, University Press, 1912.

Book Reviews: "Divine Transcendence and its Reflection in Religious Authority" (by J. R. Illingworth); "The Realm of Ends" (by J. Ward); "Problems in the Relation of God and Man" (by C. C. J. Webb): In *The Journal of Theological Studies,* XIII, 310, 447, 453. 1911–12.

Articles: "The Services of Philosophy to Theology"; "The Philosophy of Religion as an Autonomous Subject"; "The Aim and Scope of the Philosophy of Religion": In *The Expositor,* 8th ser., VI, 140, 250, 342. 1913.

Book Review: "The Philosophy of Religion" (by G. Galloway): In *The Journal of Theological Studies,* XVI, 122. 1914–15.

Book Reviews: "Belief and Practice" (by W. Spens); "The Commonitorium of Vincent Lerins" (by R. S. Moxon); "God and Freedom in Human Experience" (by C. F. D'Arcy); "Theism and Humanism" (by A. J. Balfour): In *The Journal of Theological Studies,* XVII, 203, 414, 198, 193. 1915–16.

Lectures: "Problem of the Existence of Moral Evil"; "The Problem of Suffering"; in *Elements of Pain and Conflict in Human Life.* Cambridge, University Press, 1916.

Articles: "Perfection in God and in Man"; "The Possible Meanings of 'Eternal' in the New Testament": In *The Expository Times,* ed. by James Hastings, XXIX, 202, 265. 1917–18.

Articles: "The New Realism and its Bearing on Theism," No. 1, p. 57; "The New Realism and its Bearing on Theism," No. 2, p. 246: In *The Constructive Quarterly*, VI. 1918.

Book Reviews: "Evolution and The Doctrine of the Trinity" (by S. A. McDowall); "Moral Values and the Idea of God" (by W. R. Sorley); "Psychological Principles" (by J. Ward); "Reconciliation and Reality" (by W. F. Halliday); "Suffering, Punishment and Atonement" (by E. W. Johnson): In *The Journal of Theological Studies*, XX, 261, 253, 370, 370. 1918–19.

Articles: "The Concept of the Infinite in Theology"; "The Concept of Perfection as Applied to God"; "Eternity": In *The Expositor*, XV, 161, 260, 447. 1918.

Article: "The Doctrine of Trinity; in Dogmatic Theology": In *The Expositor*, XVI, 270. 1918.

Articles: "Divine Love and the World's Evil," p. 128; "The Trial of Faith Involved in Theological Reconstruction," p. 701: In *The Constructive Quarterly*, VII. 1919.

Article: "The Doctrine of Trinity; In Philosophy": In *The Expositor*, XVII, 447. 1919.

Article: "The Development of Doctrine": In *The Expositor*, XVIII, 140. 1919.

Articles: "The Theological Significance of the Early Chapters of Genesis"; "Moral Arguments for the Existence of God"; "The Psychology of Sin"; "The Problem of Pain and Suffering"; "The Existence of Moral Evil": In *The Expository Times*, XXX, 297, 358, 411, 473, 519. 1918–19.

Articles: "Divine Omnipotence"; "The Conception of a Finite God"; "Creation and the Origin of the Soul": In *The Expository Times*, XXXI, 34, 89, 185. 1919–20.

Book Reviews: "The Construction of the World in Terms of Fact and Value" (by C. T. H. Walker); "Interpretation of the Spiritual Philosophy" (by J. Gurnhill); "The Problem of Evil" (by P. Green); "Science and Theology" (by F. W. Westway); "Some Religious Implications of Pragmatism" (by J. R. Geiger): In *The Journal of Theological Studies*, XXI, 365, 359, 363. 1919–20.

Articles: "Questions Preliminary to Critical Reconstruction in Theology," p. 19; "The Present Condition of Some Fundamental Christian Doctrines," p. 466; "The Present Condition of the Doctrine of the Incarnation and the Trinity," p. 261: In *The Constructive Quarterly*, VIII. 1920.

Article: "The Central Problem of Faith": In *The Expository Times*, ed. by James Hastings, XXXII. 1920–21.

Article: "The Present Relations of Science and Theology: (1) The

Theological Bearings of Empirical Science": In *The Constructive Quarterly*, IX, 578. 1921.

Book Review: "Recent Theistic Discussion" (by W. L. Davidson): In *The Journal of Theological Studies*, XXIII, 204. 1921–22.

Article: "The Present Relations of Science and Theology: (2) The Theological Bearings of Theoretical Science": In *The Constructive Quarterly*, X, 274. 1922.

Book Reviews: "Belief, Faith, and Proof" (by J. H. Beibitz); "The Christian Idea of Sin and Original Sin" (by E. J. Bicknell); "Christian Philosophy" (by J. Gurnhill); "The Spiritual Philosophy" (by J. Gurnhill): In *The Journal of Theological Studies*, XXIV, 99, 195, 101, 101. 1922–23.

Article: "Recent Theories as to the Cause of Universal Sinfulness": In *The Expository Times* (ed. by James Hastings), XXXV, 503. 1923–24.

Article: "Faith, Hope and Knowledge in 1 Corinthians XIII": In *The Expositor*, 9th ser., II, 108. 1924.

Controversy: Paper, "The Reign of Law"; read by F. R. Tennant at a conference of modern churchmen and published in *The Modern Churchman*, XIV, pp. 305–321. Discussion and criticism by D. R. W. Macan, Master of University College, Oxford; published in *The Modern Churchman*, XIV, 208–213. Correspondence—Dr. Tennant's reply; published in *The Modern Churchman*, XIV, 477–478; Dr. Macan's reply, *ibid.*, XIV, 478–482. 1924.

Book Reviews: "The Appearance of Mind" (by J. C. McKerrow); "Cristus Veritus" (by W. Temple); "Is God Limited" (by F. J. McConnell); "Knowledge and Virtue" (by P. N. Waggett); "Metaphysical Grounds of the Science of Nature" (by K. F. Fobel): In *The Journal of Theological Studies*, XXVI, 303, 295, 298, 300, 302. 1924–25.

Book: *Miracle and Its Philosophical Presuppositions;* Three Lectures Delivered in the University of London, 1924. Cambridge, University Press. 1925.

Book Reviews: "The Nature of Religion" (by W. P. Paterson); "Personality and Reality" (by J. E. Turner); "Le Probleme du Miracle dans le Christianisms Primitif" (by A. Fridrichsen); "Science and the Modern World" (by A. N. Whitehead): In *The Journal of Theological Studies*, XXVII, 434, 438, 438, 427. 1925–26.

Book Review: "Religion in the Making" (by A. N. Whitehead): In *Mind*, XXXVI, 221–228. 1927.

Book Reviews: "God and Reality" (by M. B. Stewart); "The Metaphysics of Evolution" (by T. Whittaker): In *The Journal of Theological Studies*, XXVIII, 307, 304. 1926–27.

Book Reviews: "Essays in Philosophy" (by J. Ward, ed. by O. W. Campbell); "An Experiment with Time" (by J. W. Dunne); "Faith and Reason in Religion" (by G. Galloway); "First Steps in the Philosophy of Religion" (by C. Harris); "Purposive Evolution" (by E. Noble); "Relativity and Religion" (by H. D. Anthony); "Réalitè et Relativité" (by G. Rabeau); "Religious Assent" (by M. Pontifex): In *The Journal of Theological Studies*, XXIX, 182, 191, 187, 193, 192, 414, 412, 303. 1927–28.

Article: "Causality": In *Encyclopædia of Religion and Ethics* (ed. by James Hastings), III, 261. 1928.

Article: "Force": In *Encyclopædia of Religion and Ethics* (ed. by James Hastings), VI, 69. 1928.

"Magnum Opus," *Philosophical Theology*, I. The Soul and Its Faculties (cf. Vol. II below), Cambridge, University Press. 1928.

Articles: "Agnosticism"; "Faith"; "Sin"; "Theology": In *Encyclopædia Britannica* (14th ed.) I, 351–352; IX, 40–41; XX, 702–703; XXII, 61–66, respectively. 1929.

Book Reviews: "The Psychological Approach to Reality" (by F. Aveling); "Ourselves and Reality" (by E. G. Braham); "The Intelligible World; Metaphysics and Value" (by W. M. Urban); "Kant's Philosophy of Religion" (by C. C. J. Webb): In *The Journal of Theological Studies*, XXXI, 299, 298, 79, 75. 1929–30.

"Magnum Opus," *Philosophical Theology*, II. The World, The Soul, and God (cf. Vol. I above), Cambridge, University Press. 1930.

Book Reviews: "Studies in Philosophy of Religion" (by Pringle-Pattison): In *Mind*, XL, 93–97. 1931.

Book Reviews: "Kant's Conception of God" (by F. E. England); "The Quest for Certainty" (by J. Dewey); "The Problem of Time" (by J. A. Gunn); "Man and the Universe" (H. Driesch to W. H. Johnson); "The Logic of Religious Thought" (by R. G. Milburn); "Die Methoden und Grundauffassungen der Religionsphilosophie der Gegenwart" (by C. Niemeir); "Der Kausale Gottesbeweis bei Herveus Natalis" (by J. Santeler): In *The Journal of Theological Studies*, XXXII, 78, 81, 86, 84, 219, 429, 428. 1930–31.

Book: *Philosophy of the Sciences* or The Relations Between the Departments of Knowledge, Tarner Lectures, Trinity College, Cambridge, for the year 1931–32. Cambridge, University Press. 1932.

Book Reviews: "Ideas: General Introduction to Pure Phenomenology" (by E. Husserl); "Novius Organum" (by J. C. McKerrow); "The Revelation of Deity" (by J. E. Turner): In *The Journal of Theological Studies*, XXXIII, 210, 215, 212. 1931–32.

Book Reviews: *Mind and Matter* (by G. F. Stout), "Die Idea der

Sunde" (by G. Mensching); "The Psychological Teaching of St. Augustine" (by Morgan); "The Nature of Belief" (by C. C. D'Arcy); "Religion and Revelation" (by A. J. Lilley); "The Philosophy of Descartes" (by A. R. Gibson); "Scientific Theory and Religion" (by E. W. Barnes); "In Job's Balance" (by L. Chestov, tr. by C. C. and C. A. Macartny); "Berkeley" (by G. D. Hicks): In *The Journal of Theological Studies,* XXXIV, 93, 286, 397. 1933.

Book Reviews: "The World and God" (by H. S. Box); "The Problem of Error in Plato and Kant" (by L. W. Keeler); "Das Wunderproblem der Deutschen Prostanteschen Theologie die Gegenwart" (by P. G. Marquardt); "Essentials in Development of Religion" (by J. E. Turner); "Quest of Reality" (by Walsche): In *The Journal of Theological Studies,* XXXV, 403, 317, 320, 401, 318. 1934.

Book Reviews: "Religious Thought in the 18th Century" (by J. M. Creed and J. S. Boys-Smith); "Nature, Man and God" (by Wm. Temple): In *The Journal of Theological Studies,* XXXVI, 213, 313. 1935.

Book Review: "The World and God" (by H. H. Farmer): In *Mind,* XLV, 241–246. 1936.

REVIEWS OF *PHILOSOPHICAL THEOLOGY*[1]

Important:
1. C. D. Broad, *Mind,* XXXVIII, 94 ff.; XXXIX, 476 ff. (Tennant considers this to be the most important review of his book and has answered it point for point in his unpublished lectures.)
2. W. G. De Burgh, *The Journal of Philosophical Studies,* III, 537 ff.; V, 615 ff. (Tennant objects to statements of one or two writers who describe Volume I of *Philosophical Theology* as "an exposition of such a psychology and epistemology as its author deems theism to require"; cf. II, 249. This remark is made by De Burgh in this review. De Burgh's review is second to Broad's in extent and in critical comment. De Burgh is opposed to Tennant's psychology and epistemology but in agreement with Tennant's theism.)
3. Robert Mackintosh, *The Congregational Quarterly,* VI, 493 ff.; VIII, 374 ff. (This review brings out important relations between Tennant and Ward. It describes Tennant as semi-Pelagian.)

1. The reviews of Tennant's *Philosophy of Sciences* are inconsequential and hence excluded. The reviews of *Philosophical Theology* are listed according to the extent of criticism and importance.

4. R. L. Calhoun, *The Journal of Religion,* XI, 461 ff. (This review points out three central matters of difference between the reviewer and the author. It raises difficulties with respect to Tennant's position on self-knowledge.)

5. John Oman, *The Journal of Theological Studies,* XXXI, 403 ff.; XXXIII, 281 ff. (Dr. Oman's review is important insofar as it indicates the divergence of his own view of the cognitive value of feeling and of value from that of Tennant.)

6. G. Dawes Hicks, *The Hibbert Journal,* XXVIII, 174 ff.; XXIX, 370 ff. (Dr. Hicks criticizes Tennant's "phenomenalism" from his own realistic standpoint. At other points his review is expository and appreciative.)

7. A. C. Knudson, *The Methodist Quarterly,* CXI, 935 ff.; CXIII, 614 ff. (Dean Knudson interprets the first volume of *Philosophical Theology* in personalistic fashion making special reference to Kant. In his later review of Volume II, he discovers that Tennant is not an orthodox personalist.)

Of lesser importance:

8. M. D'Arcy, *The Month,* CLIII, 181 ff.; CLV, 466 ff. (D'Arcy's review is aggressively hostile. He charges Tennant with complete failure in theology.)

9. H. Maurice Relton, *Theology,* XVIII, 167 ff.; XXI, 239 ff. (Relton, lecturer in Dogmatic Theology, Kings College, London [Oxford man], gives an exposition of central points with all of which he is in exact agreement.)

10. Rufus Jones, *Philosophical Review,* XXXIX, 96 ff. (Rufus Jones omits all critical comment with disappointing brevity.)

11. Anonymous, *The Expository Times,* XXXIX, 541 ff.; XLI, 348 ff. (This review is brief and complimentary. It refers to Tennant's "Pelagian tendency.")

12. Anonymous, *The London Quarterly Review,* CLI, 110 ff. (Brief and unimportant.)

IMPORTANT REFERENCES TO TENNANT[2]

(a) An extensive summary of Tennant's thought is supposedly set forth in Rannie Belle Baker's *The Concept of a Limited God,* Washington, D.C. Shenandoah Publishing House, Inc., 1934. Miss Baker is incorrect in making Tennant a personal idealist. Tennant is a Kantian and an agnostic with respect to the meta-

2. NOTE: Though the references to Tennant's various writings in books are too numerous to list, the more important are here designated.

physical quality of the thing-per-se. It is incorrect to place him in exactly the same category as Ward and Bowne.

(b) An important critical refutation of the type of design argument of which Tennant is declared representative is to be found in N. K. Smith's lecture, "Is Divine Existence Credible"; cf. *The Proceedings of the British Academy,* XVII (1931), 209 ff. An important extension of Professor Smith's thought on the argument from design may be found in his introduction to *Hume's Dialogues Concerning Natural Religion,* 1935. Cf. N. K. Smith, *A Commentary on Kant's Critique of Pure Reason,* pp. 538 ff., and translation of Immanuel Kant's *Critique of Pure Reason,* pp. 518 ff. Professor Smith rejects the argument from design and attempts to sustain the "fact of design" by immediate religious experience. This position is diametrically opposed to Tennant's.

(c) H. Osborne, *Foundations of the Philosophy of Value,* chap. viii, Cambridge, University Press, 1933. Osborne rejects Tennant's theory of value.

(d) J. C. Bennett, *Social Salvation,* New York, Scribner's, 1935. Bennett employs Tennant's definition of sin and Tennant's definition of the limitations of God. (In bibliography of *Christianity and Our World,* p. 65, Bennett makes the following comment on Tennant's *Philosophical Theology:* "The most persuasive statement of the intellectual basis for Christian faith which I know.")

(e) P. A. Bertocci, *The Empirical Argument for God in Late British Thought.* Cambridge, Massachusetts, Harvard University Press, 1938. Bertocci accepts Tennant's empirical type of philosophical theology and also Tennant's analysis of value. From this standpoint, Bertocci rejects the moral arguments for God as developed by Martineau, Pringle-Pattison, Ward, and Sorley. He does not deal with Tennant's conception of religious experience. He rejects Tennant's analysis of the pure ego, Tennant's metaphysical agnosticism (and dualism), and Tennant's solution of the problem of evil. Bertocci follows Brightman in these matters.

GENERAL BIBLIOGRAPHICAL BACKGROUND OF THIS BOOK[3]

*ALEXANDER, SAMUEL. *Space, Time and Deity.* London, Macmillan Co., 1920.

ALIOTTA, ANTONIO. *The Idealistic Reaction against Science.* Tr. by Agnes McCaskill. London, Macmillan Co., 1914.

3. An asterisk (*) indicates quotation of a reference in text of this book.

AMES, EDWARD SCRIBNER. Religion. New York, Holt & Co., 1929.

—— Psychology of Religious Experience. Boston, Houghton Mifflin Co., 1910.

*BALMFORTH, HENRY. Is Christian Experience An Illusion? London, Student Christian Movement Press, 1923.

BARNES, ERNEST WILLIAM. Scientific Theory and Religion. Cambridge, University Press, 1933.

BENNETT, CHARLES ANDREW A. Dilemma of Religious Knowledge, ed. by William Ernest Hocking. New Haven, Yale University Press, 1931.

—— The Philosophical Study of Mysticism. New Haven, Yale University Press, 1931.

BIXLER, JULIUS SEELYE. The Nature of Religious Experience. New York, Harpers, 1937.

BOODIN, JOHN ELOF. God and Creation. New York, Macmillan Co., 1934. 2 vols.

BRIGHTMAN, EDGAR SHEFFIELD. Religious Values. New York, Abingdon, 1925.

—— The Problem of God. New York, Abingdon, 1930.

—— The Finding of God. New York, Abingdon, 1931.

BROAD, CHARLIE DUNBAR. Five Types of Ethical Theory. London, K. Paul, Trench, Trubner & Co.; New York, Harcourt, Brace & Co., 1930.

*—— Examination of McTaggart's Philosophy. New York, Macmillan Co., 1933–38. 2 vols. in 3 pts.

*—— Mind and its Place in Nature. London, Kegan Paul, 1925.

—— Scientific Thought. London, Kegan Paul, 1923.

BROWN, WILLIAM. Mind and Personality. New York, Putnam's Sons, 1927.

BROWN, WILLIAM ADAMS. Beliefs that Matter. New York, Scribner's 1928.

BUCKHAM, JOHN WRIGHT. The Humanity of God. New York, Harpers, 1928.

CAIRNES, DAVID SMITH. The Faith that Rebels. New York, Doubleday, 1928.

—— The Riddle of the World. London, Student Christian Movement Press, 1937.

CALDECOTT, ALFRED. The Philosophy of Religion in England and America. New York, Macmillan Co., 1901.

CALHOUN, ROBERT LOWRY. God and the Common Life. New York, Scribner's, 1935.

CLARKE, WILLIAM NEWTON. *The Christian Doctrine of God.* New York, Scribner's, 1909.

—— *An Outline of Christian Theology.* New York, Scribner's, 1898.

COE, GEORGE ALBERT. *The Psychology of Religion.* Chicago, University of Chicago Press, 1917.

*CONKLIN, EDMUND SMITH. *Psychology of Religious Adjustment.* New York, Macmillan Co., 1929.

DAVIDSON, ANDREW BRUCE. *The Theology of the Old Testament,* ed. by S. D. F. Salmond. Edinburgh, T. & T. Clark, 1904.

DEWAR, LINDSAY. *Man and God.* London, S.P.C.K.; New York, Macmillan Co., 1935.

*DIMAN, JEREMIAH LEWIS. *The Theistic Argument.* Boston, Houghton, Mifflin & Co.; Cambridge, The Riverside Press (4th ed.), 1886.

DRAKE, DURANT. *Problems of Religion.* Boston, Houghton, Mifflin & Co., 1916.

—— and others. *Essays In Critical Realism.* London, Macmillan Co., 1921.

EDDINGTON, ARTHUR STANLEY. *The Nature of the Physical World.* New York, Macmillan Co., 1929.

—— *Science and the Unseen World.* New York, Macmillan Co., 1929.

*EDWARD, KENNETH. *Religious Experience: Its Nature and Truth.* Edinburgh, T. & T. Clark, 1926.

EDWARDS, DAVID MIALL. *Christianity and Philosophy.* Edinburgh, T. & T. Clark, 1932.

—— *The Philosophy of Religion.* New York, George H. Doran, 1924.

FARMER, HERBERT HENRY. *Experience of God.* Garden City, Doubleday, Doran, 1929.

*—— *The World and God.* London and New York, Harpers, 1935.

FLINT, ROBERT. *Anti-Theistic Theories.* Edinburgh, W. Blackwood, 1879.

—— *Agnosticism.* New York, Scribner's, 1903.

—— *Theism.* Edinburgh, W. Blackwood, 1878; New York, Scribner's, 1898.

GALLOWAY, GEORGE. *Faith and Reason in Religion.* New York, Scribner's, 1928.

—— *The Philosophy of Religion.* New York, Scribner's, 1914.

GAMERTSFELDER, WALTER SYLVESTER; EVANS, D. LUTHER. *Fundamentals of Philosophy.* New York, Prentice-Hall, 1930.

GARVIE, ALFRED ERNEST. *The Christian Belief in God in Relation to Religion and Philosophy.* London, Harpers, 1932.

—— *The Christian Doctrine of the Godhead.* New York, George H. Doran, 1926.

GOGUEL, MAURICE. *Life of Jesus,* tr. by Olive Wyon. New York, Macmillan Co., 1933.

*GRIFFITHS, REES. *God in Idea and Experience.* Edinburgh, Clark, 1931.

GWATWIN, HENRY MELVILL. *Knowledge of God and its historical development.* Edinburgh, T. & T. Clark, 1906. 2 vols.

HEFELBOWER, SAMUEL GRING. *The Relation of John Lock to English Deism.* Chicago, University of Chicago, 1918.

*HEILER, FREIDRICH. *Prayer,* tr. and ed. by Samuel McComb. London, Oxford University Press, 1932.

HICKMAN, FRANKLIN SIMPSON. *Introduction to the Psychology of Religion.* New York, Abingdon, 1926.

*HICKS, GEORGE DAWES. *The Philosophical Bases of Theism.* London, Allen & Unwin, 1937.

HOCKING, WILLIAM ERNEST. *Human Nature and its Remaking.* New Haven, Yale University Press, 1918.

*—— *The Meaning of God in Human Experience.* New Haven, Yale University Press, 1912.

—— *Types of Philosophy.* New York, Scribner's, 1929.

HÖFFDING, HAROLD. *The Philosophy of Religion,* tr. from the German edition by B. E. Meyer. London, Macmillan Co., 1906.

HOLLINGSWORTH, HARRY LEVI. *Psychology: Its Facts and Principles.* New York, Appleton, 1928.

HOPKINS, EDWARD WASHBURN. *History of Religions.* New York, Macmillan Co., 1918.

—— *Origin and Evolution of Religion.* New Haven, Yale University Press, 1923.

*HORTON, WALTER MARSHALL. *Contemporary English Theology.* New York, Harpers, 1936.

—— *Theism and the Modern Mood.* New York, Harpers, 1930.

—— *A Psychological Approach to Theology.* New York, Harpers, 1931.

HOUF, HORACE THOMAS. *What Religion Is And Does.* New York, Harpers, 1935.

*HÜGEL, BARON FRIEDRICH VON. *Essays and Addresses on the Philosophy of Religion.* 1st ser. (reprinted ed. 1931 used), New York, E. P. Dutton, 1921. 2d ser. (reprinted ed. 1933 used), 1926.

—— *The Mystical Element of Religion.* New York, E. P. Dutton, 1909. 2 vols.

—— *The Reality of God and Religion and Agnosticism,* ed. by Edmund G. Gardner. New York, E. P. Dutton, 1931.

*HUGHES, THOMAS HYWEL. *The New Psychology and Religious Experience.* New York, P. Smith, 1933.

*HUME, DAVID. *Dialogues of Natural Religion,* ed. by N. K. Smith. Oxford, Clarendon Press, 1935.

HUME, ROBERT ERNEST. *The World's Living Religions.* New York, Scribner's, 1924.

*INGE, WILLIAM RALPH. *Christian Mysticism.* New York, Scribner's, 1899.

—— *Faith and Its Psychology.* New York, Scribner's, 1910.

—— *Personal Idealism and Mysticism* (3d ed. 1924). New York, Longmans, Green & Co., 1907.

*JAMES, WILLIAM. *The Varieties of Religious Experience* (35th impression used, 1925). New York, Scribner's, 1902.

—— *The Will to Believe.* New York, Longmans, Green & Co., 1897.

JEANS, JAMES HOPWARD. *The Universe Around Us.* New York, Macmillan Co., 1929.

JOAD, CYRIL EDWIN MITCHINSON. *Matter, Life and Value.* New York, Oxford, 1929.

KANT, IMMANUEL. *The Critique of Pure Reason,* tr. by Norman Kemp Smith. London, Macmillan Co., 1929.

*KNUDSON, ALBERT CORNELIUS. *The Doctrine of God.* New York, Abingdon, 1930.

—— *The Doctrine of Redemption.* New York, Abingdon, 1933.

*—— *Present Tendencies in Religious Thought.* New York, Abingdon, 1924.

*—— *The Philosophy of Personalism.* New York, Abingdon, 1927.

*—— *The Validity of Religious Experience.* New York, Abingdon, 1937.

*LAIRD, JOHN. *Problems of the Self.* London, Macmillan Co., 1917.

LEIGHTON, JOSEPH ALEXANDER. *Man and the Cosmos.* New York, Appleton, 1922.

LEUBA, JAMES HENRY. *Psychological Study of Religion.* New York, Macmillan Co., 1912.

LEWIS, CLARENCE IRVING. *Mind and the World-Order.* New York, Scribner's, 1929.

LOVEJOY, ARTHUR ONCKEN. *Revolt against Dualism.* New York, Norton, 1930.

LYMAN, EUGENE WILLIAM. *The Meaning and Truth of Religion.* New York, Scribner's, 1933.

McCONNELL, FRANCIS JOHN. *Is God Limited?* New York, Abingdon, 1924.

MACINTOSH, DOUGLAS CLYDE. *The Pilgrimage of Faith in the World of Modern Thought*. Calcutta, University Press; New York, Longmans, Green & Co., 1931.

—— *The Problem of Knowledge*. New York, Macmillan Co., 1915.

—— *The Reasonableness of Christianity*. New York, Scribner's, 1925.

*—— *Religious Realism*. New York, Macmillan, 1931.

*—— *Theology as an Empirical Science* (reprinted ed. used, April 1927). New York, Macmillan Co., 1919.

*MASON, FRANCIS, ed. *The Great Design*. New York, Macmillan Co., 1934.

MATTHEWS, WALTER ROBERT. *God in Christian Thought and Experience*. London, Nisbet & Co., 1930.

—— *Our Faith in God*. 2d ed., London, Student Christian Movement Press, 1937.

—— *The Purpose of God*. New York, Scribner's, 1936.

MELAND, BERNARD EUGENE. *Modern Man's Worship*. New York, Harpers, 1934.

METZ, RUDOLF. *A Hundred Years of British Philosophy*. Tr. by J. W. Harvey, T. E. Jessop, Henry Sturt; ed. by J. H. Muirhead; New York, Macmillan Co., 1938.

MONTAGUE, WILLIAM PEPPERELL. *Belief Unbound*. New Haven, Yale University Press, 1930.

—— *Ways of Knowing*. New York, Macmillan Co., 1925.

MOORE, EDWARD CALDWELL. *An Outline of the History of Christian Thought Since Kant*. New York, Scribner's, 1912.

MOORE, GEORGE FOOT. *The Birth and Growth of Religion*. New York, Scribner's, 1924.

—— *History of Religions*. New York, Scribner's, 1913–19. 2 vols.

MORRIS, CHARLES WILLIAM. *Six Theories of Mind*. Chicago University of Chicago, 1932.

*NEEDHAM, JOSEPH, ed. *Science, Religion and Reality*. New York, Macmillan Co., 1926.

*OMAN, JOHN WOOD. *The Natural and the Supernatural*. New York, Macmillan Co., 1931.

*OTTO, RUDOLF. *The Idea of the Holy*. Tr. by John W. Harvey. London, Oxford University Press, 1926.

—— *Mysticism East and West*. Tr. by B. L. Bracy, R. C. Payne; New York, Macmillan Co., 1932.

POVAH, JOHN WALTER. *The New Psychology and the Hebrew Prophets*. London, Longmans, Green & Co., 1925.

PRATT, JAMES BISSETT. *The Psychology of Religious Belief*. New York, Macmillan Co., 1907.

—— *The Religious Consciousness.* New York, Macmillan Co., 1920.

*PRICE, HENRY HABBERLEY. *Perception.* New York, McBride, 1933.

*PRINGLE-PATTISON, ANDREW SETH. *The Idea of God in the Light of Recent Philosophy.* 2d ed. London, Oxford University Press, 1920.

*RAVEN, CHARLES EARLE. *The Creator Spirit.* London, Hopkinson, 1929.

*—— *Jesus and the Gospel of Love.* New York, Holt, 1931.

ROBINSON, DANIEL SOMMER. *The God of the Liberal Christian.* New York, Appleton, 1926.

ROGERS, ARTHUR KENYON. *Religious Conception of the World.* New York, Macmillan Co., 1907.

*—— *What is Truth?* New Haven, Yale University Press, 1923.

ROYCE, JOSIAH. *Sources of Religious Insight.* New York, Scribner's, 1912.

*SANTAYANA, GEORGE. *Scepticism and Animal Faith.* New York, Scribner's, 1923.

SELBIE, WILLIAM BOOTHBY. *Psychology of Religion.* Oxford, Clarendon Press, 1924.

SELLARS, ROY WOOD. *Critical Realism.* New York, Rand, 1916.

SELWYN, EDWARD GORDON, ed. *Essays Catholic and Critical.* New York, Macmillan Co., 1930.

SMITH, GERALD BIRNEY, ed. *Religious Thought in the Last Quarter Century.* Chicago, University of Chicago Press, 1927.

*SMITH, NORMAN KEMP. *A Commentary to Kant's "Critique of Pure Reason."* London, Macmillan Co., 1918.

*—— *Hume's Dialogues Concerning Natural Religion.* Ed. with an Introduction. Oxford, Clarendon Press, 1935.

*—— *Prolegomena to an Idealist Theory of Knowledge.* London, Macmillan Co., 1924.

SORLEY, WILLIAM RITCHIE. *Moral Values and the Idea of God.* Cambridge, University Press, 1918.

STEPHEN, SIR LESLIE. *History of English Thought in the 18th Century.* New York, Putnam's, 1876.

STOLZ, KARL RUF. *The Psychology of Religious Living.* Nashville, Cokesbury Press, 1932.

*STOUT, GEORGE FREDERICK. *Mind and Matter.* New York, Macmillan Co., 1931.

*—— *Studies in Philosophy and Psychology.* London, Macmillan Co., 1930.

STRATTON, GEORGE MALCOLM. *Psychology of the Religious Life.* London, Allen & Co., 1911.

STREETER, BURNETT HILLMAN. *The God Who Speaks.* New York, Macmillan Co., 1936.

—— *Reality.* New York, Macmillan Co., 1926.

*STRONG, AUGUSTUS HOPKINS. *Systematic Theology.* Rochester, Press of E. R. Andrews, 1886.

*TAYLOR, ALFRED EDWARD. *The Faith of a Moralist.* London, Macmillan Co., 1930.

THILLY, FRANK. *History of Philosophy.* New York, Holt, 1914.

THOMSON, JOHN ARTHUR. *Science and Religion.* New York, Scribner's, 1925.

*THOULESS, ROBERT H. *An Introduction to Psychology of Religion.* Cambridge, University Press, 1923.

TURNER, JOHN EVAN. *The Nature of Deity.* London, Allen & Unwin, 1927.

*—— *Essentials in the Development of Religion.* London, Allen & Unwin, 1934.

UNDERHILL, EVELYN. *Mysticism.* London, Methuen, 1911; 3d ed. rev., 1912.

—— *Worship.* New York, Harpers, 1937.

UNDERWOOD, ALFRED CLAIR. *Conversion: Christian and Non-Christian.* New York, Macmillan Co., 1925.

UREN, A. RUDOLPH. *Recent Religious Psychology.* Edinburgh, T. & T. Clark, 1928.

VAN DUSEN, HENRY PITNEY. *Plain Man Seeks for God.* New York, Scribner's, 1933.

WARD, JAMES. *Naturalism and Agnosticism.* New York, Macmillan Co., 1899. 2 vols.

*—— *Psychological Principles.* Cambridge, University Press, 1918. (2d ed. 1920.)

—— *The Realm of Ends.* Cambridge, University Press, 1911.

*WATERHOUSE, ERIC STRICKLAND. *Philosophy of Religious Experience.* London, Epworth Press, 1923.

*WEBB, CLEMENT CHARLES JULIAN. *Divine Personality and Human Life.* New York, Macmillan Co., 1920.

*—— *God and Personality.* London, Allen & Unwin, 1918.

—— *Group Theories of Religion.* London, Allen & Unwin, 1916.

*—— *Religion and Theism.* New York, Scribner's, 1934.

—— *Studies in the History of Natural Theology.* Oxford, Clarendon Press, 1915.

—— *A Study of Religious Thought in England From 1850.* Oxford, Clarendon Press, 1933.

*WIDGERY, ALBAN GREGORY. *The Comparative Study of Religions.* London, Williams and Norgate, 1923.

WIEMAN, HENRY NELSON. *American Philosophies of Religion.* Chicago, Willett, Clark, 1936.

—— *The Issues of Life.* New York, Abingdon, 1930.

—— *Methods of Private Religious Living.* New York, Macmillan Co., 1929.

—— *Normative Psychology of Religion.* New York, Crowell, 1935.

—— *Religious Experience and Scientific Method.* New York, Macmillan Co., 1926.

—— *The Wrestle of Religion with Truth.* New York, Macmillan Co., 1927.

*WILM, EMIL CARL, ed. *Studies in Philosophy and Theology.* New York, Abingdon, 1922.

WRIGHT, HENRY WILKES. *The Religious Response.* New York, Harpers, 1929.

WRIGHT, WILLIAM KELLEY. *A Student's Philosophy of Religion.* New York, Macmillan Co., 1922.

ARTICLES DIRECTLY USED

BROAD, C. D. "Belief In A Personal God," *The Hibbert Journal,* XXIV, 1925–26.

BURNS, C. D. "The Contact of Minds," *Proceedings of the Aristotelian Society,* XXIII, 1923.

DUDDINGTON, N. A. "Our Knowledge of Other Minds," *Proceedings of the Aristotelian Society,* XIX. 1919.

HICKS, G. D. "Prof. Ward's Psychological Principles," *Mind,* XXX. 1921.

JEWELL-LAPAN, W. "A Naturalistic View of 'Numinous' Experience," *The Review of Religion,* II. 1937.

PRICE, H. H. "Our Knowledge of Other Minds," *Proceedings of the Aristotelian Society,* XXXII. 1932.

WEBB, C. C. J. "The Nature of Religious Experience," *The Hibbert Journal,* XXXII. 1933–34.

—— "Our Knowledge of One Another," *Proceedings of the British Academy,* XVI. 1930.

—— *Religion and the Thought of Today:* Riddell Memorial Lectures, 1st ser. London, Oxford University Press, 1929.

YOUNGHUSBAND, FRANCIS. "Religious Experience and Philosophy," *Proceedings of the Aristotelian Society* (new ser.), XXVIII. 1928.

INDEX OF PROPER NAMES

Note: Owing to the detailed character of the Contents, an index of topics has been omitted. Cf. supra, p. ix ff.

ACKNOWLEDGMENTS

THE author wishes to express his appreciation to the following for permission to quote from the sources indicated:

Abingdon Press: Albert C. Knudson, The Validity of Religious Experience (1937).

George Allen & Unwin, Ltd.: G. Dawes Hicks, The Philosophical Bases of Theism; C. C. J. Webb, God and Personality.

British Institute of Philosophy, Sydney E. Hooper, ed.: *The Journal of Philosophical Studies,* Vol. III.

British Academy and Oxford University Press: C. C. J. Webb, Our Knowledge of One Another; N. K. Smith, Is Divine Existence Credible? in *The Proceedings of the British Academy,* Vols. XVI and XVII, respectively.

Cambridge University Press: F. R. Tennant, Philosophical Theology, and also Philosophy of the Sciences; James Ward, Psychological Principles.

T. & T. Clark: R. Griffiths, God in Idea and Experience; A. B. Davidson, Theology of the Old Testament.

Constable & Company, Ltd., and Dr. L. P. Jacks: C. D. Broad, Belief in a Personal God; C. C. J. Webb, The Nature of Religious Experience, in *The Hibbert Journal,* Vols. XXIV and XXXII, respectively.

E. P. Dutton & Company, Inc.: Baron F. Von Hügel, Essays and Addresses.

The Epworth Press: E. S. Waterhouse, Philosophy of Religious Experience.

Harper & Brothers: W. M. Horton, Contemporary English Theology.

Harrison & Sons, Ltd., and A. H. Hannay, Esq., Honorary Secretary of The Aristotelian Society: N. A. Duddington, Our Knowledge of Other Minds, in *The Proceedings of the Aristotelian Society,* Vol. XIX.

Martin Hopkinson, Ltd.: C. E. Raven, The Creator Spirit.

Houghton Mifflin Company: J. L. Diman, The Theistic Argument.

Longmans, Green & Co.: W. R. Inge, Personal Idealism and Mysticism.

The Macmillan Company and Cambridge University: C. D. Broad, Examination of McTaggart's Philosophy; D. C. Macintosh, Religious Realism; J. Needham, ed., Science, Religion and Reality; J. Oman, The Natural and the Supernatural; N. K. Smith, Prolegomena to an Idealistic Theory of Knowledge; G. F. Stout, Mind and Matter.

Oxford University Press: A. S. Pringle-Pattison, The Idea of God in the Light of Recent Philosophy.

Charles Scribner's Sons: W. R. Inge, Christian Mysticism; G. Santa-
    yana, Reason and Animal Faith; C. C. J. Webb, Religion and Theism.
Student Christian Movement Press, Ltd.: H. Balmforth, Is Christian
    Experience an Illusion?
Yale University Press: W. E. Hocking, The Meaning of God in Human
    Experience; A. K. Rogers, What Is Truth?

YALE STUDIES IN RELIGIOUS EDUCATION